Pricing:
Making Profitable
Decisions

McGraw-Hill Series in Marketing

CONSULTING EDITOR

Charles Schewe, *University of Massachusetts*

Pricing:
Making Profitable
Decisions

Kent B. Monroe
Professor of Marketing
Department of Business Administration
College of Business
Virginia Polytechnic Institute and State University

McGraw-Hill Book Company

New York   St. Louis   San Francisco   Auckland   Bogotá   Düsseldorf
Johannesburg   London   Madrid   Mexico   Montreal   New Delhi
Panama   Paris   São Paulo   Singapore   Sydney   Tokyo   Toronto

Library of Congress Cataloging in Publication Data

Monroe, Kent B.
  Pricing: making profitable decisions.

  (McGraw-Hill series in marketing)
  Includes bibliographies and index.
  1. Price policy. I. Title.
HF5416.5.M66   658.8'16   78-16027
ISBN 0-07-042780-1

PRICING: MAKING PROFITABLE DECISIONS

    4 5 6 7 8 9 0 KPKP   8 3 2

This book was set in Press Roman by Allen Wayne Technical Corp.
The editor was William J. Kane; the cover was designed by Albert M. Cetta;
the production supervisor was Charles Hess.
Kingsport Press, Inc., was printer and binder.

Contents

1
INTRODUCTION

2
PRICES AND DEMAND

3
DEVELOPING INTERNAL COSTS FOR PRICING

4

PRICING DECISIONS AND PRICE ADMINISTRATION

5
SPECIAL TOPICS ON PRICING

6

RECOMMENDATIONS

Preface

This book is designed to provide the reader with an integrative framework for making pricing decisions. The book synthesizes economic and marketing principles with accounting and financial information to provide a basis for analyzing pricing alternatives within legal and corporate constraints.

Pricing is a multidisciplinary and multifunctional subject. From a corporate viewpoint, it is a responsibility of top management that encompasses financial, marketing, and legal considerations. However, there are conceptual and operational conflicts in theory and practice between economists, accountants, and marketing managers. Because of these conflicts and the many disciplines involved, pricing has not usually been taught as a separate course for business students, nor has a practical and informative book been written for students or practitioners. Indeed, the author's experiences with executives involved with the pricing function indicate that they are often frustrated by the lack of a good, informative source on pricing principles. Further, executives lament the fact that MBA and undergraduate business students lack training in the area of pricing.

BACKGROUND

This book is the result of 10 years of effort in designing both an undergraduate and a graduate business course on pricing. The materials and examples were subjected to considerable testing; some were dropped, others changed or expanded as experience indicated. Moreover, a substantial amount of the material included has already been presented to business executives across the country in pricing seminars. Every technique presented and illustrated in the text is being used by companies in relation to their pricing function, and some of the material was developed at the suggestion of business executives.

CONCEPTUAL PLAN OF THIS BOOK

The objectives of this book are to provide a systematic presentation of the factors to be considered when setting price, and to show how pricing alternatives can be developed. As observed in Chapter 1, many contemporary pricing practices are short-run reactions to environmental pressures that have been building for some time, and may not be generalizable. Moreover, such practices are often based on faulty perceptions. This book clarifies many of these issues.

As is well known, price directly affects the quantity that can be sold in the marketplace. Hence, after the introductory chapter, Chapters 2 and 3 carefully review the effect of price on demand. Given a firm's selling objectives, the demand variable provides an upper limit on the pricing discretion of the firm, which is the willingness of buyers to purchase at a stated price. On the other hand, the cost variable sets a floor to a firm's pricing discretion. If prices are too low in comparison with costs, volume may be high but profitless. Thus, Chapters 4 to 8 review the effect of costs on pricing decisions.

The pricing discretion afforded by the upper limit (demand) and the lower limit (cost) is narrowed by a number of constraints and considerations. For example, some consideration must be given to the age of the product, the role the product plays in the product line, the competition, the nature of the discount structure, and the cooperation of salespersons and channels. Hence, Chapters 9 to 12 consider the problems of determining a base or list price and the problems of administering such a price. These four chapters utilize the demand and cost framework developed in Chapters 2 to 8 to show how pricing alternatives can be developed and analyzed.

Additional constraints on the firm's pricing discretion may arise as the result of financial objectives, capacity constraints, or the need to consider legal, regulatory, or buyer resistance to price differentials. Chapters 13 to 16 consider these special problems that face the decision maker and present ways to handle them. Finally, Chapter 17 reviews the material presented in Chapters 1 to 16 by offering some prescriptions for improving the overall pricing function of the firm.

Schematically, the organization of the book is as follows:

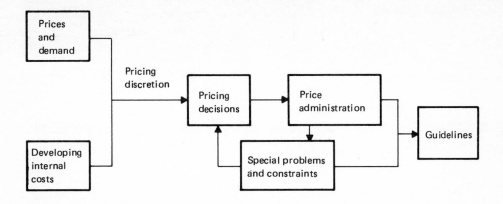

ACKNOWLEDGMENTS

Over the past few years, many individuals both encouraged and supported the development of this book, and it is not easy to acknowledge every contribution. The reviewers of the text were positive and helpful, and the book reflects many of their suggestions. Charles Schewe of the University of Massachusetts both encouraged the writing of the book and helped shape it with his careful reviews and material suggestions. Jack Nevin, University of Wisconsin, Avraham Shama, Baruch College, and William Dillon, University of Massachusetts, not only tested an earlier draft of the text in the classroom, but also provided useful suggestions for improving the manuscript. Richard N. Cardozo, University of Minnesota, Herbert Katzenstein, St. John's University, Thomas D. Giese, University of Richmond, and Gary M. Grikscheit, University of Utah, also provided valuable suggestions.

A special thanks goes to the students of the University of Massachusetts and of Virginia Polytechnic Institute and State University for their helpful comments and suggestions, and their willingness to evaluate various textual arrangements of the book. The students at the University of Massachusetts not only helped evaluate the material, but did so under the guidance of two different instructors.

Three very special assistants, Mary Dunn, Margaret Opeka, and Blair Smith, provided invaluable help with typing, material collection, and manuscript revisions. They provided excellent assistance while the manuscript was being put into final form, and their dedication and cooperation are sincerely appreciated.

As is always the case, some unsung heroes quietly and unselfishly make their contribution. My wife, Norma, and my children, Scott and Karen, allowed me often to escape to my study to work on the book. I am grateful for their help and understanding while the book was being developed.

Kent B. Monroe

Section One

Introduction

The purpose of Section 1 is to introduce the topic of pricing and to develop the strategic importance of the pricing variable. Chapter 1 defines price and illustrates seven ways price may be changed. After discussing some important environmental pressures on pricing decision makers, a number of approaches that have been used to cope with these pressures are presented. Chapter 1 concludes with a brief overview of the implications of these current pricing practices.

What for what?

"Hey!"

"Hey yourself."

"You wanna buy this?"

"Let's see it."

"Can't. You might drop it."

"Me?"

"Promise?"

"Well, no . . ."

"No assurance, no bird in the hand."

"I promise."

"Ok. Here it is."

"What is it?"

"Give it back to me."

"Why? I just got it."

"You don't appreciate it."

"I don't even know what it is."

"I can't tell you."

"I don't want it."

"I'll give you a hint."

"OK."

"It's late."

"Late? For what? Dinner?"

"Late. Old. Don'cha get it?"

"You mean late 18th or 19th Century?"

"Slow but right."

"Hmmmmm. It's heavy."

"Right again."

"And expensive?"

"Depending . . ."

"On what?"

"The value of it."

"To me?"

"To you."

"$2.98."

"Bandit. Give it back."

"Relax, I like it."

"So do I. $10 or nothing."

"Give me another hint."

"Geology."

"Geology? It's a disguised rock."

"You have no shame."

"But I have questions."

"It has value."

"$3.98."

"Out of the question!"

"I give up. What is it?"

"It's a . . . no, I can't."

"You really don't know."

"Does a lawyer know law?"

"*You* have no shame."

"But I have answers."

"Answer then."

"Ok. It's a rare Odonsplit."

"What's an Odonsplit?"

"That's it. In your hand."

"What's it for?"

"That's the wrong question."

"That's the only question."

"I have a suggestion."

"What?"

"Take it home and try it."

"Try it? How? What? Where?"

"That's up to you."

"I don't want it."

"Why not?"

"It's a mystery."

"Then it has value."

"Well, yes, but . . ."

"$8.98?"

"$4.98."

"$8.75?"

"$5.25."

"Forget it. I'll keep it."

"I can't forget it now."

"Then you'll take it?"

"On two conditions."

"Speak."

"If I can't use it, I return it."

"Agreed. The other?"

"If I like it, we trade."

"What for what?"

"This."

"What is it?"

"It's a very rare Tickfaw."

David Holmstrom

Chapter 1

Contemporary Pricing Practices

The pricing decisions for a modern organization are complex and important. Traditionally, these decisions have been determined by following the pricing practices of another organization, or by following pricing practices established in the past. Today, business firms are encountering foreign competitors who often set prices that are lower than comparable prices set by American businesses. Also, the federal government has taken an increasing and active interest in the prices established. Firms are also faced with inflation, raw-material shortages, decreasing liquidity, increasing labor and material costs, high interest rates, uncertain exchange rates, and inadequate depreciation charges for replacing plant and equipment.[1]

The economic and competitive pressures mentioned above are forcing new marketing approaches and strategies, particularly in the area of pricing. However, careful analysis and research for pricing decisions have not been the traditional policy of American businesses. Hence, many firms have not been prepared to change pricing strategies. Moreover, many of the popular pricing strategies discussed in contempory general business periodicals are often simplistic reactions to complex forces and may produce unanticipated consequences.

[1]For a detailed analysis of these problems, see "The 1970's: A Second Look," *Business Week*, September 14, 1974, pp. 50-162.

3

Oxenfeldt has suggested that pricing practice remains largely intuitive and routine, and that the pricing literature has produced few new insights or approaches that would stimulate most business people to change their methods of setting prices.[2] While there may be many reasons for this lack of creative development of new approaches to solving pricing problems, two reasons are illustrative: (1) for a lengthy period of time the economists' theory of price has dominated despite the obvious lack of realism in the theoretical structure; and (2) until recent environmental changes in the markets for goods and services, the seller's problem was not price but rather demand stimulation using promotional activities. Thus, there was little "payoff" in studying how buyers respond to prices and price changes or how a set of prices that would lead to an optimal position for the firm is determined.

The purpose of this chapter is to define price and illustrate the complexities of pricing decisions. To amplify the increasing importance of these decisions, a number of environmental pressures influencing business management and pricing will be discussed. Then the chapter will review how businesses have attempted to cope with these environmental pressures, and the implications of these current pricing strategies.

THE ROLE OF PRICE

The basic problem of an economic society is to allocate resources among the members of the society so as to maximize the welfare of the society as a whole. To achieve this welfare objective each resource should be used to perform the function that it contributes most efficiently to society. But what is the mechanism which seeks to achieve this objective? In a planned economy the central planning agency develops plans for allocating resources. In a market economy the price system allocates resources. That is, prices furnish the guideposts that indicate how resources should be used. Prices determine *what* products and services should be produced and in what amounts. Prices determine *how* these products and services should be produced. And prices determine *for whom* the products and services should be produced.

Thus, prices affect incomes *and* spending behavior. For business people, profits are determined by the difference between their revenues and their costs; and their revenues are determined by multiplying price per unit sold by the number of units sold. For the consumer with a given income level, prices influence what to buy and how much of each product to buy.

Price changes also play a major role in a market economy. When demand for a product or service is greater than the supply available, buyers bid the price up. If costs remain the same per unit sold, the higher price leads to greater profits and an incentive to invest in resources to produce even greater quantities of the product. Thus, the producers are able to bid more for raw material resources, thereby directing these resources into that industry. In addition, higher prices may also stimulate a greater rate of innovation and the development of new technology. On the other hand, if available supply is greater than demand there are pressures to decrease prices and reduce output.

[2] Alfred Oxenfeldt, "A Decision-Making Structure for Price Decisions," *Journal of Marketing*, 37 (January 1973), 48–53.

These pressures lead producers to convert their resources to alternative uses. Thus, rising prices direct resources to the bidder of greatest desire (stimulating supply), and rising prices curtail demands of the least urgent bidders (rationing supply). Declining prices have the opposite effects.

THE MEANING OF PRICE

Within this economic context, it is usual to think of price as the amount of money we must sacrifice to acquire something we desire. That is, we consider price as a formal ratio indicating the quantities of money needed to acquire a given quantity of goods or services. Or

$$\text{Price} = \frac{\text{quantity of goods and services provided by the seller}}{\text{quantity of money or goods and services given up by the buyer}}$$

Thus, when the price of a box of cereal is quoted as $0.89, the interpretation is the seller provides *one* box of cereal and the buyer gives up $0.89. Similarly, the price quotation of two shirts for $15 indicates the seller provides two shirts and the buyer gives up $15. Now, suppose the seller wishes to change the price quotation. To illustrate the complexity of pricing, there are several ways to change the above ratio.

Several years ago a shortage of cocoa beans resulted in a shortage of chocolate for candy manufacturers. This shortage of chocolate, as discussed above, also resulted in an increase in the price of chocolate. Prior to this shortage, a multipack of candy bars was priced at 6 for $0.89. The Mars Candy Company changed price by increasing the quantity of money to be given up by the buyer and quoted their candy at 6 for $1.19. Thus, one way to change price is to *change the quantity of money or goods and services given up by the buyer.*

However, the Peter Paul Candy Company changed the price of their multipack by decreasing the number of candy bars in a multipack to five and quoted their candy at 5 for $0.89. Therefore, a second way to change price is to *change the quantity of goods and services provided by the seller.* A seller may change the quantity of goods and services by changing the number of items as did Peter Paul, or the quantity of goods and services may be changed by changing the weight (contents). For example, a box of cereal may be reduced from 16 oz to 14 oz for the same amount of money.

A third way a seller can change price is by *changing the quality of goods and services provided.* If the quantity ratio remains unchanged, but the quality has been decreased, then the price has actually increased because the buyer actually receives less. If quality is raised without changing the quantity ratio, then the price has decreased.

Price can be changed by *changing the premiums or discounts to be applied for quantity variations.* Suppose a seller quotes a 5 percent discount for all quantity purchases of 100 units or more. If each unit sells for $4.00, then anyone who purchases 1 to 99 units pays $4.00 per unit. However, if someone buys 150 units, then he or she actually pays $3.80 per unit. Price can also be changed by offering premiums with purchases, such as trading stamps, toys, glasses. In each case, if the quantity ratio remains constant, a premium serves to reduce the actual price paid, because the buyer receives additional goods or services.

Changing the time and place of transfer of ownership is a fifth way to change price. A new concept in the retailing of furniture provides for a complete inventory to be stored at the retail store, thereby allowing the buyer to take immediate possession instead of waiting several months for delivery. These new furniture stores generally have three different price tags on the furniture. If the buyer wishes to pay cash and take the item home, he or she pays a lower price than the buyer who pays cash and has the store deliver it. The buyer who prefers an installment purchase and delivery pays the highest price. These different price tags explicitly recognize the differences in selling costs and services, and the furniture store, in effect, transfers the delivery costs to the buyer. However, if a buyer can find a similar product choice at another store with the same lowest price tag and free delivery, then the actual price he or she pays is even lower.

Often the actual price is changed if the *place and time of payment are changed*. Being able to purchase a product and having 90 days to pay without interest is an actual reduction in price over paying at the time of purchase. Many retail revolving charge accounts provide for no interest charges if the balance is paid within 30 days. Since money has a time value, permitting customers to have the merchandise for a time without paying for it is a reduction in price. In addition, many business firms give discounts for cash payments made within a short period of time after purchase. For example, if payment is received by the 10th of the month, a 2 percent discount may be allowed.

Changing the acceptable form of payment is a seventh way of changing price. Some stores do not accept checks, other stores operate on a cash only basis, while other stores accept credit charges for regular customers. As indicated above, being able to buy on credit without interest being charged may be a price reduction if the formal ratio does not change because of the additional service. Thus, *price is the amount of money and services (or goods) the buyer exchanges for an assortment of products and services provided by the seller*. The variety of ways to change price makes pricing a very important marketing decision.

IMPORTANCE OF PRICE DECISIONS

Pricing a product or service is one of the most vital decisions made by management. Price is the only marketing strategy variable that generates income. All the other variables in the marketing mix generate costs—advertising, product development, sales promotion, distribution, packaging—all involve expenditures. Often firms determine prices by marking up cost figures supplied by the financial division, and, therefore, are left with only their promotion and distribution decisions. But, the pressures of adapting to today's economic environment are placing additional burdens on the profits of a firm.[3] Six of these environmental pressures are discussed next.

Faster Technological Progress

The revolution in industrial science has several important impacts on pricing. First, accelerating technological progress has reduced the gap between invention and innovation, that is, the time lag between invention and commercialization. Today, it is only a matter of a very few years before a new idea is translated into a commercial product. In fact, many of the inventions for space exploration have already been adapted for industrial and consumer use.

Technological progress also has reduced the average age of products. A few years ago new products were expected to show complete profitability within 30 months after introduction; today, new products must be profitable within 18 months after introduction.[4] Thus, a new product does not have much time to become profitable, and any pricing mistakes made during introduction will make it more difficult to become profitable.

Finally, alternative uses of the buyer's money and time are increasing rapidly. In our affluent and technologically advanced society people are spending more time and money on skiing, weekend trips to resorts, or camping.[5] One result of this intensified competition is that demand is more sensitive to relative prices and shifts in prices.

Proliferation of New Products

Product innovation has also resulted in a literal population explosion of new products. One clear result is that product lines have been widened, and often the distinctiveness of products has been blurred. The widening of the range of choice has blurred market segments, and made it possible for small price differentials to produce large shifts in demand. Thus, the ability to determine prices for an entire product line has become more delicate, more complex, and more important.

Increased Demand for Services

During the 1960s the United States became a service-oriented economy, and the demand for services is still increasing. In virtually all instances this rapid increase in demand has led to rapid increases in prices, because pure services consist mainly of labor, and productivity gains have been low. Such price increases for services (many of which are now regarded as necessities) have led to public concern and to increased governmental activity. Many of these price increases have resulted from a naive and unsophisticated approach to pricing without regard to underlying shifts in demand, the rate that supply can be expanded, prices of available substitutes, consideration of

---

[3] Joel Dean, "The Role of Price in the American Business System," *Pricing: The Critical Decision,* American Management Association Report No. 66, New York, 1961, pp. 5-11.

[4] "New Products: The Push Is on Marketing," *Business Week*, March 4, 1972, pp. 72-77.

[5] For an excellent discussion of the technological environment see David W. Cravens, Gerald E. Hills, and Robert B. Woodruff, *Marketing Decision Making: Concepts and Strategy* (Homewood, Ill.: Richard D. Irwin, 1976), pp. 97-124.

the price-volume relationship, or the availability of future substitutes. In addition, the relative ease with which prices can be increased has not produced the pressures and incentives to innovate technological substitutes.

We have also witnessed an increase in demand for services built into products. These "product-attached" services basically provide additional conveniences for the user, and reduce the effort and time needed to use the products. For example, knit fabrics, self-cleaning ovens, and computer-assisted microwave ovens all are designed to be easier to use than earlier substitute products.

These product-attached services may help protect the product from competition if the price is correct, i.e., if the prices for these services are at levels that people are willing to pay. Basically, these services must provide an economic advantage to the buyer as well as providing a source of income to the seller. And where there are varying sensitivities of demand for these attached services, there are the possibilities of differential prices for different market segments.

Increased Foreign Competition

Recently we have witnessed a substantial increase in the flow of foreign-made products into the United States, due to the liberalization of foreign trade and the reduction of trade barriers, the narrowing of our superiority in productivity, and the emergence of new industrialized nations. However, in addition to these factors, the increase in foreign competition is also due to some incorrect pricing policies and attitudes of American business. In the past, we have often felt that with our superior technology and product quality we had a shelter from foreign competition, and, therefore, additional pricing discretion.

In late 1977, the United States steel industry was provided some help from foreign competition. The government set up a reference price schedule which effectively set lower price limits for foreign steel sold in the United States. Foreign competitors selling their steel products in the United States below these reference prices were faced with the possibility of prosecution. Thus, the inflexible pricing practices of the steel industry have led to the need for government protection from foreign competition.

The Changing Legal Environment

Many of the above environmental changes have caused substantial amounts of public concern, resulting in new legislation and new forms of regulation. Concern with the increased cost of medical services, automobile insurance, legal services, repair services, education, foreign competition, and product proliferation has led to new and proposed legislation at the federal, state, and local levels. Business firms are criticized for putting too much emphasis on competing through advertising, promotion, and product modification and development and not competing on the basis of price. Often these complaints can be reduced to the feeling of paying more and getting less satisfaction for the same products and services. Whether or not all these complaints are justified, this does not remove the implication of more governmental involvement in the conduct of business affairs.

Material Shortages and Inflation

Beginning in the mid-1970s our economy has been beset with recurring and persistent inflation, coupled with periodic shortages of basic materials. Both of these economic factors have placed additional pressures on the costs of producing products and services. In addition, material shortages often have forced firms to reduce their product lines and to reevaluate their efforts to develop new products. Firms have found that across-the-board price increases encounter increased customer resistance, and often exacerbate a tenuous demand relationship. As a result, many firms have rediscovered the need for new approaches to developing pricing strategies.

Summary

The need for correct pricing decisions is becoming ever more important as competition is becoming more intense and public and governmental concern more profound. Due to the increasing rate of technological progress, the time lag between invention and commercial innovation has shortened the average life of new products, and has provided for quicker competitive imitative responses. Technological progress has widened the alternative uses of buyers' money and time and has led to a greater density of substitute products and services. The demand for pure and product-attached services has exceeded the supply of these services, resulting in rapidly increasing prices and increased public concern. Foreign competition has shown that there is demand for lower-priced products, particularly as buyers' priorities shift to leisure amd recreational activities. A major impact of these environmental pressures has been to make product and service pricing more delicate, more complex, more important.

> More and more, today's pricing environment demands better, faster, and more frequent pricing decisions than ever before. It is also forcing companies to take a new look at pricing and its role in an increasingly complex marketing climate.[6]

> Above all, though, an ability to adapt to the new pricing environment will characterize those companies that succeed in competing over the next decade.[7]

"Current Pricing Strategies," which follows, briefly reviews how a number of firms have attempted to cope with today's pricing environment. Implications of these pricing strategies will also be discussed.

CURRENT PRICING STRATEGIES[8]

To cope with these environmental pressures, many sellers are placing relatively greater emphasis on costs, profits, and availability of raw materials, and less emphasis on

---

[6]"Pricing Strategy in an Inflation Economy," *Business Week*, April 6, 1974, p. 43.

[7]"Flexible Pricing, Industry's New Strategy to Hold Market Share Changes the Rules for Economic Decision-Making," *Business Week*, December 12, 1977, p. 78.

[8]This section is adapted from Joseph P. Guiltinan and Kent B. Monroe, "Making Sound Pricing Decisions in the Current Economic Environment," *Executive Scene*, 3 (Fall 1974), 11-16.

building sales and satisfying customers. If anything, there is almost a return to a production or cost orientation, and the decision objectives seem to be (1) reduce the risk of low-margin products, (2) avoid bottlenecks, and (3) improve cash flows.[9] The strategies evolving from these objectives can be categorized as cost-based strategies, or selling strategies.

Cost-based Strategies

Many of the current pricing strategies and the related product decisions have their origins in cost considerations, and, in general, ignore demand factors. Among these strategies are

1 Dropping high-volume, low-margin products
2 Increasing the emphasis on cost-plus pricing
3 Delaying price quotations until after the order is completed
4 Increasing prices "across-the-board" on a firmwide average increase in costs
5 Minimizing new product additions, and adopting skimming or high price policies for new products

These strategies provide strong indication of a sellers' market as well as a retreat from the marketing concept.

Selling Strategies

Other strategy changes affect the role of price in selling activities. Among the changes are

1 Dropping marginal customers or sending them to distributors
2 Assigning more accounts to fewer salespeople and assigning salespeople to larger geographical territories
3 Pricing attendant services separately from the major product, or pricing related products separately
4 Reducing or eliminating cash and quantity discounts
5 Removing the capability of salespeople to quote prices different from the price list, except by prior approval from a price administrator
6 Placing more emphasis on long-term contracts to reduce selling, production scheduling, and inventory costs

IMPLICATIONS OF CURRENT PRICING DECISIONS

Before deciding on a new price policy or strategy, there are a number of factors that should receive careful thought. Management should analyze the effect of proposed

---

[9] For example, see "Pricing Strategy in an Inflation Economy," *Business Week*, April 6, 1974, pp. 43–49; "The Squeeze on Product Mix," *Business Week*, January 5, 1974, pp. 50–55; "Coping with Shortages," *Business Week*, September 14, 1974, pp. 98–100; Daniel Nimer, "Pricing Capital Goods," *Industrial Marketing*, 56 (March 1971), 53–55; Joseph P. Guiltinan, "Risk-Aversive Pricing Policies: Problems and Alternatives," *Journal of Marketing*, 40 (January 1976), 10–15.

prices on demand, costs, competition, and the other elements of the marketing and distribution strategy.

Demand Implications

How the firm's buyers respond to a change in price is a fundamental consideration, for the eventual effect on sales volume and revenue is determined by the degree buyers' demands are sensitive to price. However, price setters often misunderstand or overlook some basic factors. Four such factors are discussed below.

Market versus Firm Elasticity Price elasticity of demand is a measure of the degree buyers are sensitive to price changes. In any market characterized by several functionally substitutable products there are actually two demand schedules: (1) demand for the general product (*primary demand*) and (2) demand for the firm's specific offering (*secondary demand*). Generally, it would be expected that secondary demand would be more responsive to price changes, or more price elastic. Hence, there is the danger that a seller may mistake relatively inelastic market or primary demand as inelastic secondary demand.

The problems encountered by a Texas manufacturer of metal home improvement products illustrates this danger. Usually when new-home construction is slow, the demand for home improvement products is high, and demand is relatively price inelastic. However, in mid-1974, because of increased prices for steel and aluminum, this manufacturer raised prices of the home improvement products. Despite the fact that new housing starts remained low, the firm's sales fell quickly when prices were increased.[10]

Demand for Buyers' Output The market for buyers' products may actually be price-elastic, and a reduction in price in their market would heighten demand for the seller in the first instance. Hence, manufacturers selling to such buyers, and whose product represents a significant portion of these buyers' product costs, may curtail sales opportunities by eliminating discounts or low-margin products.

Likelihood of Competitive Entry An emphasis on high-price strategies may encourage the entry of competitors when entry barriers are minor and when demand is actually price-elastic. Moreover, continued high prices or rapidly increasing prices may force buyers to reconsider their needs and, perhaps, actively seek out competitive substitutes.

Demand Consequences of a Product Line Most firms sell a wide variety of products requiring a variety of differing marketing strategies. Generally, the firm has several product lines, i.e., groups of products that are related because they are used or marketed together. Within a product line there are usually some products that are functional substitutes for each other and some products that are functionally

[10] Joseph P. Guiltinan, "Risk-Aversive Pricing Policies: Problems and Alternatives," *Journal of Marketing*, 40 (January 1976), 12.

complementary. For example, a photographic product line would include cameras, film, flashbulbs, projectors, screens, and other accessories. Because of the demand interrelationships and because there are usually several price-market targets, the product-line pricing problem is one of the major challenges facing a marketing executive.

Compounding the pricing problem is that complementarity is likely to exist even if the products are functionally substitutable. For example, one researcher discovered that a substitute relation existed for the product-line brand versus competitors' brands, but that a complementarity relationship existed between brands within the product line.[11] In addition, by adding new items or reducing certain prices, a firm may increase demand for already existing products. Finally, it is known that the lowest- and highest-priced products are more frequently remembered and perceived, implying a further complementarity.[12] The low-end price usually is the most frequently remembered price and probably has considerable influence on the marginal buyer (the buyer doubtful about buying, but still seriously considering making the purchase). Hence, the lowest-priced product often is used as a traffic-builder. On the other hand, the highest-priced product also is quite visible and possibly through quality connotations may also stimulate demand.

Emphasis on weeding out low-volume and/or low-margin products may have unanticipated consequences depending on the effect a full line has on demand. Even though a particular product's direct profit contribution is small, it may actually "build traffic" for higher-margin products. As indicated above, there is evidence that functionally substitutable products within a product line actually complement sales of each other. Furthermore, prices at the low end (and often the lowest-margin product) positively affect buyers' perceptions of the entire product line. Thus, product-line decisions based only on cost considerations may result in a weakening of demand for the seller's product line.

Cost Implications

It is important for the firm to know the composition and behavior of product costs in order to know when to accelerate cost recovery, how to evaluate a change in selling price, how to profitably segment a market, when to add or delete products from the product line. Even so, *cost plays a limited part in pricing.* Costs indicate whether the product can be made and sold profitably at any price, but not the amount of markup or markdown on cost buyers will accept. Proper costs serve to guide management in the selection of a profitable product mix and in the determination of how much cost can be incurred without sacrificing profit.

Many current pricing responses are cost-oriented and simplistic, and they elevate the role of costs in pricing decisions, while diminishing the role of demand. This emphasis on costs and profit margin may lead to additional crises.

---

[11] Glen Urban, "A Mathematical Modeling Approach to Product Line Decisions," *Journal of Marketing Research*, 6 (February 1969), 40–47.

[12] Alfred Oxenfeldt, "Product Line Pricing," *Harvard Business Review*, 44 (July–August 1966), 135–143.

Cost-Plus Pricing Adopting escalator pricing or other cost-plus pricing methods ignores the consideration of price-volume-cost relationships. The "experience curve" indicates that as cumulative production volume doubles, costs decline by a constant, predictable percentage.[13] One way to build volume is to reduce price and place managerial pressure on forcing costs down. Thus, volume-oriented pricing may lead to additional reductions in cost and the maintenance or actual increase in profit margins.[14]

Maximizing Margins Unbundling or eliminating low-margin products should be considered in terms of its incremental effect on costs. Many of the costs associated with a product or service are joint or common costs and these costs will remain when the product or service is deleted. Hence, the only costs relevant for the deletion decision are those costs that are directly traceable to the product or service that may be deleted. Unless the deletion decision permits increased production of other products, the net change in profit contribution may be negative.

Pricing with Scarce Resources When a critical production resource is in short supply, the firm must allocate the resource across its various products. Paying strict attention to profit margins may lead to a less profitable position, because high-margin items may require disproportionate amounts of the critical resource, and production capacity will be underutilized. In such circumstances, pricing should encourage sales of those products which *maximize the contribution per resource unit* used. Often, low-margin products may achieve this objective better than high-margin products.

Marketing and Distribution Strategy Implications

Rarely does the pricing decision occur in isolation. Generally, price interacts with other elements of the marketing strategy, and, therefore, several additional implications are important.

The Product Life Cycle As products go through the product life cycle of introduction, growth, maturity, and decline, the role of price and promotion varies to meet buyer, competitive, and technological changes. As the product enters the maturity stage, and competitive price differences become important to buyers, a seller's discount and service policies become important marketing strategies. Routinely eliminating or cutting back of discounts or services without regard to the product's life cycle stage could be detrimental to the seller. Further, eliminating discounts could produce negative distributor reactions and cost the manufacturer a portion of the reseller's support.

Sales Force Management Centralizing pricing authority and eliminating a salesperson's ability to quote prices consistent with local competition reduces the flexibility of the sales force. Further, as prices are increased and discounts and services

[13]*Perspectives on Experience* (Boston: Boston Consulting Group, 1970).
[14]See "The Semiconductor Becomes a New Marketing Force," *Business Week*, August 24, 1974, pp. 34-42.

curtailed, the salesperson must smooth over adverse reactions while explaining product shortages and order backlogs. In effect, the sales job is significantly altered and may lead to increased sales force dissatisfaction and personnel turnover.

SUMMARY

Pricing is one of the most important marketing decision variables. It is also a very complex and difficult decision. Traditionally, business firms and educators have paid relatively little attention to developing new approaches to making price decisions. Although many of the environmental pressures discussed in this chapter were discussed by Joel Dean and others as early as 1960, few people paid much concern to their arguments. Yet, in the 1970s the full effect of these environmental pressures became apparent and firms were ill-prepared to develop new pricing strategies.

However, business leaders and educators have begun to search for new approaches to solving pricing problems. Some firms have been quite successful in developing new strategies and in organizing for the price decision. Unfortunately, other firms have imitated these successful strategies and, often, have discovered that the overall situation is not similar; thus some undesired consequences occurred.

This chapter has reviewed many of the contemporary environmental pressures and current pricing practices that have been tried to cope with these pressures. It has been suggested that many of the current pricing practices need to be based on additional analyses, particularly in the development of cost and demand information. The next seven chapters develop approaches to obtaining better cost and demand information.

DISCUSSION QUESTIONS

1 The chapter cites two reasons for the lack of new approaches to pricing. Can you think of any additional reasons why pricing has been a neglected marketing decision variable?

2 The chapter provides the example of two candy companies changing the price of the multipack of candy bars. Assume that the strategy used by Mars resulted in a 50 percent decrease in volume during the first year after the price change, but that during the second year volume was down only 30 percent from predecision levels. Assume further that late in the second year chocolate is again scarce and expensive. If you were the price administrator for Mars, what pricing alternatives would you consider?

3 Assume for the situation described in Question 2, that you are the price administrator for Peter Paul. During the first 2 years after the price change described in the chapter, your multipack candy volume remained at predecision levels. Now you are faced with the same scarcity of chocolate. What pricing alternatives would you consider? Are any of these alternatives different from those listed in Question 2? Why, or why not?

4 Before making a final decision for either Mars or Peter Paul as described in Questions 2 and 3, what additional information would you want? If the information were available, how would you use it?

5 What do you think should be the role of a price administrator? What type of education or training should a price administrator have?
6 In Question 5, would your answer be different if you assumed the price administrator worked for a retail store? Why, or why not?

SUGGESTED READINGS

"Coping with Shortages," *Business Week*, September 14, 1974, pp. 98–100.

Dean, Joel: "The Role of Price in the American Business System," *Pricing: The Critical Decision*, American Management Association Report No. 66, New York, 1961, pp. 5–11.

"Flexible Pricing," *Business Week*, December 12, 1977, pp. 78–88.

Guiltinan, Joseph P.: "Risk-Aversive Pricing Policies: Problems and Alternatives," *Journal of Marketing*, 40 (January 1976), 10–15.

———, and Kent B. Monroe: "Making Sound Pricing Decisions in the Current Economic Environment," *Executive Scene*, 3 (Fall 1974), 11–16.

Oxenfeldt, Alfred: "A Decision-Making Structure for Price Decisions," *Journal of Marketing*, 37 (January 1973), 48–53.

"Pricing Strategy in an Inflation Economy," *Business Week*, April 6, 1974, pp. 43–49.

Section Two

Prices and Demand

One of the most important cornerstones of price determination is demand. In particular, the volume of a product that buyers are willing to buy at a specific price is that product's demand. To be able to analyze alternative pricing decisions, the price setter must estimate the amount that will be demanded at each alternative price. These volume estimates can then be used to provide both a revenue estimate and a cost estimate for each price alternative.

The discipline of economics provides the basic theory of how prices should be set. However, despite the analytical pricing solutions provided by economic theory, the theory has limited practicality. Most of the limitations of economic theory arise because of the many necessary assumptions that do not represent the real world. Nevertheless, economic theory does provide some important analytical concepts for practical pricing decisions.

There are two chapters in this section. Chapter 2 provides a brief description of the traditional economic theory of price determination. In the chapter, a number of concepts are introduced that are used throughout the book: revenue, elasticity, marginal revenue, and marginal costs. These concepts are important in any discussion on price.

One of the most important factors in the price-demand relationship is how buyers use price in their purchase decision processes. As Chap. 3 demonstrates, the behavioral dimension of price is complex and different than assumed in the economic theory of price determination. Many of the behavioral principles discussed in Chap. 3 are used in the decision chapters of Section 4.

Chapter 2

The Economics of Price Determination

In the area of pricing there is a large body of literature describing how business organizations should determine their selling prices. This literature has a rich tradition and, although theoretical in nature, provides some important analytical concepts for practical pricing decisions. This chapter has two purposes: (1) to summarize the economic theory of price determination and (2) to delineate useful concepts for actual pricing decisions.

PRICE DETERMINATION IN THEORY

In our economy, pricing decisions are made by a complex of private and public institutions. Many of these decisions are made within large, multifaceted, and complex business organizations. The way these pricing decisions are made is considerably different from the decision process described by economic theory. The essentials of the economic theory of the firm tell us how a firm will decide which production technique (or method) to use and what the particular input proportions will be to produce the desired product. Given its production method and its decision as to what to produce, the firm seeks to minimize its input costs. The firm then decides the quantities of each product it plans to sell and the price per unit at which it hopes to sell each product. The input purchase plans and the sales plans the firm will choose will depend on

1 The objectives of the firm
2 The time span of the plans

Economic analysis uses three time periods: (1) market period—plans cannot be changed, (2) short run—some input plans can be varied, and (3) long run—all input plans are variable. The objective of the firm is assumed to be profit maximization.

The Profit-Maximizing Firm

Figure 2-1 illustrates how a firm interested in maximizing profits determines how much to produce in the short run when price is constant. Since price is constant the total revenue curve must go through the origin, but being in the short run some costs are fixed, and the total cost curve does not go through the origin. Since the firm is assumed to know its costs for each possible output level, determining how much to produce is not a difficult task. As long as revenue received from the sale of an additional unit of output (marginal revenue) is greater than the additional costs of producing and selling that unit (marginal cost), the firm will expand output. Since price is constant, marginal revenue equals price, and the firm will produce at the quantity level where marginal revenue (price) equals marginal cost. (In economic analysis marginal is defined as the change resulting from a unit increase in effort.) Thus, in Fig. 2-1 maximum profits are where total revenue minus total cost is the greatest, or where the slope of the total revenue curve equals the slope of the total cost curve.

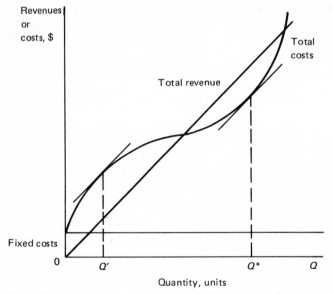

Figure 2-1 Output determination for a profit-maximizing firm—short run (constant prices).

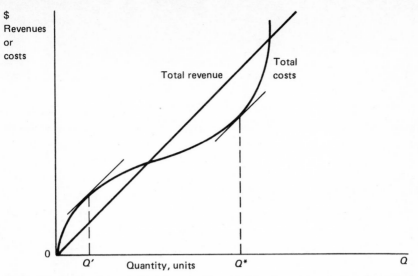

Figure 2-2 Output determination for a profit-maximizing firm—long run (constant prices).

[In quantitative analysis slope measures the amount of change in the dependent variable (revenue or costs) produced by a unit increase in the independent variable (quantity).] Note that for profits to be at a maximum, the total cost curve must lie below the total revenue curve. Thus, maximum profits can be obtained when the quantity produced is Q^* units. Whereas, at Q' units losses are at a maximum. Should the firm produce more units than Q^*, its total cost curve is increasing faster than the total revenue curve, implying that marginal costs are now greater than marginal revenues.

As shown in Fig. 2-2, the same conditions hold in the long run, but now the total cost curve goes through the origin, as does the total revenue curve. Maximum profits are still where marginal revenue equals marginal cost.

Figure 2-3 shows the situation when prices vary. Now the firm determines its output on the basis of where marginal revenue equals marginal cost, but the price it receives for its output is determined by the demand curve. That is, price is set at the level where the firm can sell its entire output. The long-run solution as shown in Fig. 2-4 is similar to the constant-price situation except when prices may vary the total revenue curve is not linear.

Challenges to the Profit Maximization Objective

The assumption of profit maximization has been challenged for two basic reasons.[1] First, profits do not appear to be the only objective of the firm. And second, when concerned about profits, does the firm really attempt to maximize?

---

[1] Richard M. Cyert and James G. March, *A Behavioral Theory of the Firm* (Englewood Cliffs, N.J.: Prentice-Hall, 1963), p. 8.

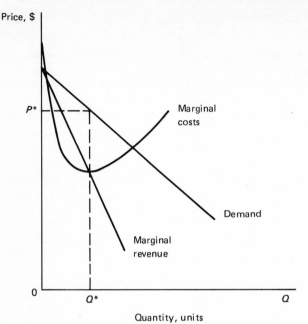

Figure 2-3 Output determination for a profit-maximizing firm—short run (varying prices).

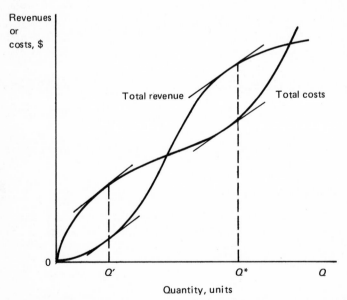

Figure 2-4 Output determination for a profit-maximizing firm—long run (varying prices).

It can be argued that a business firm is a complex organization and comprises individuals with a set of individual motives. That is, some people are working solely for the money they may earn, others are also concerned with the social relationships that evolve among themselves, others are interested in obtaining greater amounts of authority and responsibility. In addition, the participants within the organization are also probably very much concerned with long-run survival, and, hence would be interested in maintaining a given level of security for the organization (i.e., the chances the organization will still exist in the indefinite future). Generally, the key to long-run survival is the ability of the organization to adapt to environmental pressures and constraints. Hence, the actual objectives of the business organization (or for any organization) are determined through an interaction of a wide range of personal objectives and pressures and constraints from the organization's external environment.

The second challenge to the profit maximization assumption accepts the importance of profits, but questions whether firms really do attempt to maximize profits. It suggests instead that the firm's real goal is to attain satisfactory profits. *Satisfactory* profits represent a level of aspiration that the firm uses to assess alternative strategies. In essence, if a strategy is predicted to generate a minimal acceptable level of profits, then the strategy is good enough and is implemented.

ECONOMIC THEORY OF BUYER BEHAVIOR

We now turn to discussing how it is believed price affects demand. We begin first with the economic theory of buyer behavior which provides the framework for most of the social criticisms of pricing practices by manufacturers and retailers. (In Chap. 3 we will enlarge this theory by introducing the results of recent behavioral research on the influence of price on buyer behavior.) Finally, we will discuss various measures of demand sensitivity to price and methods of estimating these measures.

Essentially, the buyer has two decisions to make: (1) what products should be purchased and (2) how much should be purchased of each product. The quantity of each product to buy depends on (1) the price of that product, (2) the prices of all other products, (3) the income of the buyer, and (4) the buyer's tastes and preferences. Given the prices of all products, and given their income, buyers make their purchases according to their own tastes and preferences. The consumer is assumed to be rational and to choose among alternative products so as to maximize satisfaction (utility).

Assumptions

As indicated above, utility means want-satisfying power, resides in the mind of the buyer, and is common to all products and services. Utility is subjective, not objective, and it is assumed that a choice of product A over product B means the buyer perceives product A as having more utility than product B. The theory of buyer behavior based on the assumption of rational behavior and utility maximization involves several additional assumptions about the buyer.

1   The buyer calculates deliberately and chooses consistently.

2   Deliberate choice rules out habit or impulse buying.

3   Consistent choice rules out vacillating and erratic behavior; the buyer acts predictably.

4   If the buyer prefers product A to product B, and prefers product B to product C, then consistency requires that he or she prefers A to C.

5   Within these conditions of behavior, the buyer chooses so as to maximize utility.

6   To maximize utility the buyer knows all alternatives and is not ignorant about any aspect of his or her purchase.

7   Because of this perfect knowledge, there never is a gap between the satisfaction the buyer expects from a purchase and the actual fulfillment realized from the purchase.

8   Want and subjective utilities are not influenced by prices, i.e., higher-priced products do not provide additional utility simply because of their higher prices.

9   Finally, it is assumed that total utility increases at a diminishing rate as more of a product or service is acquired.

Solution

The solution to the question of how much of a product a buyer will purchase is illustrated in Fig. 2-5. The total utility curve illustrates the assumption of diminishing marginal returns to utility as quantity purchased increases. The quantity purchased is where total utility is maximized. An alternative approach to the quantity decision is to use marginal utility. Recall that marginal means the change resulting from a unit increase in effort; hence, marginal utility is the change in total utility due to one additional unit purchased. In Fig. 2-5 the marginal utility curve indicates that when total utility is maximized, marginal utility is zero.

Since prices are given to buyers (i.e., buyers do not negotiate price with the seller) and they have a fixed income, how do buyers determine the total assortment they will

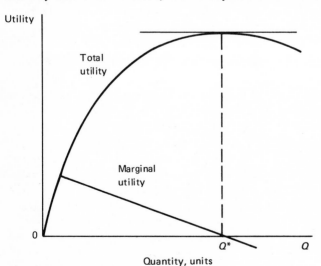

Figure 2-5   Quantity purchase determination by a utility-maximizing buyer.

purchase from the wide array of alternatives available to them? Since it is assumed that prices serve only to indicate the amount of money buyers must give up to acquire a product, how much to acquire of a particular product depends on the relation between the marginal utility of acquiring an additional unit and the price of that additional unit. Further, the assumption of diminishing marginal utility implies that buyers are capable of ranking all alternatives in terms of increasing preference, and that they purchase first the most preferred product. Buyers will continue to buy additional units of the preferred product until the marginal utility of acquiring an additional unit becomes equal to or less than the marginal utility realized from purchasing a unit of the second most preferred product. This decision process continues until the amount allocated for the shopping trip has been exhausted. The result of this decision process indicates that the marginal utility obtained from the last penny spent on product A must equal the marginal utility obtained from the last penny spent on product B and so on for all products purchased. The mathematical solution to the consumer's decision problem is

$$\frac{MU_A}{P_A} = \frac{MU_B}{P_B} = \ldots = \frac{MU_N}{P_N} \qquad\qquad (2\text{-}1)$$

where MU is marginal utility and P is price.

To summarize, in economic theory, price is assumed to influence buyer choice because price serves as an indicator of product cost. Assuming the buyer has perfect information concerning prices and want satisfaction of comparable product alternatives, he or she can determine a product mix that maximizes satisfaction within a given budget constraint. Further, if the buyer does not act to maximize want satisfaction, he or she is acting irrationally. The implication is that buyers should choose the low-price alternative if there is a choice between at least two differentially priced, but similar products.

However, buyers really do not have complete and accurate information about the utility received from a set of products nor the prices of these products. Somehow buyers do acquire sufficient information about products and about the satisfaction received from these products to decide which products to purchase with a given budget. Lacking complete information about the utility associated with the product, the buyer assesses the product on the basis of known information. Generally, one piece of information available to the buyer is the product's price. Other pieces of information about anticipated purchases are not always known, or are known less frequently than price, and the buyer cannot be sure how reliable and how complete this information is. And information not always available may introduce uncertainty about the buyer's ability to predict correctly the want satisfaction available through purchasing the product. *Hence, buyers may use price both as an indicator of product cost as well as an indicator of product quality (want satisfaction attributes).* This attractiveness attribute of a product's price will be amplified in Chap. 3. We now turn to discussing some concepts useful when analyzing price alternatives.

SOME USEFUL CONCEPTS FROM PRICE THEORY

Demand Elasticity

During our discussions in Chap. 1 and this chapter we have occasionally referred to the concept of demand sensitivity. That is, we have been concerned with the responsiveness of demand to price changes. *Price elasticity of demand* measures the responsiveness of the quantity demanded for a product or service to a change in the price of the product or service. Specifically, price elasticity of demand is defined as the rate of percentage change in quantity demanded relative to the percentage change in price.

$$E_d = \frac{(Q_1 - Q_2)/Q_1}{(P_1 - P_2)/P_1} = \frac{\Delta Q/Q_1}{\Delta P/P_1} = \left(\frac{\Delta Q}{\Delta P}\right) \times \left(\frac{P_1}{Q_1}\right) \tag{2-2}$$

where E_d = price elasticity of demand
 ΔQ = quantity change in demand
 ΔP = change in price
 Q_1, P_1 = original quantity demanded and price, respectively

If it is assumed that quantity demanded falls as price increases, then $E_d < 0$; if there is a positive relation between demand and price change then $E_d > 0$, that is, demand increases as price is increased. For the generally assumed case of a downward sloping demand curve, Fig. 2-6 depicts the concept of price elasticity.

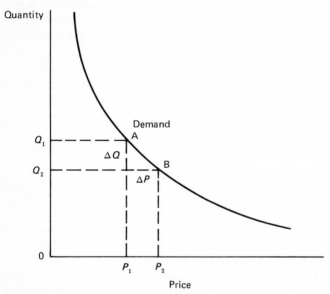

Figure 2-6 Concept of price elasticity. (NOTE: The reader will note that traditional economic texts place price on the vertical axis and quantity on the horizontal axis. However, assuming that quantity demanded depends on price, then the correct procedure is to place price on the horizontal axis and quantity on the vertical axis. We will follow the more correct procedure throughout this book.)

To illustrate the concept of price elasticity, assume that the price of a video tape recorder was $1,200, and annual sales at this price were 5,000 units. In January 1978, the price was dropped to $1,050 and annual sales were 5,500 units. In January 1979, the price again was dropped to $990, and annual sales were 10,000 units. Using Eq. (2-2) we may compute the price elasticity for each of these price changes. For these price changes, we have

$$E_{d1} = \frac{(5,000 - 5,500)/5,000}{(\$1,200 - \$1,050)/\$1,200} = \frac{-500/5,000}{\$150/\$1,200} = \frac{-500}{\$150} \times \frac{\$1,200}{5,000} = -0.80$$

$$E_{d2} = \frac{(5,500 - 10,000)/5,500}{(\$1,050 - \$990)/\$1,050} = \frac{-4,500/5,500}{\$60/\$1,050} = \frac{-4,500}{\$60} \times \frac{\$1,050}{5,500} = -14.3$$

With the exception of the special kinds of demand curves shown in Fig. 2-7 the price elasticity of demand is not the same at all prices; nor is the elasticity of demand in any particular range of prices the same as the slope of the demand curve for it over that range of prices. In Fig. 2-6 the slope of the demand curve between points A and B is $\Delta Q/\Delta P$, which is not the formula for the elasticity given in Eq. (2-2). Secondly, the higher the price the product is sold at, the smaller will be the quantity demanded, and the greater will be the value of E_d, i.e., E_d approaches zero in value. Furthermore, if the value of the price elasticity of demand is less than -1, that is, $-\infty \leqslant E_d < -1$, then demand is elastic and sellers' revenues will rise if there is a small reduction in price. Table 2-1 summarizes the elasticity measures and their relationships to total revenue.

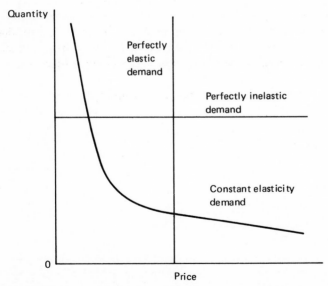

Figure 2-7   Demand curves for special cases.

Table 2-1 Relationship of Price Elasticity of Demand to Total Revenues

Value of E_d	Description	Effect on total revenues of	
		Small price rise	Small price reduction
0	Perfectly inelastic	Increase	Decrease
$-1 < E_d < 0$	Inelastic	Increase	Decrease
-1	Unitary elastic	No change	No change
$-\infty < E_d < -1$	Elastic	Decrease	Increase
$-\infty$	Perfectly elastic	Decrease	Increase

Often other measures of demand sensitivity are used to explore the implications of change. *Income elasticity of demand* is the responsiveness of the quantity demanded of a product or service to a change in personal income.

$$E_I = (\frac{\Delta Q}{\Delta I}) \times (\frac{I}{Q}) \qquad (2\text{-}3)$$

where E_I = income elasticity of demand
ΔQ = quantity change in demand
ΔI = change in personal income

If E_I is negative, this implies that the product is an inferior good. That is, as income goes up fewer units are demanded. For example, as income goes up, some households may switch some of their meat purchases from hamburger to steak and actually consume less hamburger. If E_I is positive then demand increases as income increases, but there are two different possibilities. If $0 < E_I < 1$ then the product becomes less important in the households' consumptions plans even though total expenditures increase, e.g., necessities such as food and clothing tend to comprise less of the family's total expenditures as income increases. Finally, if E_I is greater than 1, then the product becomes more important as income increases, e.g., leisure and recreational activities.

A third measure of demand sensitivity is *cross price elasticity of demand* that measures the responsiveness of demand for a product, Q_A, to a change in price of another product, Q_B.

$$E_c = (\frac{\Delta Q_A}{\Delta P_B}) \times (\frac{P_B}{Q_A}) \qquad (2\text{-}4)$$

where E_c = cross price elasticity of demand
ΔQ_A = change in demand for product A
ΔP_B = change in price for product B

If E_c is negative, then in general the two products are complementary; if E_c is positive, then in general the two products are substitutes. For example, razor blades are complements to razors, but different brands of razors are substitute products. Cross price elasticity is often used as a measure of the effects of competitive price changes.

For example, assume the price of a Kodak instant camera is $45.00, and a comparable Polaroid is $49.00. Further, assume the quantity demanded for the Kodak camera is 50,000 units, and the quantity demanded for the Polaroid is 100,000 units. Suppose Kodak reduces the price of its camera to $42.00. The quantity demanded for the Kodak camera increases to 60,000 units, and the quantity demanded for the Polaroid decreases to 95,000. (Because of overall increases in market demand for instant cameras, the demand increase experienced by Kodak is not all at the expense of demand for the Polaroid camera.)

The cross price elasticity of demand for the Polaroid camera can be computed using Eq. (2-4).

$$E_c = \frac{-5,000}{-\$3} \times \frac{\$45}{100,000} = 0.75$$

Revenue Concepts

As mentioned in our discussion of price elasticity of demand, there is a relationship between sellers' revenues and the elasticity of demand for their products. To establish this relationship we need to define the concepts of total revenue, average revenue, and marginal revenue. *Total revenue* is the total amount spent by buyers for the product or service.

$$TR = PQ \tag{2-5}$$

where TR = total revenue
       P = price of the product
       Q = quantity demanded at price P

Average revenue is the total outlay by buyers divided by the number of units sold, or the price of the product.

$$AR = \frac{TR}{Q} = P \tag{2-6}$$

where AR is average revenue. The average revenue curve and the demand curve are the same. *Marginal revenue* refers to the total change in total revenue resulting from a change in sales volume.

$$MR = \frac{\Delta TR}{\Delta Q} \tag{2-7}$$

Price and Marginal Revenue The normal, downward sloping demand curve reveals that to sell an additional unit of output, price must fall. The change in total revenue—marginal revenue—is the result of two forces: (1) the revenue derived from the additional unit sold, which is equal to the new price; and (2) the loss in revenue which results from marking down all prior salable units to the new price. If force (1) is greater than force (2), total revenue will increase; and total revenue will increase only if marginal revenue is positive. This relationship between total revenue and marginal revenue can be illustrated using Fig. 2-8. As shown in Fig. 2-8, $\Delta Q = Q_2 - Q_1$ and $\Delta P = P_1 - P_2$ where P_1 is the initial price, P_2 is the new (lower) price, Q_1 is the (smaller) sales quantity at P_1, Q_2 is the (larger) sales quantity at price P_2, ΔQ is the unit increase in sales as price falls from P_1 to P_2, and ΔP is the decrease in price necessary to increase sales by ΔQ. It can be shown that marginal revenue is

$$\text{MR} = P_2 - Q_1 \Delta P \tag{2-8}$$

Thus we see that MR is positive only when the revenue generated from the new price is greater than the loss in revenue resulting from marking down all previously salable items.

Price Elasticity and Marginal Revenue It can also be shown that the relation between marginal revenue and price elasticity of demand is given by

$$\text{MR} = P_1 \left(1 + \frac{1}{E_d}\right) = P_1 \left(\frac{E_d + 1}{E_d}\right) \tag{2-9}$$

This relation between marginal revenue and price elasticity of demand has been used by the United States Postal Service to justify its postage rates. When applied to rate setting, this relation has been called the *inverse elasticity rule*. Historically, first class mail has been the most price inelastic class of mail, with estimates ranging from -0.1 to

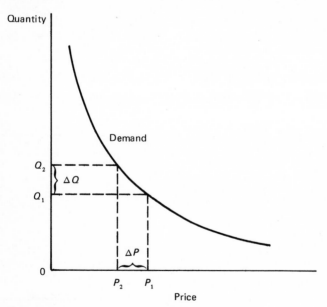

Figure 2-8 Price–quantity demanded relationship.

-0.3. Since all classes of mail have been price inelastic, then price increases will result in increases in total revenue (positive marginal revenue) as shown in Table 2-2. Because first class mail is the most inelastic then a $0.03 price increase per ounce will produce most of the needed new mail revenues. As a result, the postage rates for other classes of mail have not had as large a percentage increase as first class mail during the 1970s.

Thus, marginal revenue varies with price and with the price elasticity of demand. Table 2-2 shows the relationship between revenues and price elasticity for both the negative price-demand relationship and the implied positive price-demand relationship from the price-quality studies discussed in Chap. 3.

As Table 2-2 indicates for the generally assumed negative price-quantity demanded relationship, revenues will increase if price is increased and demand is price inelastic; and revenues will fall if price is increased and demand is price elastic. But, if buyers use price to impute quality into the product or service and thereby perceive a higher-priced item as more attractive, a positive price–quantity demanded relationship ensues and any increase in price will increase revenues. To be able to determine the effects on demand from changing price requires a method of estimating the price-volume relationship. Some commonly used methods of demand estimation are discussed next.

METHODS OF ESTIMATING DEMAND

Throughout this chapter we have stressed the importance of demand in determining the price of a product or service. Thus, there has been an implicit assumption that there are ways to determine the responsiveness of demand to alternative prices. As we have indicated the measure of the responsiveness of demand to price changes is the price elasticity measure. Assuming the key to optimal price decisions is the determination of price elasticities, how can one go about determining the price elasticity of demand?

Surveys

The basic objectives of a survey approach to demand estimation is to administer a questionnaire either through personal interviews, telephone interviews, or through the mail to elicit facts and opinions from respondents relating either to a prediction of the quantity they would be willing to pay at various prices, or an indication of their intent to buy in the near future. In a brand preference study housewives were asked to indi-

Table 2-2 Relationship between Revenues and Price Elasticity

Price-demand relationship	Value of E_d	Marginal revenue when price increases	Marginal revenue when price decreases
Negative	$-1 < E_d < 0$	Positive	Negative
Negative	$E_d = -1$	Zero	Zero
Negative	$-\infty < E_d < -1$	Negative	Positive
Positive	$0 < E_d < 1$	Positive	Negative
Positive	$E_d = 1$	Positive	Negative
Positive	$1 < E_d < \infty$	Positive	Negative

cate the amounts they would be willing to buy at selected prices.[2] It was concluded from the responses that baking powder was price inelastic and that higher prices could be charged. Analyzing a set of consumer questionnaires, another company determined that their product was primarily being purchased by high-income households, implying that sales could be increased at lower prices (demand was elastic).[3] This conclusion was verified when prices were lowered. Another approach would be to adapt the methodology of Gabor and Granger[4] and ask consumers to indicate price ranges they would be willing to pay for a given product. Comparing the acceptable price ranges with the actual price last paid provides an indication of willingness to pay higher or lower prices, and an estimation of the size of these price market segments. As indicated in Chap. 9, the Gabor and Granger approach is particularly suitable for estimating new-product demand.

A different approach is used by the Survey Research Center at the University of Michigan. Periodically, they ask a representative sample of consumers about their attitudes toward spending, saving, credit, prices, and other economic matters. From this information, they develop an index of consumer sentiment toward the economy in general, and a measure of intentions to buy certain types of consumer durables. Although there is some controversy among some economists about the predictive accuracy of the intentions approach, the intentions survey does provide a gross estimate of demand for automobiles and other durables for a number of months ahead. It does provide information useful in predicting consumers' reactions to changes in the price level, but it does not provide information on specific price elasticities for specific products.

Laboratory Experimentation

Most of the research reported in the next chapter on buyers' perception of prices was the result of controlled manipulations of prices and price situations. The primary advantage of such approaches is the ability to isolate and control various market factors that affect demand and then to observe buyers' reactions to changes in one or more of these factors. The disadvantage is that the laboratory is not the natural shopping environment and thus whether such findings from a laboratory study could be replicated in a natural environment is a serious question.

Pessemier[5] has developed a technique for introducing some realism into laboratory experiments by having respondents go on simulated shopping trips. Each participant was told how much money he or she had to spend, the assortment of goods available in each product category, and the price of each choice. Using a questionnaire that provided for several alternative pricing situations, Pessemier was able to determine price

---

[2] Edward R. Hawkins, "Methods of Estimating Demand," *Journal of Marketing*, 21 (April 1957), 428–438.

[3] Ibid., p. 430.

[4] Andre Gabor and Clive Granger, "Price as an Indicator of Quality, Report on an Enquiry," *Economica*, 46 (February 1966), 43–70.

[5] Edgar M. Pessemier, *Experimental Methods for Analyzing Demand for Branded Consumer Goods with Applications to Problems of Marketing Strategy* (Pullman, Wash.: Washington State University Press, 1963).

elasticities and the effects of price changes on brand shares. In another study, subjects were confronted with an actual array of products and were asked to purchase a brand from each category.[6]

Field Experimentation

A more logical way to measure demand responsiveness to price and price changes is to manipulate store prices and observe the effect on sales. Although reactions to price are observed in the natural environment, the lack of control over other factors that affect sales—advertising, competition, weather—makes it difficult to know exactly whether the changes in responses are the result of the price manipulations. However, the most serious problems associated with field experimentation are the time and expense required to change prices and monitor sales for the particular items. Because of these factors it is difficult to obtain estimates for more than a few products at a time. Careful application of experimental research designs, sampling methods, and statistical tests to evaluate the results will help to control and measure the effects due to extraneous factors. Nevin[7] has demonstrated a way to use field experimentation to validate laboratory experiments for estimating consumer demand.

Statistical Methods

Recently attempts have been made to estimate the price-quantity relations by deriving a set of demand equations from a number of observations. Some *econometric* attempts have developed a single equation that relates demand for an item to several variables such as price, income, store location, and consumer density. Collecting data on the dependent variable, demand, and on the independent variables simultaneously, an attempt is made to derive an equation that measures the relationships between the independent and dependent variables. Often, however, there are several variables that may affect demand, but which are themselves affected by demand, and a single-equation model would produce biased estimates. To overcome this estimation problem, a multiple-equation model is developed. For either model, once the parameters are estimated from empirical data, it is possible to predict the effect on demand of a change in price or any other independent variable.[8]

An Operational Approach[9]

Each of the above techniques for estimating demand relies on objective statistical data. Primarily, these statistical approaches are historical in that they rely on data collected

[6]Edgar M. Pessemier and Richard D. Teach, "Pricing Experiments, Scaling Consumer Preferences, and Predicting Purchase Behavior," in *Proceedings*, Fall Conference, American Marketing Association, Chicago, 1966, pp. 541-557.

[7]John R. Nevin, "Laboratory Experiments for Estimating Consumer Demand: A Validation Study," *Journal of Marketing Research*, 11 (August 1974), 261-268.

[8]For a good review of the application of econometric methods to marketing see Leonard J. Parsons and Randall L. Schultz, *Marketing Models and Econometric Research* (New York: North-Holland Publishing Co., 1976).

[9]Bill R. Darden, "An Operational Approach to Product Pricing," *Journal of Marketing*, 32 (April 1969), 29-33.

before the pricing decision is to be made. Moreover, these statistical approaches do not provide for executive experience, intuition, or judgment, nor do they consider future buyer and competitor responses to prices. However, the price setter must consider the role of the other variables of the marketing plan; he or she must consider competitor reactions; and he or she must use his or her experience and judgment to develop operational hypotheses about market reaction to price changes.

To formalize the executive's judgment, the operational approach asks the price setter to estimate for each price alternative three possible levels of demand.

Estimate 1: A very high estimate such that there is only 1 chance in 100 that a larger quantity will be sold—Q_o, the *optimistic estimate*.

Estimate 2: A very low estimate such that there is only 1 chance in 100 that a smaller quantity will be sold—Q_p, the *pessimistic estimate*.

Estimate 3: An estimate that reflects the pricer's judgment of the *quantity most likely to be sold*—Q_m.

Given these three estimates, the "largest expected volume," or the volume that has a 50-50 chance of being reached can be computed.

$$Q_e = \frac{Q_p + 4Q_m + Q_o}{6} \qquad\qquad (2\text{-}10)$$

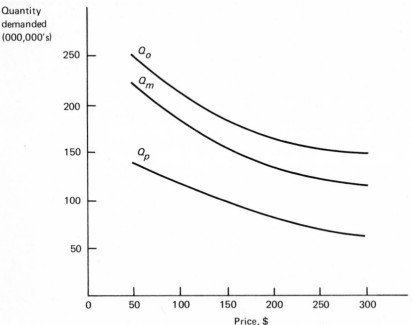

Figure 2-9 Subjectively estimated demand curves.

And the estimate of the volume variance is

$$\sigma^2 = \frac{(Q_o - Q_p)^2}{36} \tag{2-11}$$

By repeating this estimate procedure for each price alternative, three demand curves can be obtained—D_o, optimistic demand; D_m, medium demand; and D_p, pessimistic demand (see Fig. 2-9). These estimates can then be incorporated into the analysis for making the price decision. Applications of this operational approach will be discussed in later chapters.

SUMMARY

This chapter has briefly reviewed the economic theory of price determination and has discussed some economic concepts useful for analyzing pricing alternatives. The reader should remember that these concepts, in and of themselves, have limited usefulness for price determination. However, when these concepts are extracted from their theoretical domain and applied within the constraints of reality, they are important analytical tools. The concepts of elasticity and marginal revenue are very important, but they must be applied to decisions affecting the future, where uncertainty prevails. Hence, it is vitally important to provide the price setter with useful analytical techniques, techniques that permit executive judgment and experience to systematically become a part of the decision technique. Future chapters will clarify and apply this important point.

DISCUSSION QUESTIONS

1 If the business firm does not seek to maximize profits, what are some alternative objectives?
2 For each profit objective listed in Question 1, what do you think is the role of price?
3 Assume a firm makes three products A, B, C. Assume the profit equation for this firm is given by

$$\text{Profits} = (P_A - c_A)Q_A + (P_B - c_B)Q_B + (P_C - c_C)Q_C - f$$

where P is price, c is variable cost, Q is volume sold at price P, and f is fixed costs.
   If the firm wishes to increase profits, what things in the equation can it attempt to change? List as many changes as possible.
4 A manufacturer of video-TV games sold 50,000 units in 1978 at a price of $50 each. In 1979, the price was reduced to $39, and 70,000 units were sold. In 1980, the price was reduced to $25 and 120,000 units were sold. Calculate the historical price elasticity of demand for each price change.

5 What do you think happened to the cost of producing a unit of the video-TV game of Question 4 when annual production increased from 50,000 units in 1978 to 120,000 in 1980? Explain your reasoning.
6 Can you think of some products for which demand would be
   a Income elastic
   b Income inelastic
7 In Question 6, what would be the role of price for a product which is income elastic?

SUGGESTED READINGS

Abrams, Jack: "A New Method for Testing Pricing Decisions," *Journal of Marketing*, 28 (July 1964), 6-9.

Bell, Carolyn Shaw: "On the Elasticity of Demand at Retail," *The American Journal of Economics and Sociology*, 20 (October 1960), 63-72.

Cyert, Richard, and Charles Hedrick: "Theory of the Firm: Past, Present, and Future; an Interpretation," *Journal of Economic Literature*, 10 (June 1972), 398-412.

Dalrymple, Douglas J.: "Estimating Price Elasticity," *Journal of Retailing*, 42 (Winter 1966-1967), 1-4.

Darden, Bill R.: "An Operational Approach to Product Pricing," *Journal of Marketing*, 32 (April 1968), 29-33.

Hawkins, Edward R.: "Methods of Estimating Demand," *Journal of Marketing*, 21 (April 1957), 428-438.

Nevin, John R.: "Laboratory Experiments for Estimating Consumer Demand: A Validation Study," *Journal of Marketing Research*, 11 (August 1974), 261-268.

Pessemier, Edgar A.: "An Experimental Method for Estimating Demand," *Journal of Business*, 33 (October 1960), 373-383.

Sampson, Richard T.: "Sense and Sensitivity in Pricing," *Harvard Business Review*, 42 (November-December 1964), 99-105.

Silbertson, Aubrey: "Surveys of Applied Economics: Price Behavior of Firms," *The Economic Journal*, 80 (September 1970), 511-582.

Chapter 3

Price as an Index of Value

INTRODUCTION

Do we know how price influences individual buyers in their purchase decisions? As discussed in Chap. 2, it has generally been assumed that the behavior underlying the decisions of what to buy and how much to buy was embodied in the downward sloping demand curve. That is, as the price of a product increased, fewer buyers would decide to purchase the product, and those buyers who still purchased the product would be disposed to purchase fewer units than before. Hence, it has been assumed that price serves only as a measure of purchase cost (sacrifice) to the buyer. However, recent research evidence indicates that the role of price is more complex than that of a simple indicator of purchase cost to buyers. In this chapter, the traditionally assumed role of price as a determinant of buyer behavior is contrasted with the emerging evidence of the complexity of price as an influence on purchase decisions.

Traditional Model

The traditional model of buyer behavior leading to the downward sloping demand curve assumes that the decisions of what to buy and how much to buy depend on (1) the prices of all goods, (2) the level of income or amount of purchasing power, and (3) the tastes and preferences of the buyer. Assuming perfect information about prices, a fixed level of income (budget), and knowledge about tastes and preferences, the buyer maximizes satisfaction by minimizing the price paid for each good.

Criticisms of the Model

The assumption of "rational behavior" implies

1 Perfect information about prices.
2 The buyer is capable of perfectly processing information.
3 Prices do not affect subjective wants or satisfactions.
4 Perfect information about tastes and preferences.

In the real world, assumptions 1, 2, and 4 are clearly not present. Further, value may be defined as the number of units of quality per dollar expenditure, or

$$\text{Value} = \frac{\text{quality}}{\text{price}} \qquad (3\text{-}1)$$

Available research evidence indicates that buyers generally are not able to assess perfectly a product's quality (the ability of the product to provide satisfaction). Rather, *perceived quality* is the relevant variable, and under appropriate conditions, the perceived quality in a product is positively related to price. Thus, the model of value becomes

$$\text{Value} = \frac{\text{perceived quality as a function of price}}{\text{price}} \qquad (3\text{-}2)$$

Hence, price may have both attracting and repelling attributes. For example, a new mustard was recently packaged in a crockery jar. Significant sales did not develop until the price was increased from $0.49 to $1.00 a jar.

MULTIDIMENSIONAL ROLE OF PRICE ON BUYERS' PERCEPTIONS

Recognizing this dual, conflicting nature of price leads to the question of how to determine the way price actually affects purchase decisions. It has been common to refer to the "irrational" way that price affects behavior as *psychological price*—this term includes the concepts of customary prices, odd prices, price lines. Theoretically, the phenomenon of psychological price would indicate that the customer is perceptually sensitive to certain prices, and that departure from these prices in either direction would result in a decrease in demand. Despite the apparent acceptance of these "psychological" phenomena, there is little evidence to support this "magical" nature of prices. As the brief review in the next section indicates, these pricing practices have their origins in traditional ways of retailing, and of restraining the salesclerk from pocketing money from the sales transaction. Moreover, buyers are accustomed to these pricing practices and might be uncomfortable if products were not priced this way.

Traditional Psychological Pricing

Customary pricing is the method of pricing where all price alternatives are excluded except a single price point. The traditional example has been the former 5-cent candy bar or package of gum. With customary prices, sellers adapt to changes in costs and market conditions by adjusting the product size or quality, assuming the buyer would consider paying only one price. Moreover, common experience suggests that some sellers do use certain prices more frequently than others.

Odd price is used to refer to a price ending in an odd number (e.g., 1, 3, 5, 7, 9), or to a price just under a round number (e.g., 99, 98). Research evidence for the justification of such prices has largely been of an anecdotal nature. Ginzberg[1] imposed experimental patterns of odd and even prices on selected items in a large mail-order catalog and could not discover any generalizable result of the study. Later, Gabor and Granger[2] concluded that the dominance of pricing below the round figure in some markets may be largely an artifact. That is, if sellers use odd pricing, then some buyers will consider the odd price as the real price and the round figure price as incorrect and respond accordingly. A study of pricing in the food industry revealed that retail food prices show

1 Prices ending in 9 are most popular.
2 Prices ending in 5 are second most popular. Over 80 percent of the retail prices ended in 9 or 5.[3]

Marketing people who use these prices apparently assume a jagged demand curve as shown in Fig. 3-1. Such an assumption implies that buyers will buy less as prices are lowered until a "critical price point" is reached. In the vicinity of this critical point, buyers would purchase greater quantities.

Price lining controls the entire price and merchandise is offered at a number of specific but limited prices, usually three. Once the lines are set, prices may be held constant over a period of time, and changes in market conditions are adapted to by adjusting the quality of the merchandise in each line. For example, a clothier may traditionally offer three lines of sportcoats priced at either $90, $75, or $60.

Such a retailer apparently assumes most people will pay between $60 and $90 for a sportcoat. Further, this price policy assumes that most people perceive prices for sportcoats between $60 and $75 as roughly equivalent. Hence, price cuts within this range would not increase the quantity sold. Figure 3-2 illustrates the demand curve assumed by the policy of price lining. The horizontal areas of the curve indicate the price ranges that are perceived by buyers as equivalent. (Such a perceptual phenomenon has been referred to by psychologists as stimuli being not noticeably different.)

Ad hoc explanations of traditional pricing practices suggesting critical prices or magical numbers have not been supported by the limited research available. However, retailers have found some pricing practices work better than others, thereby suggesting there are some buyer-perceptual phenomena underlying observed response patterns.

[1] Eli Ginzberg, "Customary Prices," *American Economic Review*, 26 (June 1936), 296.
[2] Andre Gabor and Clive Granger, "Price Sensitivity of the Consumer," *Journal of Advertising Research*, 4 (December 1964), 40-44.
[3] Lawrence Friedman, "Psychological Pricing in the Food Industry," In Almarin Phillips and Oliver E. Williamson (eds.), *Prices: Issues in Theory, Practice, and Public Policy* (Philadelphia: University of Pennsylvania Press, 1967), pp. 187-201.

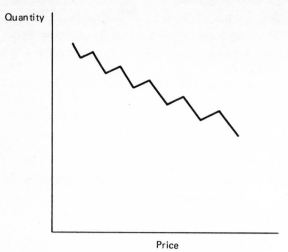

Figure 3-1 Assumed demand curve for odd pricing.

Price Awareness and Price Consciousness

Do buyers search for the lowest-priced alternatives and do they know the prices they pay? According to economic theory, the buyer is assumed to have perfect information concerning prices and want satisfaction of comparable product alternatives. For example, buyers are assumed to know the prices they pay. Furthermore, it is also assumed that buyers are price sensitive in that they will search for lower-priced choices. The term *price awareness* refers to the ability of the buyer to remember prices, whereas *price consciousness* denotes the buyer's sensitivity toward price differentials.

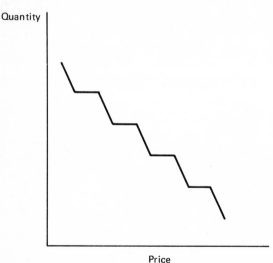

Figure 3-2 Assumed demand curve for price lining.

A buyer is characterized as price conscious to the degree he or she is unwilling to pay a higher price for a product, and if the price is greater than what is acceptable to pay, the buyer may refrain from buying. Moreover, the price conscious shopper will not be willing to pay for distinguishing features of a product, if the price difference for these features is too large. Conversely, a shopper who is relatively not price conscious may be willing to pay more for a product in a "high price" store, or for a product whose features are appealing.

Very little evidence is available to determine the extent of buyers' price awareness. In general, price awareness seems to be negatively associated with income (with the exception of the poor), and price awareness seems to be lower for typically branded products.[4] Other research suggests that although buyers may find it difficult to name correctly the exact prices paid, they have a general knowledge of the current price range of fast-selling items.[5]

Until recently it has been generally believed that increasing affluence tends to make buyers less price-conscious, particularly for grocery products. In fact, some recent research indicates that price does not usually rank as the primary attribute shoppers consider when making purchase decisions. One study found that concern for price was exhibited by 13, 17, and 25 percent of shoppers purchasing cereal, candy, and detergent respectively.[6] Finally, very price-conscious shoppers seem to be more valid perceivers of price than non-price-conscious shoppers.[7]

The Price-Quality Relationship

Finding some degree of price awareness and price-consciousness among buyers does not necessarily imply that price is used solely as a measure of cost (sacrifice). Buyers may also use price as an indicator of product quality.

Several studies have investigated the price-quality relationship. Originally, these investigations considered situations in which the only differential information available to respondents was price. These studies, as shown by Eq. (3-2), did find that product-quality perception was a function of price. Moreover, they have found that buyers tend to prefer higher-priced products when price is the only information available, when there is a belief that the quality of available brands differs significantly, and when the price differences between choices is large.[8]

A frequent criticism of these studies is that when price is the only information available, people naturally will relate product quality to price. Hence other price-quality studies have experimentally varied other cues in addition to price. The findings

[4] Andre Gabor and Clive Granger, "On the Price Consciousness of Consumers," *Applied Statistics*, 10 (November 1961), 170–188.

[5] "How Much Do Customers Know about Retail Prices?" *Progressive Grocer*, 43 (February 1964), C104–C106.

[6] William Wells and Leonard Lo Sciuto, "Direct Observation of Purchasing Behavior," *Journal of Marketing Research*, 3 (August 1966), 227–233.

[7] F. E. Brown, "Who Perceives Supermarket Prices Most Validly?" *Journal of Marketing Research*, 8 (February 1971), 110–113.

[8] Kent B. Monroe, "Buyers' Subjective Perceptions of Price," *Journal of Marketing Research*, 10 (February 1973), 70–80.

of multi-cue studies have been mixed, in that some studies have observed positive price-perceived quality relationships while other studies have not found this relationship to be significant.[9]

Thus, the available evidence precludes any generalization about a price-quality relationship. The single-cue studies unanimously observed a price-quality relationship, but the multi-cue studies often found little direct price-quality relationships. One reason for the lack of clear-cut evidence is that the limited amount of research has tested different products and prices. However, the price-perceived quality studies do suggest that brand name is important—possibly is more important than price—for relatively inexpensive grocery products and beverages. Price is apparently increasing in importance in the case of clothing, but buyers may still prefer to purchase according to brand name.

Price Thresholds

Our discussion so far has been directed toward the questions of whether buyers are aware of prices they pay and whether buyers may use price as an indicator of quality. But to gain further insight into how price may influence purchase behavior we need to examine the evidence available to us from the field of psychology.

Theoretical Framework   It has been established that humans have upper and lower limits of responsiveness to physical stimuli such as sound and light. For example, those of us who have taken hearing tests are aware that some sounds are either too low or too high for us to hear. The low and high sounds that we can just barely hear are called our lower and upper *absolute* hearing *thresholds*. Originating much of the interest in thresholds, Weber's law suggests that small, equally perceptible changes in a response correspond to proportional changes in the stimulus.

$$\frac{\Delta S}{S} = K \qquad\qquad\qquad (3\text{-}3)$$

where S = magnitude of the stimulus
ΔS = change in S corresponding to a defined change in response
K = constant

Weber's law applies to the perception of changes in a stimulus, i.e., *to perceived differences between two intensities of a stimulus.* For example, Weber's law suggests that if a product's price being raised from $10 to $11 is sufficient to deter us from buying the product, then another product originally priced at $20 would have to be repriced at $22 before we would become similarly disinterested. That is,

$$\frac{\$1}{\$10} = \frac{\$2}{\$20} = 0.10 = K \qquad\qquad\qquad (3\text{-}4)$$

Later, Fechner reformulated Weber's law, and derived what is now known as the Weber-Fechner law.

[9] Ibid.

$$R = k \log S + a \tag{3-5}$$

where R = magnitude of response

S = magnitude of the stimulus

k, a = constants

The importance of the Weber-Fechner law to pricing is that it provides an expression between price (stimulus) and a response. In particular, the Weber-Fechner law advances the hypothesis that a buyer has lower and upper price thresholds, which implies that a buyer has a range of acceptable prices for a purchase. Furthermore, the existence of a lower price threshold implies that there are positive prices greater than $0, which are unacceptable because they are considered to be too low.

Research conducted in Europe and the United States using a variety of methods has consistently confirmed the existence of a range of prices buyers are willing to pay.[10] As expected, the research has also determined that the acceptable price range for a product shifted downward as buyers' income declined. Moreover, as income fell, the upper price threshold dropped less than the lower price threshold, implying that a low price is a more powerful deterrent to higher-income groups than is a high price to lower-income groups.

Thus, people apparently may refrain from purchasing a product not only when the price is considered to be too high, but also when the price is considered to be too low. It may be that people suspect the quality of a product if its price is too much below what they consider to be an acceptable price to pay. This phenomenon of refusing to buy if the price is too low is not considered in the economic theory of consumer behavior we reviewed in Chap. 2.

Differential Price Thresholds   Usually a buyer has alternative choices available for a contemplated purchase and normally selects from among these choices. The prices of these alternative choices may provide cues that facilitate this decision process. However, even if the numerical prices are different, it cannot be assumed that the prices are *perceived* to be different. Hence, the problem becomes one of determining the effect of perceived price differences on buyer choice.

Weber's law has often been cited as the basis for inferences concerning perceived price differences. As Weber's law would indicate, it has been suggested that the perception of a price change depends on the magnitude of the change. It has also been discovered that people are more sensitive to price increases than to decreases.[11] Moreover, the value of K in Eq. (3-3) varies for different products.[12] The immediate implication is that buyers will be more sensitive to price changes for some products, i.e., have lower differential price thresholds. In other words, for some products, a price increase or decrease may not be perceived, thereby suggesting that these products have a relatively high K value.

[10] Ibid.

[11] Joseph U. Uhl, "Consumer Perception of Retail Food Price Changes," paper presented at Association for Consumer Research Conference, Amherst, Mass., August 1970.

[12] Peter Cooper, "Subjective Economics: Factors in Psychology of Spending," and "The Begrudging Index and the Subjective Value of Money," in Bernard Taylor and Gordon Wills (eds.), *Pricing Strategy* (Princeton, N.J.: Brandon/Systems, 1970), pp. 112-131.

Adaptation-Level Theory Various researchers have suggested that price perception, and, therefore, behavioral response, are relative to the present price level, actual or perceived. This price perception hypothesis has a theoretical foundation in *adaptation-level theory*, which suggests that an individual's behavior represents an adaptation to three classes of stimuli, *focal, contextual*, and *organic*.[13] In price perception, immediate interest focuses on the two external stimuli, focal and contextual. *Focal stimuli* are the stimuli the individual is directly responding to. *Contextual* or *background stimuli* are all other stimuli in the behavioral situation. *Organic stimuli* refer to the inner physiological and psychological processes affecting behavior. In our point of view, the comparative purchase offers, including price, are the focal stimuli, while available resources, purpose of purchase, and store environment are the contextual stimuli. In a pricing context, adaptation-level theory suggests that price perception depends on the actual price and the individual's reference price or adaptation level (AL).

Some important implications of adaptation-level theory on price perception are[14]

1 Price perceptions are relative to other prices and to associated use-values.
2 There is a reference price for each discernible quality level for each product category and this price influences judgments of other prices.
3 There is a region of indifference about a reference price such that changes in price within this region produce no change in perception.
4 The reference price will be some average of the range of prices for similar products, and need not correspond to any actual price nor the price of the leading brand.
5 Buyers do not judge each price singly; rather each price is compared with the reference price and the other prices in the price range.

In the past few years, evidence has emerged confirming the existence of a reference price serving as an AL for price judgments.[15] It has been suggested that price will not serve as an indicator of product quality unless there is a perceptible difference in price from the reference price. For example, in the mustard example at the beginning of this chapter, the original price, $0.49, was not perceptually different from the price of other brands. Other researchers have observed that buyers use as a reference point the *range of prices last paid* or the current market price to judge prices.

Assimilation-Contrast Effects Several pricing studies have suggested that the prevailing range of prices affects the buyer's reference price.[16] Since the magnitude of the price range is affected by the lowest and highest price (end prices) in the range, we would expect that these two end prices also affect price judgments. That is, we have isolated three different price cues as affecting price judgment: the reference price, the

---

[13] Harry Helson, *Adaptation-Level Theory* (New York: Harper & Row, 1964).
[14] Fred E. Emory, "Some Psychological Aspects of Price," in Bernard Taylor and Gordon Wills (eds.), op. cit., pp. 98–111.
[15] Monroe, op. cit.
[16] Kent B. Monroe, "Objective and Subjective Contextual Influences on Price Perceptions," in P. D. Bennett, J. N. Sheth, and A. G. Woodside (eds.), *Consumer and Industrial Buying Behavior* (New York: Elsevier North-Holland, 1977), pp. 287–296.

lowest price, and the highest price. Prices used by individuals to make perceptual judgments (AL, end prices) are called *anchoring stimuli*. By *price judgment* is meant the individual's assessment of whether a price is too low, just right (acceptable), or too high. And, as indicated above, buyers compare each price to the reference (anchor) prices and to the other prices in the range. Hence, the research question is: What happens when these reference or anchor prices change?

When a new price is introduced at or near the end (high or low) of a current series of prices (price range), the buyer's judgment is displaced toward this new price and a new reference price is *assimilated* into the price series; the buyer will then consider the new product-price offering as a reasonable substitute for the present product-price offerings. However, when this new end reference price is too remote from the current price series, the price is perceived as belonging to another product-price category— the *contrast effect*. We now consider some implications of this multidimensional nature of price perception.

IMPLICATIONS FOR PRICING DECISIONS

Although the theoretical concepts and research findings reviewed generally apply to consumer marketing, the experiences of some industrial marketing firms affirm that often industrial buyers also perceive prices as outlined above. For example, a purchaser of water pipes for a community in Iowa considered the highest-priced pipes as the best pipes: "the Cadillac" of the industry. But, beyond the applicability of these findings and concepts to different markets, there are some important implications for pricing decisions.

When pricing a product line, the evidence suggests that the lowest and highest prices in the product line are more noticeable, and hence, *anchor* buyers' judgments. These end prices, along with the reference price, may accentuate the perceived value for a given product (a bargain), or may diminish the perceived value (too expensive), depending on where the product's price lies in the product line. Similarly, these same phenomena may occur when a single product is compared with a number of competitive products. Further, if either or both end prices are outside the acceptable price range, a contrast effect may develop, and the products would be evaluated within a different context. This decision implication is discussed further in Chap. 10.

The perception of a sale price may depend on the position of the price in the range. If the price is below other offerings, buyers may perceive a bargain (assimilation effect), or buyers may not believe that the sale price is a reduction from the advertised original (contrasting effect). For example, buyers might react more favorably if a $600 television set were on sale for $450 than if this set were advertised as being on sale at $299.

If the price range is narrowed by shifting the end prices toward the middle of the range, or if there is little variation in prices, price becomes less dominant in purchase decisions. One reason for this result is that buyers will have greater difficulty discriminating among alternative choices leading to assimilation effects (no perceived price differences). Where there are few price differences, buyers tend to base their choices on other factors, such as brand name.[17]

The order in which buyers are exposed to alternative prices affects their perceptions. Buyers who are exposed initially to high prices will perceive subsequent lower prices as less expensive than they would if they were initially exposed to low prices.[18] Evidence available indicates that the strategy of introducing a new product to the market using a short-term "introductory low sale price" produces lower long-run volume than if the product is introduced at its regular price.[19] Magazines find it particularly difficult to trade subscribers up to regular subscription rates if the first subscription term is bought at a discount price. It is easier to reduce price than to raise price. Pricing new products is discussed in Chap. 9.

SUMMARY

Perception basically involves the process of categorization. That is, we tend to place new experiences into existing classifications of familiar experiences. Thus, when buyers are confronted by a price different from what they believe they have previously paid, they must decide whether the difference between the new and old prices is significant to them. If the price difference is insignificant, they may classify the two prices as similar and act as they have in the past. However, if the price difference is perceived as significant, they may classify the new price in a new price-product category and change their purchase behavior.

During this process of categorization buyers make heavy use of cues or clues. Some of these cues are price cues which influence buyers' judgments of whether the price differences are significant. The review of some of the behavioral phenomena underlying this perceptual process has perhaps raised more questions than we currently can answer. However, as buyers we can become more sensitive to the way price may influence our judgments about products that we are considering buying. At the same time, *the price setter must be concerned with identifying the cues used by buyers, so that he or she can act to secure accurate perceptions of the offering.*

DISCUSSION QUESTIONS

1 **a** Listed below are two sets of prices. Without calculating the differences, which pair of prices, set A or set B, *appears* to be further apart?

	A		B	
$83	$67		$87	$71

[17] Kent B. Monroe, "The Influence of Price Differences and Brand Familiarity on Brand Preferences," *Journal of Consumer Research*, 3 (June 1976), 42–49.

[18] Albert J. Della Bitta and Kent B. Monroe, "The Influence of Adaptation Levels on Subjective Price Perceptions," in S. Ward and P. Wright (eds.), *Advances in Consumer Research* (Boston: Association for Consumer Research, 1974), vol. 1, pp. 359–369.

[19] Anthony Doob, et al., "Effect of Initial Selling Price on Subsequent Sales," *Journal of Personality and Social Psychology*, 11 (1969), 345–350.

b In the next set of prices, which pair of prices, set A or set B, *appears* to be most different?

	A			B	
$79	$93		$75	$89	

c If you followed the directions and did not calculate the differences, what strategies or rules did you use?

2 a Listed below are three sets of prices. Without performing any calculations, which set of prices *appears* to have the highest average?

A	$87	$81	$75	$69
B	$89	$79	$73	$71
C	$84	$81	$75	$72

b Which set of prices *appears* to have the lowest average?

c What strategies or rules did you use to make your judgments?

3 In Chap. 1, the pricing problem of the Mars and Peter Paul Candy Companies was considered. Assume you are the price administrator for Peter Paul. As you consider how to change the price of your multipack candy from 5 for $0.89, are there any behavioral implications of your alternative strategies? (Refer to your answer to Discussion Question 3 of Chap. 1.) In what way do you think the concept of a reference price (AL) applies to this decision problem?

4 a Assume you are interested in purchasing a pair of pants (slacks) to go to a football game or a rock concert. In a store, you find five different pairs that are acceptable in terms of style, fit, fabric, and color. The prices of these pants are $7, $9, $15, $21, and $29. Which price do you find most acceptable? Why? Are there any prices unacceptable? Why?

b Suppose the prices were $17, $19, $25, $31, and $39. Which price do you find most acceptable? Why? Are there any prices unacceptable? Why?

c Assume the purpose of your purchase is to buy a pair of pants to go to church, a cocktail party, or to a symphony. Would your answer to part **a** change? Why? Would your answer to part **b** change? Why?

SUGGESTED READINGS

Brown, F. E.: "Who Perceives Supermarket Prices Most Validly?" *Journal of Marketing Research*, 8 (February 1971), 110–113.

Cooper, Peter: "Subjective Economics: Factors in Psychology of Spending" and "The Begrudging Index and the Subjective Value of Money," in Bernard Taylor and Gordon Wills (eds.), *Pricing Strategy* (Princeton, N.J.: Brandon/Systems, 1970), pp. 112–131.

Doob, Anthony et al.: "Effects of Initial Selling Price on Subsequent Sales," *Journal of Personality and Social Psychology*, 11 (1969), 345–350.

Emory, Fred E.: "Some Psychological Aspects of Price," in Bernard Taylor and Gordon Wills (eds.), *Pricing Strategy* (Princeton, N.J.: Brandon/Systems, 1970), pp. 98–111.

Gardner, David M.: "The Role of Price in Consumer Choice," *Selected Aspects of Consumer Behavior* (Washington, D.C.: National Science Foundation, 1977), pp. 415–433.

Monroe, Kent B.: "Buyers' Subjective Perceptions of Price," *Journal of Marketing Research*, 10 (February 1973), 70–80.

_____, Albert J. Della Bitta, and Susan Downey: "Contextual Influences on Subjective Price Perceptions," *Journal of Business Research*, 5 (December 1977), 277–291.

Olson, Jerry: "Price as an Informational Cue: Effects on Product Evaluations," in A. G. Woodside, J. N. Sheth, and P. D. Bennett (eds.), *Consumer and Industrial Buying Behavior* (New York: Elsevier North-Holland, 1977), pp. 267–286.

Section Three

Developing Internal Costs for Pricing

Perhaps the one topic within the pricing function that most concerns business executives is that of developing valid and useful cost information. The purpose of this section of the book (Chaps. 4 to 8) is to present methods of developing valid cost information for the pricing function. The focus of the material will be on the decisions to be made, not on cost accounting theory.

Chapter 4 discusses cost concepts and classifications, the different ways these different types of costs behave, and ways to identify patterns of cost behavior.

Chapter 5 develops the key cost analysis methods and explores ways of using the data for analyzing pricing alternatives; it also discusses the effect of changing the underlying cost structure, and shows how break-even analysis can be used in a dynamic price-volume-profit situation. An important problem when analyzing pricing alternatives is to estimate the effect on demand (volume) when prices are changed. Since the price setter cannot know prospective price elasticity of demand, the chapter develops a way to compute implied price elasticities for a given profit objective.

One of the least developed areas of costing is the analysis of the marketing effort and the determination of profit contribution by product line, customer account, order, sales territory, and salesperson. However, proper costs for pricing must include all costs that may change when activities are changed or redirected. Chapter 6 explores additional costing approaches to obtain data for analyzing the marketing effort.

Chapters 4, 5, and 6 present methods for determining relative contributions to covering fixed costs and profits by various profit segments. However, nondirect costs such as factory overhead and general selling expenses are also present, and are not directly traceable to profit segments. Over time a variety of formulas have been used to allocate these costs to products and other profit segments of the business. Unfortunately, the fixed costs allocated by these formulas are illogical even though quick and easy to calculate. Chapter 7 explores the disadvantages of these methods of assigning overhead and presents a method of assigning the cost burdens to those segments of the business that are responsible for incurring the particular burden. A clear advantage of the more systematic approach is its utility for justifying cost differences, a topic further developed in Chap. 16.

In many pricing decision contexts it is vitally important to forecast the trend in market prices for the products concerned. Since competitive prices tightly constrain the firm's pricing discretion in these markets, it is common practice to forecast prices. Drawing on industrial examples, Chap. 8 reviews various approaches to price forecasting. Since price forecasting is also important in pricing products over their life cycles, Chap. 8 provides a transition from the demand and cost analysis given in Chaps. 2 to 7 to the determination of pricing decisions. Currently, the strategy of dominant market share is believed to be a basis of sales and profit growth. The experience curve phenomenon is often used to justify such a marketing strategy. Chapter 8 illustrates how the experience curve may be used in pricing.

The Role of Costs
in Pricing Decisions

INTRODUCTION

As is well known, profits are the difference between revenues and costs. Price directly affects the quantity that can be sold in the marketplace, hence Chaps. 2 and 3 have analyzed the effect of price on demand. Given the selling objectives of a firm, the demand variable provides an upper limit on the pricing discretion the firm has; this limit is the willingness of buyers to purchase at a stated price. On the other hand, the other variable directly affecting profits, cost, sets a floor to a firm's pricing discretion. If prices are too low in comparison with costs, volume may be high but profitless.

Objective cost data are essential for deciding what price to set. Only by determining the difference between costs and the price under consideration and then balancing that margin against the capacity necessary to produce the estimated volume can the seller determine the value of the product in terms of its contribution to recovering the seller's initial investment. When considering the cost aspect of a pricing decision, the crucial question is what costs are relevant to the decision. When cost-plus methods of pricing are used, and the cost portion of the formula is arbitrarily determined, the resultant price is erroneous in that the pricing formula does not allow for demand or for competition.

It is important for the seller to know the determinants and behavior of product costs in order to know when to accelerate cost recovery, how to evaluate a change in selling price, how to profitably segment a market, and when to add products to or eliminate products from the product line. Even so, costs play a limited part in pricing. They indicate whether the product can be made and sold profitably at any price, but they do not indicate the amount of markup or markdown on cost buyers will accept. Proper costs serve to guide management in the selection of a profitable product mix and to determine how much cost can be incurred without sacrificing profit.

Costs for pricing must deal with the future. Current or past information probably will not provide an adequate basis for profit projections unless it is valid to assume that the future is a mirror of the past. Product costs must be based on expected purchase costs of raw materials, labor wage rates, and other expenses to be incurred. In addition, information about development, promotion, and distribution costs is needed. Information on product costs should be regularly developed to determine whether changes have occurred that may affect the relative profitability of the company. It is planned costs that are important, not past costs, since profit planning necessarily deals with the future.

The purpose of this chapter is to discuss different concepts of costs and ways of classifying costs. As has been observed, it is important for the seller to know both the determinants or causes of product costs as well as their behavior. This chapter also discusses ways of identifying patterns of cost behavior.

COST CONCEPTS AND CLASSIFICATIONS

To determine profit at any volume, price level, product mix, or time, proper cost classification is required. Some costs vary directly with the rate of activity, while others do not. When these different costs are mixed together in a total unit cost, it is not possible to relate volume to costs, and the pricing decision is likely to be reduced to a formula that can lead to serious errors. However, if the cost data are properly classified into their fixed and variable components and properly attributed to the activity causing the cost, the effect of volume becomes readily apparent and sources of profit are revealed.

It is important to emphasize the concept of activity. Commonly, costs that vary with production rate, such as labor or materials, have been classified as variable costs, and all other costs, including marketing and distribution costs, have been classified as fixed. However, as Chaps. 4 to 6 develop, it will be stressed that such a classification scheme is inappropriate for proper cost classification. For example, the travel costs of supporting a salesperson vary directly with number of miles traveled. Also, when a salesperson is paid on commission, then selling costs vary with sales. As shown in Chap. 6, and again in Chap. 16, order processing costs vary with the complexity of the order. Therefore, it is important to recognize that the cost concepts defined in the next section apply to marketing and distribution as well as production.

Cost Concepts

Direct Costs Direct costs (also called *traceable* or *attributable* costs) are those costs incurred by and solely for a particular product, department, program, sales territory, or customer account. These costs may be fixed or variable. Material and labor costs may be traceable to a unit of product. The administrative salaries, rent, and other office expenses may be traced to the district sales office, and, therefore, are direct costs of the sales territory.

Indirect Traceable Costs   Indirect traceable costs can be objectively traced to a product, department, program, sales territory, or customer account if the costs can be identified with that unit. These costs, although not incurred solely for a product, are objectively identified with the product. They may be fixed or variable. Materials used in the production of several products can be objectively traced to or identified by the rate of usage for the production of each different product. General plant overhead may be indirectly attributed to a product.

Common Costs   Common or general costs support a number of activities or profit segments. These costs cannot be objectively traced to a product or segment based on a direct physical relationship to that product or segment. The administration costs of a sales district is common to all units of product sold in that district. A common or general cost does not change when one of the activities it supports is discontinued. Hence, discontinuing a product in the line will not affect the administration costs of the district, nor of other general expenses such as market research or research and development.

Opportunity Costs   Opportunity cost is the marginal income foregone by choosing one alternative over another. Essentially, opportunity costs reflect the "cost" of not choosing the best alternative or opportunity. As will be developed in Chap. 15, these costs are relevant when operating at or near full capacity or when resources are in scarce supply. If a decision is made not to produce a product with the largest contribution per resource unit consumed, then the difference between the income earned and the larger income that could have been earned is income foregone (opportunity cost).

Cost Behavior

In addition to classifying costs according to ability to attribute a cost to a product or profit segment, it is also important to classify costs according to variation with the rate of activity. As noted above, unless costs can be segmented into fixed and variable costs, it is not possible to trace the effects of changes in price, volume, or product selling mix on costs.

Direct Variable Costs   Costs that vary directly with an activity level are called *direct variable costs*. As production is increased in a given time period a proportionately higher amount of labor and materials is used. Assuming no changes in scale economies as the volume is increased these direct variable costs will be constant per additional unit produced. However, there usually is a point where unit direct variable costs change due either to economies of quantity raw-material purchases or to increased labor unit costs resulting from overtime or a second shift. Figure 4-1*a* illustrates direct variable costs.

In pricing, direct variable costs are also known as *out-of-pocket costs*, since these costs are incremental to the decision to make and sell, and therefore, require an outlay of immediate cash. One test of a unit variable cost is whether it is readily discontinued or whether it would not exist if a product were not made. Direct variable costs include those costs which the product incurs unit by unit and such costs as productive labor, energy required at production centers, raw material required, sales commissions, royalties, and shipping costs. The major criterion of a direct variable cost is that it be traceably and tangibly generated by, and identified with, the making and selling of a specific product.

Semivariable Costs   Some costs vary with activity rates but are not zero at a zero activity rate. Plant supplies are needed in some minimum amount to get activities started, and then additional quantities are required as the level of activity increases. Hence these semivariable costs consist of a base amount that is constant in relation to activity and a variable amount that varies directly with changes in the activity level. Figure 4-1*b* illustrates semivariable costs.

Period Fixed Costs   Some costs, while fixed for the planning period, are assigned to specific projects by management to fulfill company objectives. These *specific programmed costs* refer to costs used to generate additional revenues such as opening a new sales district office or warehouse or a special advertising program for a specific product line. These direct fixed costs are separable because they may be charged to the product line or activity which is the recipient of the incurred cost. Other costs are also fixed for the planning period, but they are incurred for the entire company and are common to the various products or activities. Examples of these *general programmed costs* are general and administrative salaries, research and development, and general marketing expenses. Other costs are neither separable nor inescapable during the planning period. These *constant costs* are *common* and are incurred as long as the firm is in business. Included in these costs are depreciation, real estate taxes, rent, and interest payments on mortgages. In pricing, all the period fixed costs are referred to simply as fixed costs as long as the costs will be incurred in the planning period. These fixed costs are illustrated in Fig. 4-1*c*.

Table 4-1 summarizes the cost concepts and behavior discussed in this section. As the table indicates, some directly attributable costs vary directly with the activity level, and some costs, although fixed, are directly attributable to the activity level. Hence, it is important to clarify specifically what is meant by the terms *direct* and *indirect*. *The directly traceable or attributable costs are those that we can readily determine as contributing to the product cost. However, whether a direct cost is variable, fixed, or semivariable depends on properly determining the cause of that cost.*

Determinants of Cost Behavior

As Table 4-1 indicates, no cost is inherently fixed or variable. Further, whether a cost is fixed or variable depends on whether that cost varies as the organization's activity level changes. Traditionally, it has been customary to consider variable costs as those costs that vary with production volume, usually measured in terms of product units.

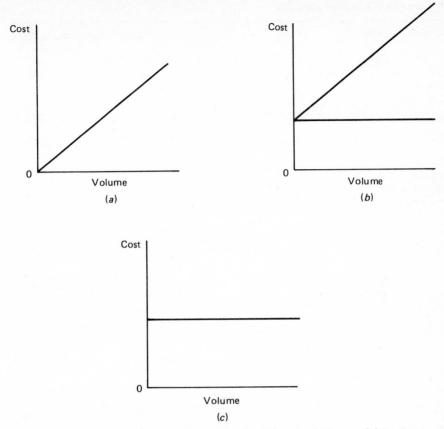

Figure 4-1 Cost behavior patterns. (*a*) Variable cost, (*b*) semivariable cost, (*c*) fixed cost.

For example, material cost is usually considered a variable cost because it varies directly with changes in production activity.

However, when analyzing costs for the purpose of setting prices, or for justifying price differences, it is important to recognize that there are other sets of activities in addition to production that are cost incurring. For example, a salesperson's travel expenses vary directly with the distance traveled (e.g., $0.18 per mile). Or, a salaried salesperson's expenses in serving an account vary directly with the amount of time spent serving a customer account. Or, the shipping department's cost of preparing an invoice may vary directly with the number of items on an invoice. For the U.S. Postal Service, the cost of providing a particular class of service varies with the number of pieces mailed, the weight, and the distance these pieces are mailed. In general, a cost is a variable cost if the cost changes because of a change in the activity causing that cost.

On the other hand, fixed costs are affected by long-range planning decisions. Some of these fixed costs are long-term lease commitments and depreciation costs that remain constant over periods of time. These general programmed costs originate in capacity decisions, whereas specific programmed costs result from decisions on how to

Table 4-1   Cost Classifications

Classified according to variation with activity rate	Cost component	Classified according to ability to trace or attribute the cost to a product or segment
Costs vary linearly with activity rate	Raw materials Utilities Shipping Royalties Sales Commissions	Directly traceable or attributable
Costs vary with activity rate, but are not zero at zero activity level	Operating labor Direct supervision Maintenance Plant supplies	
Costs do not vary with activity level	Rent Insurance Taxes Depreciation	Directly traceable or attributable, but independent of activity level
	Payroll General plant overhead Storage facilities Medical and safety expenses	Indirectly traceable or attributable to a product or segment
	General administration Sales administration Market research Research and development	Common or general costs not easily traceable or attributable to a product or segment

Source: Adapted from Donald R. Woods, *Financial Decision Making in the Process Industry* (Englewood Cliffs, N.J.: Prentice-Hall, 1975), p. 212.

use that capacity. These specific programmed costs are planned expenditures to generate a sales volume or to handle a specified level of administrative work. Thus, managers can increase the specific programmed costs whenever they decide to do so.

Different decisions may produce different levels of fixed costs. For example, shutdown fixed costs are usually lower than operating fixed costs of a plant. Required power levels are lower and security and maintenance personnel are fewer when a plant is shut down than when it is running.

Fixed costs may also differ with the extent to which a fixed cost is traceable to a specific time period. Administrative salaries, lease payments, and taxes are direct costs of the time period in which they are paid. However, other fixed costs reflect a lump-sum payment that is apportioned over a series of future time periods. Depreciation expenses are common costs apportioned over specific time periods and they vary according to the computational procedure employed. Because depreciation costs are subjective and reflect prior decisions, they are irrelevant for pricing and other planning decisions. Unfortunately, they are often lumped in with other fixed costs, unitized

Table 4-2 Cost Behavior Identification Form

Department: _____

Cost	Variable varies with	Semivariable varies with	Fixed
Direct labor	Production		
Direct materials	Production		
Supervision			(X)
Supplies		Production	
Power	Machine time		
Maintenance		Machine time	

according to some estimate of projected volume, and become a part of the cost that price is expected to recover. *Depreciation costs should be separated from other period expenses for the purpose of pricing.*

Although costs are not inherently fixed or variable, it is essential that an organization identify the behavior pattern that they follow. It is vitally important to know which costs vary with changes in activity levels and which costs remain constant.

Cost Behavior Analysis

Essentially, there are two approaches to determine how a cost behaves. One approach focuses on the decision maker, the other on accounting records. Generally, the decision maker is asked to discuss the behavior of each cost within the department. For example, department managers will know that more labor and materials are used as production increases. Further, department managers may also be able to identify different causal factors of cost besides production. Table 4-2 illustrates a typical cost behavior identification worksheet that may be used during these interviews.

Correlation and regression analysis is commonly used to identify cost behavior patterns from accounting data.[1] Such an approach, because it relies on historical data, assumes that the past reflects the future. Further, the approach assumes that the data properly describe the dynamic events producing the costs. For example, analysis of U.S. Postal Service data suggested that as first class mail volume increased the cost of stamps remained constant when comparing yearly data. However, what the data failed to show was the increasing reliance on postage meters by business customers of the U.S. Postal Service.

Regression procedures normally attempt to measure changes in costs in relation to changes in activity. Changes in materials cost are measured in relation to changes in output to determine the behavior pattern of materials cost. With the availability of high-speed computers and library programs, regression analysis is easy to use and inexpensive.

Moreover, by using computers, companies are able to monitor costs continuously across product lines, sales territories, or customer accounts. Today, virtually all

[1] See George J. Benston, "Multiple Regression Analysis of Cost Behavior," *Accounting Review*, 41 (October 1969), 657–672.

moderate-size companies use the computer to monitor costs.[2] United States Elevator uses the computer to monitor daily and monthly cost fluctuations. The cost of every raw-material component is reviewed daily by the president.[3] International Telephone and Telegraph provides the company's controller with monthly cost-monitoring reports for each operating division.[4] The Jewelry Division of Zale Corporation gets a daily computer printout showing the current relationship between cost and margin on all Zale inventory.[5] The next chapter develops the methods for analyzing the relationships between price, cost, and volume.

SUMMARY

Costs set a floor to to a firm's pricing discretion. But, when considering the cost aspect of a pricing decision, the crucial problem is to determine what costs are relevant to the decision. Moreover, it is also important to know the determinants and behavior of these costs in order to analyze the full impact of the pricing decision.

The purpose of this chapter has been to discuss cost concepts and classifications, the different ways these different types of costs behave, and ways to identify patterns of cost behavior. Today, we have sufficient knowledge about generating and analyzing cost data. With the aid of high-speed computers and statistical programs, the decision maker is able to know the relevant costs for pricing purposes. Perhaps more than anything else, managers need to exert the will to develop detailed cost studies of their operations. The next three chapters illustrate the types of analyses that can be performed if proper cost data are available.

DISCUSSION QUESTIONS

1 a Develop a comprehensive list of the different types of costs that are incurred in the manufacturing process.
  b Assuming a general situation, classify these costs as
    (1) Direct, indirect, or common costs
    (2) Variable, semivariable, or fixed costs
  c What was your rationale in making these classifications?
2 a Develop a comprehensive list of the different types of costs that are incurred by a manufacturer in the marketing and distribution of its products.
  b Assuming a general situation, classify these costs as
    (1) Direct, indirect, or common costs
    (2) Variable, semivariable, or fixed costs
  c What was your rationale in making these classifications?
3 a Develop a comprehensive list of the different types of costs that are incurred by a retailer.

[2] "Flexible Pricing," *Business Week*, December 12, 1977, p. 88.
[3] Ibid.
[4] Ibid.
[5] "Pricing Strategy in an Inflation Economy," *Business Week*, April 6, 1974, p. 43.

    b Assuming a general situation, classify these costs as
        (1) Direct, indirect, or common costs
        (2) Variable, semivariable, or fixed costs
    c What was your rationale in making these classifications?

SUGGESTED READINGS

Benston, George J.: "Multiple Regression Analysis of Cost Behavior," *Accounting Review*, 41 (October 1969), 657–672.

Brown, F. E., and Alfred A. Oxenfeldt: "Should Prices Depend on Costs?" *MSU Business Topics*, 16 (Autumn 1968), 73–77.

Corr, Arthur V.: "The Role of Cost in Pricing," *Management Accounting*, 56 (November 1974), 15–18+.

Weathers, Henry T.: "Managerial Profitability," *Management Accounting*, 56 (July 1974), 25–27, 34.

Wentz, Theodore: "Realism in Pricing Analyses," *Journal of Marketing*, 30 (April 1966), 19–26.

Woolsey, Samuel M.: "Distinguishing between Direct Costs and Fixed Costs," *Direct Costing Techniques for Industry* (Englewood Cliffs, N.J.: Prentice-Hall, 1967), pp. 63–75.

Chapter 5

Contribution Analysis for Pricing Decisions

Some 40 years ago, the president of a company asked his controller why, with a sales increase of $100,000, profits had fallen by $20,000. The controller, Jonathan Harris, devised a cost accounting system that showed profits as a function of sales. Today, his system of accounting is known as *direct costing*.[1]

As developed in Chap. 4, a direct cost is a cost that is traceable to an object, activity, sales territory, product line, or customer account. Further, it was also pointed out that direct costs are independent of cost behavior in that direct costs may be fixed costs or variable costs. A direct costing system attributes only those costs that may be objectively traced to an activity. Thus, no arbitrary cost allocations of common costs are assessed to that activity.

From a decision perspective, a direct cost system shows cost changes in production as output increases or decreases. Marketing plans can be improved when direct cost information documents the effect on contribution to profits of changes in prices, promotion expenses, product mix, or other marketing activities designed to influence demand and revenues. However, the profit impact of production and marketing changes can only be determined when both the cost and revenue changes resulting from a change in activity are determined. A direct cost approach facilitates such a determination. Contribution analysis focuses on the change in profits resulting from changes in activity levels and derives from a direct costing approach.

[1] Jonathan N. Harris, "What Did We Earn Last Month?," *NAA Bulletin*, January 1936, p. 501.

This chapter develops the key aspects of contribution analysis and shows ways in which valid cost information may be used for product management. The chapter first introduces traditional break-even analysis. Then break-even analysis is extended into a more dynamic method called *profit analysis*. After offering some useful guidelines for break-even analysis, the chapter shows in detail how profit analysis may be used to evaluate alternative price choices.

Figure 5-1 provides a view of what material we will be developing in this chapter and what is to follow in Chaps. 6 and 7. Figure 5-1 shows the building blocks—direct, indirect, variable, and fixed—explained in the preceding chapter. The concept of out-of-pocket cost was also explained in Chap. 4. In this chapter, we develop the concept of contribution and apply this concept while discussing direct labor and direct material costs. Indirect manufacturing costs refer to other manufacturing expenses, such as supplies, that are indirect, but can be objectively traced to the production activity. These costs are discussed further in Chap. 7. Marketing costs are discussed in Chap. 6. Note also the distinction between conversion costs and manufacturing costs.

BREAK-EVEN ANALYSIS

Break-even analysis is a simple and easily understandable method of examining the relationship between fixed costs, variable costs, volume, and price. Detailed analysis of break-even data will show the effect of decisions that convert costs from variable to fixed or vice versa; the effect of decisions that reduce or increase costs; the effect of

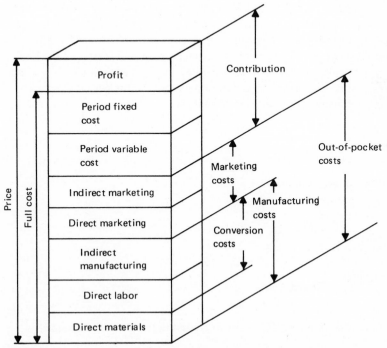

Figure 5-1 The elements of price. *(Adapted from Phillip F. Ostwald, Cost Estimating for Engineering and Management (Englewood Cliffs, N.J.: Prentice-Hall, 1974), p. 266.)*

decisions that increase sales volume and revenue; and the effect of decisions to change selling prices.

To illustrate the concept of break-even analysis and its application to pricing decisions consider the situation of a specialty retailer who buys shirts from a supplier at $8 each and sells them for $10 each. Assume that the fixed costs are $10,000 per year and that estimated sales volume is 10,000 shirts per year. The data below summarize this situation.

	One shirt	10,000 shirts per year
Sales	$10.00	$100,000
Out-of-pocket costs	$ 8.00	$ 80,000
Fixed costs	1.00	10,000
Total costs	$ 9.00	$ 90,000
Profits	$ 1.00	$ 10,000

However, the difficulty with this approach is that profit per shirt is $1 *only if* 10,000 shirts are sold during the year. If fewer shirts are sold, unit profit is less; if more shirts are sold unit profit is more. The contribution approach provides a mechanism for us to see the effect of different sales volumes on profits and to determine a break-even point.

Each time a shirt is sold, a contribution to profit of $2 is generated. The number of shirts that must be sold before the retailer breaks even is $10,000/$2 = 5,000 shirts. This figure is the retailer's break-even point: the level of sales volume which produces total contributions equal to the period fixed expenses. Only when the 5,001st shirt is sold will the retailer realize any profit for the year. The unit profit of $1 indicated above obviously is incorrect since no profits are realized until sales exceed 5,000 shirts.

The break-even *point* is when sales revenue exactly covers all costs, i.e., the level of sales revenue when profits are zero. Or, as illustrated above, the break-even point is the amount of sales revenue that generates contributions equal to the period fixed costs.

Using the shirt example, the break-even formula is

$$BEQ = \frac{FC}{P - VC} \tag{5-1}$$

where BEQ = break-even sales quantity
  FC = period fixed costs
  P = selling price
  VC = direct variable costs
Applying the shirt data we obtain

$$BEQ = \frac{\$10,000}{\$10 - \$8} = 5,000 \text{ shirts}$$

Alternatively the break-even formula can be expressed in terms of sales revenue.

$$BES = \frac{FC}{PV} \qquad (5\text{-}2)$$

where BES is the break-even sales revenue and PV is the profit-volume ratio given by the relation

$$PV = \frac{P - VC}{P} \qquad (5\text{-}3)$$

Using the shirt data we obtain

$$PV = \frac{\$10 - \$8}{\$10} = 0.20$$

and therefore

$$BES = \frac{\$10,000}{0.20} = \$50,000$$

Often it is desirable to picture the economic character of a business firm by showing the break-even analysis on a break-even chart. Essentially, there are three lines on a break-even chart. One line shows the fixed expenses over the volume range, another line shows the total costs, and the third is the revenue line. The break-even point is where the revenue line intersects the total-cost line.

We normally plot the sales revenue on the x or horizontal axis and costs are plotted on the y or vertical axis. Both are expressed in identical dollars on an identical scale. Thus, the $45°$ revenue line will indicate the same value whether referred to from either the cost or revenue scale. The point where the total-cost line intersects the revenue line is the sales volume where total costs equal total sales revenue. Figure 5-2 shows the break-even chart for the retail shirt store. How to extend break-even analysis to include an analysis of the impact on profits follows.

PROFIT ANALYSIS

Virtually every planned action or decision in an organization affects costs, and therefore, profits. Profit analysis attempts to determine the effect of costs, prices, and volume on profits in order to determine the best course of action to follow. The goal of this analysis is to provide accurate and objective data about the contributions made by each product. Knowing the relative profit contributions of each product gives management a sound basis for determining the relative selling effort allocations.

Perhaps the most important piece of data resulting from a profit analysis is the *marginal income ratio*, or the *contribution ratio*, which is usually referred to as the *profit-volume ratio* (PV). The PV ratio is the percentage of sales available to cover fixed costs and profits after deducting variable costs. Equation (5-3) gives the compu-

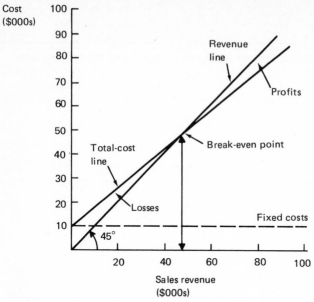

Figure 5-2 Break-even chart for the retail shirt store.

tational formula for PV. In the data below the contribution ratio or PV is the contribution of $3,500 ($10,000 - $6,500), divided by sales, or 35 percent. Thus, 35 cents out of each sales dollar contributes toward paying fixed costs and providing a profit.

Sales	$10,000
Variable costs . . .	6,500
Fixed costs	2,500
Profit	$ 1,000

Once the PV has been calculated it is possible to determine the effects on profits of additional sales volume. If $1,000 of additional sales were generated, the additional profits would be $1,000 × 0.35, or $350. Since the fixed costs of $2,500 have already been covered by the original $10,000 of sales, additional volume contributes 35 cents of every sales dollar to profits. Thus, a 10 percent increase in sales produces a 35 percent increase in profits. A second increase in sales of 10 percent will produce a 28.5 percent increase in profits [($1,100 × 0.35)/($1,000 + $350)]. It is important to note that this analysis is possible only when all direct costs have been separated into their fixed and variable components.

In multiproduct firms it is important to place emphasis on achieving the maximum amount of contribution revenue instead of attempting to maximize sales revenues. Each product faces different competition, has a different demand elasticity, and perhaps depends for its sales, at least in part, on the sales of the other products in the line. Table 5-1 shows the effect of changing product prices of a product line.[2] In the

---

[2]This example is borrowed from Spencer A. Tucker, *Pricing for Higher Profit* (New York: McGraw-Hill, 1966), pp. 86–87.

Table 5-1 Determining Contributions and Profits for a Product Line

Item	Product A	Product B	Product C	Product D	Total
Unit variable cost	$ 9.00	$ 10.00	$ 11.00	$ 12.00	
Before					
Unit selling price	$ 15.00	$ 16.00	$ 17.00	$ 18.00	
Unit contribution	$ 6.00	$ 6.00	$ 6.00	$ 6.00	
Units sold (000s)	50	60	40	30	180
Total revenue	$750,000	$960,000	$680,000	$540,000	$2,930,000
Total contribution	$300,000	$360,000	$240,000	$180,000	$1,080,000
Less: Fixed costs					$1,000,000
Net profit					$ 80,000
After					
Unit selling price	$ 14.00	$ 19.00	$ 18.00	$ 20.00	
Unit contribution	$ 5.00	$ 9.00	$ 7.00	$ 8.00	
Units sold (000s)	70	40	40	25	170
Total revenue	$980,000	$760,000	$720,000	$500,000	$2,960,000
Total contribution	$350,000	$360,000	$280,000	$200,000	$1,190,000
Less: Fixed costs					$1,000,000
Net profit					$ 190,000

before situation, the firm subjectively set its prices at a uniform contribution level and ignored competition, demand elasticity, and product-line interdependence. However, examining their pricing decisions, they discovered that product A was price elastic, implying that a price reduction would lead to a greater percent increase in sales volume. Product B was being priced below competition and increasing its price to competitive levels would leave the total contribution unchanged although revenues would decrease. Products C and D were found to be demand inelastic and therefore, prices could be increased leading to increases in revenues. As Table 5-1 indicates, the firm was able to earn twice the profit with less unit sales and about the same revenue.

Extension of Break-Even Analysis

As we have seen, the break-even chart assumes that each dollar of revenue will have the same cost, the same profit-volume ratio, and eventually, the same profit. However, in the real world of business, operations are not so uniform. In fact, over time, we would expect changes in out-of-pocket (variable) costs, fixed expenses, and prices with resultant changes in profits.

In terms of the break-even chart, a decrease in variable costs, with no corresponding change in fixed expenses decreases the slope of the total-cost line, resulting in a lower break-even point. An increase in variable costs increases the slope of the total-cost line, leading to a higher break-even point.

If prices are increased and the volume remains the same, contributions are increased. This occurs because each sales dollar has less out-of-pocket content. Thus, the effect is to lower the slope of the total-cost line, producing a lower break-even point.

Table 5-2

1.	Sales revenue (price = $10/unit)		$1,000,000
2.	Direct material cost	$400,000	
3.	Direct labor cost	400,000	
4.	Total direct variable cost (2 + 3)	$800,000	
5.	Fixed costs	100,000	
6.	Total costs (4 + 5)		900,000
7.	Contribution (1 – 4)		$ 200,000
8.	Profit-volume ratio (7 ÷ 1)		0.20
9.	Break-even sales (5 ÷ 8)		$ 500,000
10.	Unit sales ($1,000,000/$10)		100,000
11.	Unit contribution (7 ÷ 10)		$ 2.00
12.	Break-even quantity (5 ÷ 11)		50,000

Table 5-3

1.	Sales revenue	$1,000,000
2.	Variable costs	$ 600,000
3.	Fixed costs	$ 200,000
4.	Total costs (2 + 3)	$ 800,000
5.	Contribution (1 – 2)	$ 400,000
6.	Profit-volume ratio (5 ÷ 1)	0.40
7.	Break-even sales (3 ÷ 6)	$ 500,000

If only fixed costs are increased, the result is an increase in the break-even point, causing profits to start later, but at the same PV rate. Therefore, any changes in the price, volume, or cost variables can be shown on the break-even chart.

To illustrate some of the dynamics of the analysis assume the data are as shown in Table 5-2. Now assume the firm wants to consider adding new equipment. It is believed this new equipment will reduce labor costs by $200,000 per period for the same volume level. However, acquisition of the machinery will lead to an increase in fixed expenses by $100,000. As Table 5-3 and Fig. 5-3 show, the break-even points are identical for the original and the proposed situations. However, the new situation would contribute 40 cents of profit per sales dollar above the break-even point, as compared to the original situation that contributed only 20 cents of profit per sales dollar above the break-even point. This illustration provides an indication of the dynamics of break-even analysis. The guidelines below illustrate these dynamics.

Some Useful Guidelines for Break-Even Analysis

Let us return to the specialty retailer who buys shirts from a supplier at $8 each and sells them for $10 each. Fixed costs are $10,000 per year and estimated sales volume is 10,000 shirts per year. Recall that for this situation the break-even point is 5,000 shirts, or $50,000.

Now, if fixed costs are increased to $15,000 per year, the break-even point becomes

$$\text{BES} = \frac{\$15,000}{0.20} = \$75,000$$

If price is raised to $11.00, the PV becomes 0.273 ($3/$11), and

$$\text{BES} = \frac{\$15,000}{0.273} = \$55,000$$

Or, if fixed costs remain at $15,000, but the shirts are purchased for $7, the PV becomes 0.30 ($3/$10), and the break-even point is

$$\text{BES} = \frac{\$15,000}{0.30} = \$50,000$$

These three examples provide three useful guidelines.

1 A change in fixed costs affects only the break-even point.
2 A change in the price and/or variable costs affects both the break-even point and the PV.
3 An increase in prices and/or a decrease in variable costs can offset an increase in fixed expenses (assuming volume remains unaffected).

We have shown that with fixed costs at $15,000, price at $10, and variable costs at $7, the break-even point is the same as in the original example. However, are profits the same? To answer this question we need an additional formula.

$$\text{Profit} = (\text{sales revenue} \times \text{PV}) - \text{fixed costs} \qquad (5\text{-}4)$$

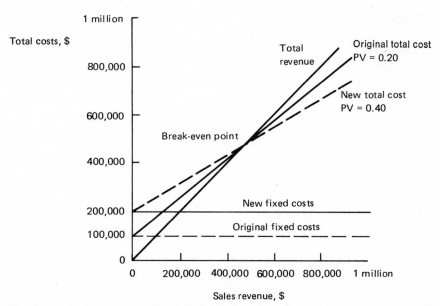

Figure 5-3 Effect of changing the cost structure.

Applying this formula to the original situation for a sales level of $70,000 we get

Profit = ($70,000 × 0.20) - $10,000 = $4,000

And for the new situation

Profit = ($70,000 × 0.30) - $15,000 = $6,000

Thus, we have three additional guidelines.

4 Two products can have identical break-even points but will still earn profits or losses at their own PV rate.

5 Above or below the identical break-even points, the ratio of two products' profits or losses will be proportionate to the rate of their PV rates, e.g.,

$$\frac{\$4,000}{\$6,000} = \frac{4}{6} = \frac{0.20}{0.30}$$

6 Above or below the break-even point, profits or losses are generated by the PV rate.

Suppose the retailer sets a target profit of $5,000 on sales of $80,000. If variable costs are $8.50 per shirt and fixed costs are $15,000, what must the shirts be priced at? To answer this question we need two additional formulas.

$$PV = \frac{\text{target profit} + \text{fixed expenses}}{\text{sales revenue}} \tag{5-5}$$

$$= \frac{(\$5,000 + \$15,000)}{\$80,000} = 0.25$$

$$Price = \frac{\text{variable costs}}{1 - PV} \tag{5-6}$$

$$= \frac{\$8.50}{(1 - 0.25)} = \$11.33$$

This example provides another guideline.

7 When the objective is to determine a price for a target PV, divide the appropriate variable costs by the complement of the PV.

These seven guidelines provide a basis for examining the effect of changes in the product's or firm's underlying cost structure. Profit analysis is an extension of break-even analysis in that it is possible to use the methodology of break-even analysis to examine the effects on profits of changes in costs or prices. The concept that allows us to perform such analyses is the PV ratio. We will now apply the PV ratio and profit analysis to evaluating pricing alternatives for an established product. Applications of profit analysis to pricing new products are developed in Chap. 9.

TESTING PRICING ALTERNATIVES

Whenever management considers changing prices it should consider the reactions of the market to the proposed changes. Moreover, the effect of any price change on volume and contribution must be explicitly evaluated. The data in Table 5-4 show the result of evaluating three pricing alternatives: (1) keep price at $10.00 per unit; (2) decrease price by 6.2 percent to $9.38 per unit; (3) increase price by 7 percent to $10.70 per unit.

The concept of demand price elasticity indicates that if demand is elastic, reducing prices will lead to increased revenues, and if demand is inelastic, increasing prices will lead to increased revenues. However, this concept of elasticity is insufficient to decide which alternative to choose, since the more important consideration is the effect of a price change on the contribution, and, therefore, on profits. Moreover, demand price elasticity is an elusive concept to measure.

The data in Table 5-4 indicates that if the firm has a desired profit objective of $5,000,000, changing price means different levels of volume and sales revenue are required because the PV changes. Thus, if the price reduction alternative is being considered in order to penetrate a new market, the relevant research question is whether the price reduction can generate additional volume by 33 percent [(3,200,000 – 2,400,000)/2,400,000]. On the other hand, a contemplated price increase of 7 percent must not result in a decline in volume of more than 22 percent [(1,870,000 – 2,400,000)/2,400,000]. Obviously, if the price reduction results in a volume increase of more than 33 percent, the firm would be in a better profit position after the price reduction,

Table 5-4

	Decision alternative		
	No price change	Decrease price 6.2%	Increase price 7%
Unit selling price	$ 10.00	$ 9.38	$ 10.70
Unit variable costs	7.50	7.50	7.50
Unit contribution	$ 2.50	$ 1.88	$ 3.20
PV	0.25	0.20	0.30
Fixed costs	$ 1,000,000	$ 1,000,000	$ 1,000,000
Desired profit	$ 5,000,000	$ 5,000,000	$ 5,000,000
Required sales revenue*	$24,000,000	$30,000,000	$20,000,000
Required unit volume†	2,400,000	3,200,000	1,870,000

*Required sales revenue = (desired profit + fixed costs)/PV.
†Required unit volume = required sales revenue/price.

assuming production capacity is available. Or, if the price increase leads to a volume decrease of less than 22 percent, the firm would be in a better profit position after the price increase. Figure 5-4 illustrates this situation.

Figure 5-4 is constructed by noting that for each price alternative, the maximum loss occurs when zero units are sold. This maximum loss equals fixed costs, or $1,000,000. The data of Table 5-4 indicate that the desired profit of $5,000,000 requires a sales revenue of $24,000,000 if price is $10.00, $30,000,000 if price is $9.38, and $20,000,000 if price is $10.70. Connecting these three points on the desired profit line with the maximum loss point at zero sales volume produces the PV break-even chart of Fig. 5-4.

Computing Necessary Volume Changes

It is possible to determine the necessary volume changes to maintain a level of profitability for any given PV value. Tables 5-5 and 5-6 give the percent volume changes necessary to offset different percent price changes. Figures 5-5 and 5-6 give an alternative way of making these calculations.

For example, suppose that a firm is considering raising price by 9 percent and its current PV ratio is 0.30. Table 5-5 and Fig. 5-5 both indicate that as long as volume does not decline more than 23 percent, the firm's profitability will be enhanced. Similarly, if the firm was considering a 9 percent price decrease, then Table 5-6 and Fig. 5-6 both indicate that volume must increase at least by 43 percent to maintain the same level of profitability as before the price change.

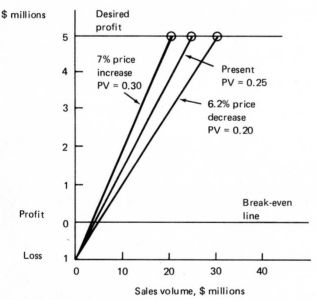

Figure 5-4 PV break-even chart: alternative pricing decisions.

Table 5-5 Permissible Volume Decrease to Offset Price Increase

Price increase, %	Percent maximum volume decrease permissible						
	PV ratio						
	0.10	0.15	0.20	0.25	0.30	0.35	0.40
1	9.09	6.25	4.76	3.85	3.23	2.77	2.44
2	16.67	11.76	9.09	7.41	6.25	5.41	4.76
3	23.08	16.67	13.04	10.71	9.09	7.89	6.98
4	28.57	21.05	16.67	13.79	11.76	10.26	9.09
5	33.33	25.00	20.00	16.67	14.29	12.50	11.11
6	37.50	28.57	23.08	19.35	16.67	14.63	13.04
7	41.18	31.82	25.93	21.88	18.92	16.67	14.89
8	44.44	34.78	28.57	24.24	21.05	18.60	16.67
9	47.34	37.50	31.03	26.47	23.08	20.45	18.37
10	50.00	40.00	33.33	28.57	25.00	22.22	20.00
15	60.00	50.00	42.86	37.50	33.33	30.00	27.27
20	66.67	57.14	50.00	44.44	40.00	36.36	33.33
25	71.43	62.50	55.56	50.00	45.45	41.67	38.46
30	75.00	66.67	60.00	54.55	50.00	46.15	42.86
35	.....	.....	63.64	58.33	53.85	50.00	46.67
40	.....	.....	66.67	61.54	57.14	53.33	50.00
45	.....	.....	.....	64.29	60.00	56.25	52.94
50	.....	.....	.....	66.67	62.50	58.82	55.56

Table 5-6 Minimum Volume Increase Required for Price Decrease

Price decrease, %	Percent minimum volume increase required						
	PV ratio						
	0.10	0.15	0.20	0.25	0.30	0.35	0.40
1	11.11	7.14	5.26	4.17	3.45	2.94	2.56
2	25.00	15.38	11.11	8.70	7.14	6.06	5.26
3	42.90	25.00	17.65	13.60	11.11	9.38	8.11
4	66.67	36.36	25.00	19.05	15.38	12.90	11.11
5	100.00	50.00	33.33	25.00	20.00	16.67	14.29
6	150.00	66.67	42.86	31.58	25.00	20.69	17.65
7	233.33	87.50	53.85	38.89	30.43	25.00	21.21
8	400.00	114.29	66.67	47.06	36.36	29.63	25.00
9	900.00	150.00	81.82	56.25	42.86	34.62	29.03
10	∞	200.00	100.00	66.67	50.00	40.00	33.33
15	.....	∞	300.00	150.00	100.00	75.00	60.00
20	.....	.....	∞	400.00	200.00	133.33	100.00
25	.....	.....	.....	∞	500.00	250.00	166.67
30	.....	.....	.....	.....	∞	600.00	300.00
35	.....	.....	.....	.....	.....	∞	700.00
40	.....	.....	.....	.....	.....	.....	∞

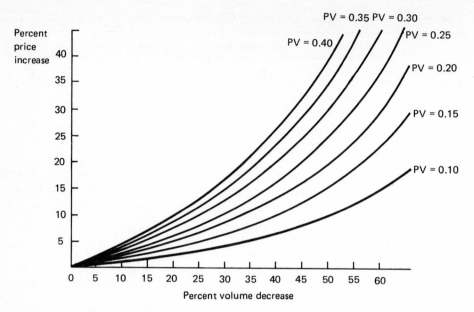

Figure 5-5 Permissible volume decrease to offset price increase.

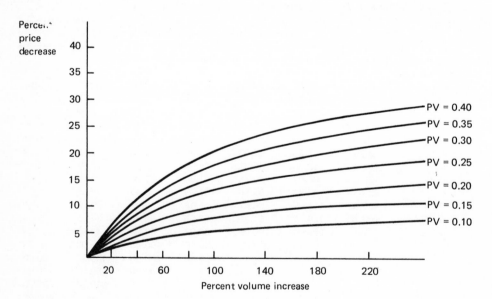

Figure 5-6 Minimum volume increase required for price decrease.

In general, for a price decrease, the necessary volume increase before profitability is enhanced is given by

$$\text{Volume increase (\%)} = \left(\frac{x}{PV - x}\right) 100 \qquad (5\text{-}7)$$

where x is the percent price decrease expressed as a decimal.

Similarly, for a price increase, the permissible volume decrease before profitability is harmed is given by

$$\text{Volume decrease (\%)} = \left(\frac{x}{PV + x}\right) 100 \qquad (5\text{-}8)$$

where x is the percent price increase expressed as a decimal.

To illustrate these two formulas consider the volume changes necessary for first, a 9 percent price decrease, and then, second, a 9 percent price increase. Further, assume the current PV ratio is 0.30. From Eq. (5-7) the percent volume increase is

$$\text{Volume increase (\%)} = \left(\frac{0.09}{0.30 - 0.09}\right) 100 = \left(\frac{0.09}{0.21}\right) 100 = 42.86\%$$

From Eq. (5-8) the percent volume decrease is

$$\text{Volume decrease (\%)} = \left(\frac{0.09}{0.30 + 0.09}\right) 100 = \left(\frac{0.09}{0.39}\right) 100 = 23.08\%$$

Computing Implied Price Elasticities

Once an alternative price proposal has been evaluated according to the volume changes necessary to enhance profitability, implied price elasticities may be computed. Recall that price elasticity of demand is defined as the percent change in volume relative to a percent change in price. From the example of Table 5-4, we have demonstrated that a proposed price decrease of 6.2 percent required a minimum volume increase of 33 percent before profits could be increased, if the current PV ratio is 0.25. This condition gives us the following implied price elasticity of demand:

$$E_d = \frac{33\%}{-6.2\%} = -5.32$$

A price elasticity of demand of -5.32 indicates that demand must be quite elastic before the price reduction can be profitable. If management does not believe that demand is sufficiently price elastic, then the alternative of reducing price by 6.2 percent is not economically justified.

Similarly, the alternative of increasing price by 7 percent produces an implied price elasticity of

$$E_d = \frac{-22\%}{7\%} = -3.14$$

When evaluating a price increase, it is important to remember that the estimated volume decrease is the maximum permissible if profits are to be enhanced. Hence, the actual price elasticity must be less elastic than the computed -3.14. For example, if management believes that price elasticity of demand is around -2, then the price increase of 7 percent will be profitable, but a price decrease of 6.2 percent will harm profits. Conversely, if management believes that price elasticity of demand is around -6, then the price decrease of 6.2 percent will enhance profits.

SUMMARY

This chapter has developed the key cost analysis method useful for evaluating pricing alternatives. A contribution approach has the advantage of forcing an analysis of costs in terms of causal factors. Those factors that are directly related to the costs incurred in the production and sale of a product are included as relevant to the cost analysis.

Break-even analysis was introduced and expanded to consider cost, demand, and profit implications of alternative prices. In addition, the analysis also permits an examination of alternative cost structures and their implications for establishing the cost bases of prices.

Expanding break-even analysis to include the profit implications of alternative price decisions provides some dynamics to an otherwise static analytical method. This chapter demonstrates how use of the PV ratio can help determine necessary or permissible volume changes for considered price changes. Moreover, since it is difficult to estimate future or prospective price elasticities of demand, the chapter also shows how to compute implied price elasticities for these necessary or permissible volume changes. Once management knows the conditions that must prevail before a price alternative will enhance profitability, it is in a position to make the best decision relative to the objectives of the firm and competitive factors.

Perhaps the main advantage of direct cost and contribution analysis is that it permits the calculation of those costs which are affected by the particular decision being analyzed. These costs, and more importantly the cost changes, can be traced to the decision, and the decision maker has a more objective basis for selection among alternative choices. Closely related, direct costing provides a way of calculating the profit contribution on various products, product lines, markets, accounts, or salespersons. Contribution data, as summarized in Table 5-7, have many additional advantages. Finally, through direct costing and the development of contribution data, management is given the opportunity to avoid arbitrary formulas to allocate common costs when establishing prices.

Table 5-7 Advantages of Contribution Data for Pricing Decisions

The use of contribution information facilitates

1. The determination of correct prices for individual products and/or orders
2. Selecting target prices for desired PV to classes of buyers or markets
3. Identifying the most profitable products, customers, markets
4. Identifying which products need management's attention
5. Selecting and improving the product mix
6. Determining the pricing floor
7. Evaluating proposals to increase profits by increasing prices and/or increasing volume
8. Clarifying the understanding of costs by company personnel responsible for pricing
9. Getting all departments to speak a common language in talking about prices and profits
10. Estimating profits from alternative future proposals
11. Establishing a better reward-for-performance basis of compensating the selling effort

Source: Adapted from Spencer A. Tucker, *Pricing for Higher Profit* (New York: McGraw-Hill, 1966), pp. 93-94.

DISCUSSION QUESTIONS

1 Assume the specialty retailer discussed in this chapter determines that fixed costs have increased to $21,000 per year. Further, assume that the shirts can now be acquired for $9 and that the retailer raises the retail price of shirts to $12. Compute
   a Contribution dollars per shirt.
   b PV ratio.
   c Break-even quantity.
   d Break-even sales (dollars).
   e Draw a break-even graph.

2 For the specialty retailer in Question 1, assume fixed costs decrease to $18,000 per year. Perform the same calculations as you did in parts **a** to **e** of Question 1. Describe the changes that have taken place.

3 For the specialty retailer in Question 1, assume the supplier raises the price of the shirts to $10. What price must the retailer charge for the shirts to obtain the same break-even point in sales dollars at this new price?

4 For the specialty retailer in Question 1, assume yearly shirt sales have been 20,000 shirts.
   a Calculate the profits earned before taxes.
   b Assume the situation depicted in Question 3. For the new price you calculated in Question 3, determine the maximum volume decrease permissible, if profits are to remain at the amount determined in part **a** of Question 4.
   c Calculate the implied price elasticity of demand for your answer in part **b**.
   d Describe the results of your calculations in parts **b** and **c**.
   e Prepare a PV break-even chart for part **b**.

5 An electronic equipment manufacturer has been producing 15,000 units of a special electronic component for one of its most important customers for the past 3 years of a 5-year contract. The contract calls for delivery of these parts at $15.00

each. Direct labor and material costs are $10.50 per unit. Direct fixed costs are $20,000. At the beginning of the fourth year, a new customer requests a 1-year contract to purchase 10,000 units of this part at a price of $11.00 per unit. The manufacturer's controller estimates that production costs at 25,000 units would be about $10.25 per unit, and that total fixed costs would increase to $30,000. Analyze this situation. Be sure to consider all implications of the situation. What action would you recommend?

SUGGESTED READINGS

Arnstein, William E.: "Relating Pricing to Costs," *Financial Executive*, 39 (December 1971), 38–47.

Böer, Germain B.: *Direct Cost and Contribution Accounting* (New York: John Wiley, 1974).

Ferrara, William L.: "Break-Even for Individual Products, Plants, and Sales Territories," *Management Advisor* (formerly *Management Services*), 1 (July–August 1964), 38–47.

Swalley, Richard W.: "The Benefits of Direct Costing," *Management Accounting*, 56 (September 1974), 13–16.

Tucker, Spencer A.: *Pricing for Higher Profit* (New York: McGraw-Hill, 1966).

Woolsey, Sam M.: "The Direct-Cost Approach to Setting Optimum Sales Prices," *Industrial Marketing*, 55 (January 1970), 35–39.

——: *Direct Costing Techniques for Industry* (Englewood Cliffs, N.J.: Prentice-Hall, 1967).

Wright, Wilmer: "Direct Costs Are Better for Pricing," *NAA Bulletin* (April 1960), 17–26.

Chapter 6

Marketing Cost Analysis

One of the least developed areas in costing is the analysis of the marketing effort and determination of profit contribution by product line, customer account, order, sales territory, or salesperson. When we reflect on the size of advertising and sales promotion budgets of most companies, we might assume that management has information on the relative profitability of marketing expenditures. Typically, this is not the case, and the marketing effort includes spending inefficiencies that are considered "unavoidable costs of marketing."[1] However, proper costs for pricing must include all costs that may change when activities are changed or redirected. This chapter expands cost analysis to include additional approaches for obtaining data when activities are changed or redirected.

As the cost components of Fig. 5-1 indicate, marketing costs may be classified as direct or indirect. And, as defined in Chap. 4, direct marketing costs may be variable or fixed. Similarly, indirect marketing costs may be variable or fixed. This chapter expands the contribution analysis of Chap. 5 to include marketing costs. Since marketing cost accounting is not a well-developed technique, emphasis is also placed on the need for and the benefits of marketing cost data for marketing decision making. The chapter also demonstrates how data may be obtained for analyzing the marketing effort.

[1]Richard A. Feder, "How to Measure Marketing Performance," *Harvard Business Review*, 43 (May–June 1965), 132–142.

NEED FOR MARKETING COST DATA

It has been estimated that the average manufacturer spends up to 5 percent of its marketing funds at a loss.[2] There are many reasons for such misdirected efforts.

Attempts to achieve too high a market share.

Failure to adjust marketing efforts to variations in demand.

Failure to adjust national marketing strategies for product or market dissimilarities.

Available data are not reported in sufficient detail to permit profitability analysis by product, market, or other meaningful profit segment.

Data are not presented on a comparative basis or are incomplete.

Product and distribution cost data are averages or outdated standards and do not reflect current and future costs in serving a market or customer group.

Marketing managers have made little effort to define their information needs.

Poor communication between marketing, accounting, and systems personnel.

Responsibilities of Marketing Management

Clearly, the major responsibility for obtaining better marketing cost information lies within the realm of marketing management. Among these responsibilities is the need to define clearly the types of decisions requiring better cost information. Management must also determine the value expected from better information. For example, one company determined that a theoretical sales effort allocation plan suggested annual savings of $500,000 over the current practice. A limited test of the new plan revealed that it would cost $50,000 to install the necessary information system, but that the annual savings would approximate $400,000. Other companies have reviewed past, costly errors to determine how better information might have prevented the errors.

Benefits of Marketing Cost Data

Today, the typical business firm, manufacturer, wholesaler, or retailer sells a relatively large number of products. Each of these products is in a different market and faces different degrees of competition. Consequently, to compete effectively, each product requires its own marketing mix. Moreover, these firms sell to different types and sizes of customers in different geographical locations. Essentially, then, marketing management is concerned with identifying and selecting alternative courses of action that lead to more profitable sales volumes. To identify profit opportunities, management needs to know the changes in profit that result when changes in sales volume occur because of marketing decisions.

It is necessary to have cost information

- By product
- By market (sales territory, shipping area, advertising area)
- By channel of distribution

[2] Ibid., p. 132.

- By class of customer (type of retailer, type of wholesaler for consumer marketing; SIC code for industrial marketing)
- By size of customer
- By key accounts
- By average order size
- By type of marketing expenditure (sales calls, discounts, advertising and promotional costs)

When analyzing alternative decisions, the proper information is the marginal or incremental profit contribution that covers fixed costs and profits after subtracting all direct and indirect traceable costs. By placing the accent on incremental profit opportunity, the firm can pinpoint the market segments with highest profit opportunities, determine the level of selling effort to achieve profit objectives, decide when to accept new orders or introduce new products, determine the costs of different distribution patterns, determine realistic prices, establish a basis for cost justification defenses against price discrimination complaints, design sales incentive plans, establish sales call patterns, and set minimum order quantities.[3]

NATURE OF MARKETING COST ANALYSIS

Marketing cost analysis involves a study of the organization's entire marketing function. The purpose of marketing cost analysis is to identify and measure marketing cost elements to determine the profitability of different market/sales segments, such as products, customers, territories, and sales order sizes; and to eliminate or reduce losses resulting from misdirected marketing efforts.

In its simplest form, marketing cost analysis can be made from five sets of data: (1) names and location of customers, (2) types of businesses of customers, (3) number of each customer's orders in a given period, (4) total sales to each customer in the same period, and (5) total sales and gross profits on each product in the line.[4] In addition, additional data frequently available include (6) number of shelf-stock and full-case orders, (7) number of deliveries, (8) method of delivery, (9) type of merchandise ordered, (10) method of payment, and (11) amount of returns. These data can be collected from customer records using a basic document such as an invoice or bill of lading.[5]

Generally, most firms' records will permit a more extensive approach to analyzing marketing costs. However, regardless of the sophistication of the firm's records, several common errors should be avoided. First, marketing costs should not be allocated to products, customers, or other profit segments on the basis of sales volume, since most

---

[3] Examples of market segment accounting are given in Leland L. Beik and Stephen L. Buzby, "Profitability Analysis by Market Segment," *Journal of Marketing*, 37 (July 1973), 48–54; and Frank H. Mossman, Paul M. Fischer, and W. J. E. Crissy, "New Approaches to Analyzing Marketing Profitability," *Journal of Marketing*, 38 (April 1974), 43–48.

[4] Charles H. Sevin, *Analyzing Your Cost of Marketing*, Small Business Administration Management Aids No. 85, reprinted April 1971.

[5] Frank H. Mossman, Paul M. Fischer, and W. J. E. Crissy, "New Approaches to Analyzing Marketing Profitability," *Journal of Marketing*, 38 (April 1974), 44.

marketing costs are not caused by sales. Second, general and administrative costs should not be arbitrarily allocated to profit segments. And, third, legitimate marketing costs should not be "lumped" into general cost categories such as manufacturing or general and administrative costs.

Alternative Approaches

Marketing cost analysis may be traced back to a book published in 1908 by a cost accountant, A. Hamilton Church.[6] Church recommended that "office and selling" expenses be apportioned among products using a method that any competent person could rationally justify. During the next 20 to 30 years, this method of arbitrarily allocating selling costs to products became known as the *traditional approach*. Primarily, the developers of this allocation approach argued that marketing costs were not like production costs and, therefore, were not readily traced to individual products or product lines.

In the early 1930s, one of the foremost marketing scholars, Wroe Alderson, developed the basis of what today we call *marketing cost analysis*.[7] (Most texts still refer to the techniques of costing marketing activities as *distribution cost analysis*. However, to avoid the possible interpretation that such costing efforts do not cover all marketing costs, we prefer the more general term marketing cost analysis.) Alderson's method was further developed by Charles Sevin and is referred to today as the *net profit approach*.

In recent years, increasing emphasis has been placed on the *direct cost-contribution approach*. As developed in Chap. 5, the contribution approach emphasizes the contribution in excess of direct variable costs and direct fixed costs made to cover fixed costs by different marketing profit segments. We will now define marketing cost classifications and then develop both the contribution and net profit approaches to marketing cost analysis.

Marketing Cost Classifications

Common fixed marketing costs are costs incurred in common for different profit segments and do not vary with the volume of sales in any profit segment. For example, costs of institutional advertising of a company's name would not be allocated to individual segments.

Direct variable marketing costs vary with sales and can be allocated to profit segments. Sales commissions, transportation costs, and some aspects of ordering and billing costs vary directly with sales and/or customer accounts.

Separable fixed marketing costs are costs that can be allocated to specific profit/sales segments. Field supervision expenses and warehousing are examples of fixed marketing costs that can be identified with specific segments.

---

[6] A. Hamilton Church, *The Proper Distribution of Expense Burden* (New York: The Engineering Magazine, 1908).

[7] An excellent history of marketing cost analysis is contained in two unpublished papers: Paul F. Anderson, "The Development of Distribution Cost Analysis Methods, 1908–1941," Virginia Polytechnic Institute and State University, 1973; and Joseph A. Hopkins, "Distribution Cost Analysis–Development during 1940–1976," Virginia Polytechnic Institute and State University, 1977.

THE CONTRIBUTION APPROACH

The contribution approach essentially extends the contribution method of cost analysis developed in Chap. 5. To illustrate the approach assume that a firm produces three types of lawn mowers: X, a gasoline-powered mower; Y, an electric-powered mower; and Z, a gasoline-powered tractor mower. Assume further that the company has three sales territories: A, B, C. Production variable costs for each product are given in Table 6-1 and include materials and labor. Product X is sold at a price of $100; Y is priced at $150; and Z is priced at $450.

Tables 6-1 and 6-2 illustrate three types of direct variable marketing costs: commissions, transportation, and order-processing costs. In Table 6-1 these variable marketing costs are directly assignable to the territories because there is a direct relationship to the sales effort activity within each territory. In Table 6-2 these same variable costs are assigned to the three products again on the basis of a sales effort activity. It is also important to note that in Table 6-2 territory direct fixed costs are not allocated to the three products since there is no objective way to allocate these common marketing costs to each product.

The main distinction between the contribution approach and the net profit approach is that the contribution method avoids arbitrary allocation of common, fixed marketing costs. As noted in Chap. 5, once the contribution of each product or profit segment is determined, then a PV ratio may be computed and alternative prices for each product may be analyzed exactly as developed in Chap. 5. For example, the PV ratio for product X in territory A is $57,500/$300,000, or 0.19. If the firm is considering raising the price of gasoline-powered lawn mowers in territory A to $110—a 10 percent price increase, then using the formula from Eq. (5-8), volume in territory A can fall no more than 34.5 percent if the territory's profit contribution from product X is to be enhanced.

$$\text{Volume decrease } (\%) = \left(\frac{0.10}{0.19 + 0.10}\right) 100 = 34.5\%$$

THE NET PROFIT APPROACH[8]

This approach is primarily of use to manufacturers and wholesalers. However, the method is adaptable for use by retailers also. In general, reference will be to profit segments and it should be understood that these segments may be individual products, product lines, customer types, specific customer accounts, sales territories, or alternative channels of distribution.

The *net profit approach* attempts to allocate all indirect costs among the profit segments. Essentially, this approach is similar to the full-costing method to be described in Chap. 7 and has the same disadvantages. Indeed, the contribution method avoids arbitrary allocation of common, fixed marketing costs. However, the Federal Trade Commission requires a full-cost allocation approach for justifying cost differences

[8]This section is based on Charles H. Sevin, *Marketing Productivity Analysis* (New York: McGraw-Hill, 1965).

Table 6-1 Marketing Cost Analysis—Contribution by Territories

	Territory			Total
	A	B	C	
Sales revenues				
Product X	$300,000	$150,000	$120,000	$570,000
Product Y	110,000	80,000	70,000	260,000
Product Z	90,000	120,000	110,000	320,000
	$500,000	$350,000	$300,000	$1,150,000
Variable costs				
Production	$350,000	$270,000	$180,000	$800,000
Marketing—commission	35,000	23,000	20,000	78,000
Marketing—transportation	9,000	7,000	6,000	22,000
Marketing—ordering	6,000	5,000	4,000	15,000
	400,000	305,000	210,000	915,000
Contribution	$100,000	$45,000	$90,000	$235,000
Direct fixed costs				
Rent	$2,000	$1,500	$2,500	$6,000
Salaries	11,000	8,500	9,500	29,000
Promotion	6,000	5,000	3,000	14,000
	19,000	15,000	15,000	49,000
Territory contribution	$81,000	$30,000	$75,000	$186,000
Common fixed costs				25,000
Total contribution				$161,000

Table 6-2 Marketing Cost Analysis—Contribution by Products
Territory A

| | Product | | | Total |
	X	Y	Z	
Sales revenue	$300,000	$110,000	$90,000	$500,000
Variable costs				
Production	$210,000	$ 80,000	$60,000	$350,000
Marketing—commissions	25,000	6,000	4,000	35,000
Marketing—transportation	4,000	3,000	2,000	9,000
Marketing—ordering	3,500	1,500	1,000	6,000
Total variable costs	$242,500	$ 90,500	$67,000	$400,000
Product contribution	$ 57,500	$ 19,500	$23,000	$100,000
Territory direct fixed costs				
Rent				$ 2,000
Salaries				11,000
Promotion				6,000
				$ 19,000
Territory contribution				$ 81,000

under the Robinson-Patman Act. (See Chap. 16.) But, perhaps more appropriately, short-run decisions would be concerned more with the profit contribution made by specific segments. Thus, either the contribution approach or the net profit approach may be appropriate depending on the purpose of the analysis.

There are two analytical steps in the net profit approach.

1 Marketing expenditures of a business are reclassified from a *natural-expense* basis into *functional-cost* groups. The functional-cost groups comprise all the costs associated with each marketing activity (function) performed by the business.

2 Functional-cost groups are assigned to profit segments on the basis of *measurable factors* that exhibit causal relationships to the functional costs.

A natural-expense item refers to the usual way expenses of a business are classified; e.g., rent, wages. However, a natural expense such as wages may *functionally* be related to direct selling, selling supervision, order assembly, order billing, and credit. Each of these activities are a part of a separate marketing function and the natural-expense item must be apportioned among several functional-cost groups.

To classify marketing costs according to functions requires a study of the marketing activities performed by the business. The assignment of natural-expense items to functional-cost groups often is accomplished by means of work-measurement studies, space measurements, managerial estimates, and statistical techniques. As suggested in Chap. 4, it is important to establish a cause-effect relationship between various marketing costs and the corresponding functional-cost grouping. The discussion of cost classifications and cost behaviors of Chap. 4 is equally appropriate here. Table 6-3 gives examples of functional-cost groups and bases of allocation.

Table 6-3 Functional-Cost Groups and Bases of Allocation

Functional-cost group	To products	To customers	To sales territories
1. Selling—direct costs: Personal calls by salespeople and supervisors on accounts and prospects; sales salaries, incentive compensation, travel, and other expenses	Selling time devoted to each product, as shown by sales-call reports or other studies	Number of sales calls times average time per call, as shown by sales-call reports or other studies	Direct
2. Selling—indirect costs: Field supervision, field sales-administration expense, sales-personnel training, sales management; market research, new-product development, sales statistics, tabulating services, sales accounting	In proportion to direct selling time or time records by projects	In proportion to direct selling time or time records by projects	Equal charge for each salesperson
3. Advertising: Media costs such as TV, radio, billboards, newspapers, magazines; advertising production costs; advertising department salaries	Direct, or analysis of space and time by media; other costs in proportion to media costs	Equal charge to each account; or number of ultimate consumers and prospects in each account's trading area	Direct analysis of media circulation records
4. Sales promotion: Consumer promotions such as coupons, premiums; trade promotions such as price allowances, point of purchase displays, cooperative advertising	Direct, or analysis of source records	Direct, or analysis of source records	Direct, or analysis of source records
5. Transportation: Railroad, truck, barge; payments to carriers for delivery on finished goods from plants to warehouses and from warehouses to customers; traffic department costs	Applicable rates times tonnages	Analysis of sampling of bills of lading	Applicable rates times tonnages
6. Storage and shipping: Storage of finished-goods inventories in warehouses; rent (or equivalent costs), public warehouse charges, fire insurance and taxes on finished-goods inventories; physical handling, assembling, and loading out of rail cars, trucks, barges	Warehouse space occupied by average inventory; number of shipping units	Number of shipping units	Number of shipping units

Table 6-3 Functional-Cost Groups and Bases of Allocation *(Continued)*

Functional-cost group	To products	To customers	To sales territories
for shipping finished products from warehouses and mills to customers, labor, equipment, space, and material costs			
7. Order processing: Checking and processing of orders from customers to mills for prices, weights, and carload accumulation, shipping dates, coordination with production planning; pricing department; preparation of customer invoices; freight accounting; credit and collection; handling cash receipts; provision for bad debts; salary, supplies, space, and equipment costs	Number of order lines	Number of order lines	Number of order lines

Source: Charles H. Sevin, *Marketing Productivity Analysis* (New York: McGraw-Hill, 1965), pp. 13–15.

As Table 6-3 indicates, there are certain types of data required before marketing costs can be assigned to products. Essentially, the data needed are

1 The average inventory value of finished goods
2 The amount of storage space required for these finished goods
3 The frequency with which the product is ordered (number of invoice lines)
4 The number of "packs" of the product sold (gross, cases, dozen)
5 The weight or number of units shipped
6 The proportion of selling time spent selling the product
7 Direct advertising costs

The data required for assigning marketing costs to customers are

1 The total number of invoice lines for the period
2 The total weight or number of units shipped
3 The number of sales calls
4 Any direct advertising or promotion costs
5 The number of orders placed by the customer
6 The average amount of accounts receivable
7 The number of invoices posted to accounts receivable
8 The amount of returns

The analysis of marketing costs by territory generally is simpler than the analysis either by products or by customers. When a firm's marketing activities are organized along well-defined geographical boundaries, a large proportion of marketing expenses is directly traceable to the territories. Hence, the problem of assigning indirect marketing expenses is less burdensome. Once functional expenses have been assigned to the marketing profit segments, a profit and loss statement is prepared for each segment.

To illustrate the application of the net profit approach, assume that the lawn mower manufacturer wishes to assign the rent, salaries, and promotion expenses of territory A to products X, Y, and Z. As indicated above, the first step is to reclassify these natural-expense items into functional marketing cost groups. The relevant marketing cost groups for territory A are selling, advertising and promotion, order processing, and storage and shipping. The reclassification of the natural indirect expenses into functional costs is shown in Table 6-4. Table 6-5 shows the basis for allocating the functional expenses to each product, which is the second step in the net profit approach.

In Table 6-4, the rent is divided evenly by the order processing, storage and shipping activities because salespeople work away from the territory office and an advertising agency handles the advertising and promotion activity. The district sales supervisor, who also sells and coordinates the territory's advertising and promotion activities, spends about 57 percent of the time in selling. Therefore, the supervisor's salary is divided proportionately between selling, and advertising and promotion. The remaining $4,000 of salaries is divided between order processing, and storage and shipping.

Once the natural expenses have been classified into functional expenses, the task is to assign each functional expense to the three products. Table 6-5 shows the allocation formulas and the data necessary to complete this task. From sales reports filed by the supervisor it is determined that 50 percent of the selling time is devoted to product X, the gasoline-powered lawn mower. Hence, 50 percent of the $4,000 fixed selling expense is assigned to product X, as shown in Table 6-6. Advertising and promotion expenses are assigned on the basis of the number of advertisements and the average cost per advertisement. Since product X was featured in 40 local advertisements, $3,600 ($90 × 40) is assigned to product X. Similarly, on the basis of average cost per order processed, and the average shipping cost per unit shipped, the remaining marketing costs are assigned to the three products.

As shown in Table 6-6, the last step is to calculate the net profit for each product. Thus, an accounting profit or loss can be computed for the profit segments, which in

Table 6-4 Classifying Natural Expenses into Functional Expenses

	Natural accounts	Selling	Advertising and promotion	Order processing	Storage and shipping
Rent	$ 2,000	$ —0—	$ —0—	$1,000	$1,000
Salaries	11,000	4,000	3,000	2,000	2,000
Promotion	6,000	—0—	6,000	—0—	—0—
	$19,000	$4,000	$9,000	$3,000	$3,000

Table 6-5 Bases for Allocating Functional Expenses to Products

Product	Selling Proportion of selling time	Advertising and promotion Number of advertisements	Order processing Number of orders	Storage and shipping Number of units shipped
X	0.50	40	300	1,000
Y	0.30	40	75	733
Z	0.20	20	50	200
Totals	1.00	100	425	1,933
Functional expenses	$4,000	$9,000	$3,000	$3,000
Allocation formula	Direct propor- tion of selling time	Cost per advertisement: $\dfrac{\$9,000}{100} = \$90$	Cost per order $\dfrac{\$3,000}{425} = \$7.06$	Cost per unit $\dfrac{\$3,000}{1,933} = \$1.55$

this example are products. The reader should note that the computation of marketing costs using the net profit approach has a distinct element of arbitrariness. When one arbitrary formula replaces another, the relative profitability of a profit segment could shift quite radically. Hence, as argued in Chap. 4, for pricing decisions the contribution approach makes it easier to analyze the profit impact of alternative prices.

SUMMARY

As discussed in Chap. 5, the role of costs for pricing decisions is limited, but nevertheless, quite important. However, there is a great tendency to lump marketing costs into a general cost category, often called administrative, selling, and general overhead. Such

Table 6-6 Territory A: Profit and Loss by Product

	Product			
	X	Y	Z	Territory
Sales revenue	$300,000	$110,000	$90,000	$500,000
Variable costs	242,500	90,500	67,000	400,000
Product contribution	$ 57,500	$ 19,500	$23,000	$100,000
Fixed costs				
Selling	$ 2,000	$ 1,200	$ 800	$ 4,000
Advertising and promotion	3,600	3,600	1,800	9,000
Order processing	2,118	529	353	3,000
Storage and shipping	1,550	1,140	310	3,000
Total expenses	$ 9,268	$ 6,469	$ 3,263	$ 19,000
Net profit	$ 48,232	$ 13,031	$19,737	$ 81,000

a classification of costs is a gross error. Marketing costs can be classified into direct traceable, indirect traceable, and common fixed costs similarly to production costs. By so classifying marketing costs, management is in a position to know the effects of price changes on volume and production and on marketing costs. Thus, given a precise measure of marketing costs, all relevant costs for pricing will be known.

Further, the firm would also be in a position to estimate the profitability of various sales/profit segments at past prices and at alternative future prices. And by knowing which products, territories, or customer accounts are unprofitable, price changes can be analyzed to discourage growth of unprofitable segments and to encourage growth of profitable ones. Control of marketing costs is enhanced and a method of re-allocating marketing efforts to more profitable segments becomes a reality. Finally, as developed in Chap. 16, marketing cost analysis provides a means of justifying price differentials.

DISCUSSION QUESTIONS

1 A wholesaler of office supplies conducted a marketing cost study. At the conclusion of the study, the main results were summarized for the manager as shown below:

	Account classification				
	A	B	C	D	E
Number of accounts	500	400	300	200	100
Average order	$ 100	$ 300	$ 500	$ 900	$ 1,200
Annual sales	$500,000	$1,500,000	$2,250,000	$2,000,000	$1,800,000
Contribution	$150,000	$ 450,000	$ 675,000	$ 600,000	$ 540,000
Selling expense	$ 60,000	$ 50,000	$ 45,000	$ 25,000	$ 20,000
Delivery expense	50,000	50,000	45,000	30,000	20,000
Credit and collection expense	40,000	20,000	15,000	10,000	5,000
Order processing expense	30,000	30,000	25,000	20,000	15,000
Total expenses	$180,000	$ 150,000	$ 130,000	$ 85,000	$ 60,000
Profit (loss)	$ (30,000)	$ 300,000	$ 545,000	$ 515,000	$ 480,000

a Identify the marketing cost approach probably used by the company.
b What are some of the possible causes of class A accounts being unprofitabale?
c Refer back to "The Meaning of Price" discussion in Chap. 1. What are some ways that price can be used to enhance the profitability of serving class A accounts?
d Can you think of any other alternative solutions to enhance the profitability of serving class A accounts?
e On what bases do you think the wholesaler allocated the four types of expenses to the account classes? Can you think of other ways to allocate these expenses?
f Consider your answers to parts c and d above. Suppose the wholesaler implemented your solutions, what changes might occur in the expense accounting? What assumptions did you make to arrive at these changes in the expense accounting?

2 A small electric appliance company made two products: a food blender and a food mixer. The company sold in two territories, A and B. Given below are the cost and revenue figures for 1979.

	Blender	Mixer
Selling price per unit	$40.00	$20.00
Sales volume in units		
Territory A	6,000	8,000
Territory B	4,000	13,000
Direct variable manufacturing costs per unit	$20.00	$ 9.00
Variable selling costs per unit	$ 2.00	$ 1.50
Variable distribution costs per unit	$ 4.00	$ 0.50
Promotion expenses per year	$2,500	$2,000

Fixed costs for territory A were $5,000 and for territory B were $5,400. Other fixed expenses for the firm amounted to $12,000.

a Perform a contribution analysis by products.

b Perform a contribution analysis by territories.

c The firm is considering an across-the-board price increase of 10 percent. What is the maximum permissible volume decrease before profitability is harmed?

d What additional information would you desire before deciding to raise prices? Why?

SUGGESTED READINGS

Beik, Leland L., and Stephen L. Buzby: "Profitability Analysis by Market Segments," *Journal of Marketing*, 37 (July 1973), 48–53.

Böer, Germain B.: "Market Reporting Systems," *Direct Cost and Contribution Accounting* (New York: John Wiley, 1974), chap. 7, pp. 91–108.

Buzby, Stephen L., and Lester Heitger: "Profit Contribution by Market Segment," *Management Accounting*, 58 (November 1976), 42–46.

Corr, Arthur V.: "A Cost-Effectiveness Approach to Marketing Outlays," *Management Accounting*, 58 (January 1976), 33–36.

Dunne, Patrick M., and Harry I. Wolk: "Marketing Cost Analysis: A Modularized Contribution Approach," *Journal of Marketing*, 41 (July 1977), 83–94.

Feder, Richard A.: "How to Measure Marketing Performance," *Harvard Business Review*, 43 (May–June 1965), 132–142.

Kirpalani, V. H., and Stanley S. Shapiro: "Financial Dimensions of Marketing Management," *Journal of Marketing*, 37 (July 1973), 40–47.

Mossman, Frank H., W. J. E. Crissy, and Paul M. Fischer: *Financial Dimensions of Marketing Management* (New York: John Wiley, 1978).

———, Paul M. Fischer, and W. J. E. Crissy: "New Approaches to Analyzing Marketing Profitability," *Journal of Marketing*, 38 (April 1974), 43–48.

Chapter 7

Developing
Full-Cost Estimates

The previous three chapters have presented methods for determining relative contributions to covering fixed costs and profits by various profit segments. However, indirect costs such as factory overhead and general administrative expenses are incurred and are not always traceable to profit segments. Over time a variety of formulas has been used to allocate these overhead costs to products and other profit segments of business. Unfortunately, the fixed costs allocated by these formulas, although quick and easy, are illogical. Indeed, the exact way and the rate at which overhead is applied to profit segments differ from one company to the next, and frequently differ within a company.

This chapter explores the disadvantages of these methods of assigning overhead and presents a functional method for assigning cost burdens to the segments of the business responsible for incurring the particular burden. One clear advantage of the functional approach is its utility for justifying price differentials, a topic developed in Chap. 16.

The primary need for developing "full costs" is to enable the decision maker to know what costs the contribution covers. Those who favor traditional full costing for pricing purposes maintain that a knowledge of direct costs and contribution may provide an excuse for price cutting. That is, since the contribution amount is usually larger than the gross profit figure, the decision maker might be tempted to reduce prices. Hence, the full-cost advocates claim that fixed or period costs must be allocated so that each product or segment "carries its proper share," "pulls its own weight," or "is charged fairly." Over time, various methods of full-cost pricing have evolved, and, as shown in this chapter, each method leads to a different price.

Price should not be conceived as the residual of the costing process. Buyers are not concerned that the seller has covered all his costs; rather they are concerned with the perceived value of the product in relation to its price. Essentially, price must be acceptable to the market and above direct variable costs.

Developing a full-cost estimate provides the price setter with a range of acceptable prices from the cost floor—the out-of-pocket cost level—to the market-determined ceiling. As the building blocks of Fig. 5-1 illustrate, a direct costing approach can provide both the direct costs and the full costs, thereby enabling the price setter to know whether the contribution covers full costs. Such information should help prevent the occurrence of unwise price reductions.

On the other hand, direct costing helps prevent the use of formulas, magic numbers, factors, percentages, or other illogical techniques for determining price. Short-cut formulas victimize the decision process and the firm rides the roller coaster of profits and losses as the formulas approach or depart from actual costs. The formula approach is like spreading period costs with a bulldozer, filling in holes and leveling peaks.[1]

We will first briefly illustrate the full-cost method of pricing and point out how the selling price is sensitive to the way in which overhead is allocated to the product. Then we will develop the concept of overhead and illustrate how different methods may be used to assign overhead or common costs to profit segments. Each method of overhead application will be presented and discussed. At the end of the chapter, it will be pointed out that many overhead costs can be classified as fixed and variable, and that a functional approach can be used to assign these costs to products. The functional approach is an adaptation of the net profit approach of assigning marketing costs discussed in Chap. 6.

FULL-COST METHOD OF PRICING

Using the full-cost (or cost-plus) method of pricing, a percentage of variable costs is added to the average variable costs to determine selling price. Presumably, this percentage or margin covers overhead costs and profit. In equation form this decision rule is

$$\text{Price} = (1 + m)(\text{variable costs}) \qquad (7\text{-}1)$$

where m is markup. As the equation indicates, the pricing decision actually reduces to determining the size of m.

Among the reasons cited for adhering to this pricing method are:[2]

---

[1] Spencer A. Tucker, *Pricing for Higher Profits* (New York: McGraw-Hill, 1966), p. 32.
[2] R. L. Hall and C. J. Hitch, "Price Theory and Business Behavior," *Oxford Economic Papers*, No. 2, May 1939.

1 Sellers do not know consumer preferences, and, therefore, are not able to determine product demand and revenue schedules.

2 Sellers do not know how rival sellers will react to price changes, but competitors are expected to follow price reductions, and not follow price increases.

3 Sellers do not know the degree to which demand is sensitive to price changes, and, therefore, do not know the effects on revenues if prices are changed.

4 There is a traditional belief that prices ought to equal full cost, that full-cost pricing produces the "right" or "fair" price.

As these reasons suggest, the full-cost method of pricing provides for some price stability, and prices change only when average variable costs change. Presumably, since labor and material cost changes would similarly affect competing sellers, competitive reaction to price changes produced by cost changes would be predictable and in the same direction. Thus, pricing decisions based on markup rules are not thought to be responsive to demand or shifts in demand.

The full-cost method is a popular method because it is easy to explain and justify to buyers and to the government. However, the main premise of the method is that all products must bear their full share of costs. Thus, the method assumes that if all the assigned costs are covered by the selling price, then all costs will be recovered.

Perhaps the greatest weakness of this pricing method is that in practice full costs refer to fully allocated costs. Fully allocated costs refer to costs assigned to products using common facilities by the firm. Multiproduct firms may produce different products using essentially the same kind of inputs and equipment. Moreover, these products may benefit from the use of common administrative, selling, and distribution facilities. Usually these common costs are allocated to the products on an expected-volume basis using arbitrary allocation rules.

To appreciate how these arbitrary allocation rules affect selling price, consider the following four formulas:

I Assign production overhead as 150 percent of direct labor and to the total of labor, material, and production overhead, add one-tenth for administrative, selling, and distribution overhead (A, S, D overhead).

II Assign all overhead as 100 percent of direct material cost.

III Assign all overhead as 200 percent of direct labor cost.

IV Assign production overhead as 100 percent of direct material costs, and all other overhead as 50 percent of direct labor cost.

Any of these formulas applied to labor and/or material costs will recover overhead *annually*. However, when applied to determine unit selling price, the results are quite different as Table 7-1 shows. Table 7-2 summarizes these very different results. Note that product A's price could range between $23.10 and $36.30 depending on the overhead allocation formula. Even more dramatically, product C's price could range between $33.00 and $71.50. The executive may wonder why the concern, "if we have been pricing this way, and everyone in the industry sets price in a similar way." The answer is that it is not possible to determine the relationship between price, volume, and costs to analyze different alternative approaches to maintaining or improving

Table 7-1 Example of Full-Cost Pricing Method

	Product		
Price computations	A	B	C
Costs			
1. Direct labor	$ 2.00	$ 5.00	$20.00
2. Direct material	15.00	10.00	5.00
Formula I			
3. Production overhead (150% of 1)	$ 3.00	$ 7.50	$30.00
4. Subtotal (1 + 2 + 3)	$20.00	$22.50	$55.00
5. A, S, D overhead (10% of 4)	2.00	2.25	5.50
6. Total cost (4 + 5)	$22.00	$24.75	$60.50
7. 10% markup (m)	2.20	2.48	6.05
8. Selling price (6 + 7)	$24.20	$27.23	$66.55
Formula II			
9. Overhead (100% of 2)	$15.00	$10.00	$ 5.00
10. Total cost (1 + 2 + 9)	$32.00	$25.00	$30.00
11. 10% markup (m)	3.20	2.50	3.00
12. Selling price (10 + 11)	$35.20	$27.50	$33.00
Formula III			
13. Overhead (200% of 1)	$ 4.00	$10.00	$40.00
14. Total cost (1 + 2 + 13)	$21.00	$25.00	$65.00
15. 10% markup (m)	2.10	2.50	6.50
16. Selling price (14 + 15)	$23.10	$27.50	$71.50
Formula IV			
17. Production overhead (100% of 2)	$15.00	$10.00	$ 5.00
18. A, S, D overhead (50% of 1)	1.00	2.50	10.00
19. Total cost (1 + 2 + 17 + 18)	$33.00	$27.50	$40.00
20. 10% markup (m)	3.30	2.75	4.00
21. Selling price (19 + 20)	$36.30	$30.25	$44.00

Table 7-2 Selling Prices from Formulas I to IV

	Formula			
Product	I	II	III	IV
A	$24.20	$35.20	$23.10	$36.30
B	27.23	27.50	27.50	30.25
C	66.55	33.00	71.50	44.00

profitability. Hence, when inflation is a way of life, some resources are scarce, and customers are unhappy with frequent across-the-board price increases, the firm has inadequate cost data to make relevant pricing and product line decisions.

A final point is that the above full-costing decision rules do not consider the different ways in which assets are combined to produce the product. For example, in Table 7-1, product A is materials-intensive, whereas product C is labor-intensive. Does product A require more fixed capital in the way of processing machinery than does product C? If so, the burden that product A places on the firm is substantially different from that of product C. Yet, none of the illustrated pricing formulas is able to reflect the different ways in which these products incur costs. (It should be noted that each of these formulas is used by industrial firms.)

THE NATURE OF OVERHEAD

The key to full-cost estimation is the method of charging period or time costs to individual products or orders. Direct product costs are generated with the product or service and exist only when the product is made or the service is offered. The period portion of variable costs does not vary directly with the product or service, but instead varies with overall output. For example, if sales increase by 30 percent during the period, additional clerical help may be hired to handle the ordering and billing. There are also fixed period costs that are not identifiable with any specific product or service. These expenses occur at the same amount regardless of volume; e.g., real estate taxes.

Overhead is that portion of period costs that cannot be objectively traced to particular operations, products, or other profit segments. To determine a full cost, this overhead must be allocated to the profit segments on some basis. *Overhead distribution* involves assigning actual overhead costs to various profit segments. *Overhead application* involves assigning overhead cost to individual units within a profit segment; e.g., products, customer accounts.

Overhead Distribution

Among the methods used to distribute overhead costs to profit segments are (1) percentage of direct labor cost or time; (2) percentage of direct labor and direct material costs; (3) percentage of conversion costs; (4) percentage of direct material costs; (5) on the unit-of-product basis; (6) on a percentage of sales volume; (7) on a machine-hour rate method; and (8) on a functional basis. Each of these methods will result in differing applications of overhead costs for the same product, and, therefore, are suspect as a means for determining price.

Some of these methods may be actual rates, as for example,

$$\text{Rate} = \frac{\text{actual overhead}}{\text{actual direct labor hours or direct labor costs}}$$

An actual overhead rate has the advantage of distributing the actual, incurred overhead cost. However, such a rate is unavailable until the end of the accounting period, it is a historical rate, and it is subject to seasonal and cyclical fluctuations as actual overhead costs and activity levels change. Normally, overhead rates are based on an operating plan or budget derived from recent and expected cost experiences.

Overhead Application

We now will review a number of the popular current methods used to determine full-cost estimates. In each case, a brief commentary on the method will be made.

On the Basis of Direct Labor Cost The method of applying overhead as a percentage of direct labor cost is one of the oldest and most popular.

$$\text{Rate} = \frac{\text{overhead charge}}{\text{direct labor cost}} \qquad (7\text{-}2)$$

For example, if total overhead to be assigned is $711,750 and total budgeted direct labor cost is $474,500, then

$$\text{Rate} = \frac{\$711,500}{\$474,500} = 1.5 \quad \text{or} \quad 150\%$$

To illustrate the direct labor cost method and the other methods to be discussed, two products will be used for comparative purposes. Product A is produced on older equipment and requires additional labor as compared to product B, which is produced on modern, relatively expensive equipment.[3] Table 7-3 provides the basic data for these two products and illustrates the application of the direct labor cost method.

This method assumes there is a direct relationship between overhead costs and direct labor and ignores the possibility that low-labor items, such as product B, require large overhead support. One result is that labor-intensive products may be overcosted, whereas low-labor products using expensive facilities may be undercosted. Hence, the expensive facilities are likely to be kept busy, perhaps even in excess of normal capacity. Consequently, this costing method may lead to unprofitable volume if price reductions are used to build volume of product B.

[3] These examples are adapted from Spencer A. Tucker, *Pricing for Higher Profits* (New York: McGraw-Hill, 1966), pp. 32–40.

Table 7-3 Overhead Costs Applied on the Basis of Direct Labor Cost

Cost element	Product A	Product B
Direct material	$ 6.00	$ 6.00
Direct labor	8.00	3.00
Overhead (150% of direct labor)	12.00	4.50
Total cost	$26.00	$13.00

On the Basis of Direct Labor Plus Direct Material Costs This method is applied using

$$\text{Rate} = \frac{\text{overhead charge}}{\text{direct labor cost} + \text{direct material cost}} \qquad (7\text{-}3)$$

Hence, if overhead charge is $711,750 and total direct labor and material costs are $1,423,500, then

$$\text{Rate} = \frac{\$711,750}{\$1,423,500} = 0.50 = 50\%$$

This method assumes a direct relationship between the sum of direct material and direct labor costs and overhead costs. Hence a relatively high-material-content product produced on inexpensive facilities will be overburdened because of the nature of its content. Thus, overhead may be assigned on the basis of two direct costs, both of which may vary without directly affecting actual overhead costs. As a result, products with the lowest combinations of materials and labor are assigned the least overhead burden, despite what the actual load on the firm may be. For example, if the low-material- and -labor-content product is frequently ordered in small shipping amounts, the ordering, billing, and shipping burden may not be reflected in its actual overhead charges and the product will be undercosted. Table 7-4 illustrates this method.

On the Basis of Direct Material Costs Now the rate is determined using

$$\text{Rate} = \frac{\text{overhead charge}}{\text{direct material cost}} \qquad (7\text{-}4)$$

Hence, if overhead charges are $711,750 and total direct material costs are $949,000 then

$$\text{Rate} = \frac{\$711,750}{\$949,000} = 0.75 = 75\%$$

As illustrated in Table 7-5, only one cost factor, materials, is used as the allocation base. Even though each product probably makes different use of the facilities, each has

Table 7-4   Overhead Costs Applied on the Basis of Direct Labor Plus Direct Material Costs

Cost element	Product A	Product B
Direct material	$ 6.00	$ 6.00
Direct labor	8.00	3.00
Total	$14.00	$ 9.00
Overhead (50% of total)	7.00	4.50
Total cost	$21.00	$13.50

Table 7-5 Overhead Costs Applied on the Basis of Direct Material Costs

Cost element	Product A	Product B
Direct material	$ 6.00	$ 6.00
Direct labor	8.00	3.00
Overhead (75% of direct material)	4.50	4.50
Total cost	$18.50	$13.50

the same overhead burden. For industries that have uniform, bulk materials such as forgings, cement, sugar, or paint, this method is easy and equitable. But if products use facilities differing considerably in capital cost, it is a faulty cost allocation method.

On the Unit-of-Product Basis The unit-of-product charge is determined by

$$\text{Overhead per unit} = \frac{\text{overhead charge}}{\text{expected total volume}} \tag{7-5}$$

If overhead costs are $711,750 and the expected volume of products A and B is 52,350 and 90,000 units respectively, then the overhead charge per unit is

$$\text{Overhead per unit} = \frac{\$711,750}{52,350 + 90,000} = \$5$$

Table 7-6 illustrates this method. Again we observe that products using the facilities differently have the same overhead charge, which is illogical. This method is frequently found in process production systems where a few products are made and where the products have common factors such as weight or volume.

On the Basis of Conversion Costs Using this method, the overhead rate is given by

$$\text{Rate} = \frac{\text{overhead charge}}{\text{direct labor cost} + \text{indirect manufacturing cost}} \tag{7-6}$$

If the overhead charge is $711,750, total direct labor cost is $474,500, and indirect manufacturing cost is $237,250, the overhead rate is

$$\text{Rate} = \frac{\$711,750}{\$474,500 + \$237,250} = 1.0 = 100\%$$

Table 7-6 Overhead Costs Applied on the Unit-of-Product Basis

Cost element	Product A	Product B
Direct material	$ 6.00	$ 6.00
Direct labor	8.00	3.00
Unit overhead	5.00	5.00
Total cost	$19.00	$14.00

Table 7-7 Overhead Costs Applied on the Basis of Conversion Costs

Cost element	Product A	Product B
Direct material	$ 6.00	$ 6.00
Conversion costs		
Direct labor	8.00	3.00
Indirect manufacturing	1.00	2.00
Period overhead (100% of conversion costs)	9.00	5.00
Total cost	$24.00	$16.00

As Table 7-7 shows, this method is similar to the direct labor method in that it assumes that overhead costs vary with direct conversion costs. However, there is a refinement in that some indirect manufacturing costs are charged directly to the products. Also, the method does not use material as a basis for allocating overhead costs. Both of these refinements are steps in the right direction.

On the Machine-Hour Rate Basis This method has the formula

$$\text{Rate per machine-hour} = \frac{\text{overhead charge}}{\text{machine-hours}} \qquad (7\text{-}7)$$

As the formula indicates, a machine-hour rate is the cost of operating a profit segment for 1 hour in the processing of orders or products. The machine-hour rate is a rate of conversion cost. Overhead is applied to a product by multiplying the rate by the number of hours involved in specific operations. The machine-hour rate is expensive and is not universally applicable. It is best used when machinery operations comprise a significant portion of the product's total cost.

For example, if the total overhead is $711,750, and the estimated machine-hours for the planning period are 71,175, then

$$\text{Machine-hour rate} = \frac{\$711,750}{71,175} = \$10 \text{ per hour}$$

Therefore, if product A requires 30 minutes of machine time and product B requires 2 hours, then the overhead charges are $10(0.5) = $5 and $10(2) = $20 respectively, as shown in Table 7-8.

The machine-hour rate represents a further refinement in allocating overhead, because it is based on the different ways in which the products use the facilities. However, even this method does not consider the different ways in which a product incurs overhead. All administrative and marketing expenses are lumped together with indirect manufacturing expenses. Hence, this method assumes a cause-effect relationship between total overhead and machine-time.

On a Functional Basis As discussed in Chap. 4, costs can be classified as either variable or fixed with respect to changes in activity levels. Materials and direct labor

Table 7-8 Overhead Costs Applied by the Machine-Hour Rate

Cost element	Product A	Product B
Direct material	$ 6.00	$ 6.00
Conversion costs		
Direct labor	8.00	3.00
Total overhead	5.00	20.00
Total cost	$19.00	$29.00

generally are classified as variable costs. As Table 4-1 indicates, other costs may also be classified as variable. Hence, it would seem sensible to classify traditional overhead accounts also as variable or fixed. Indeed, as developed in Chap. 6, many marketing costs are variable and, even if fixed for the period, are directly or indirectly traceable to products, territories, or customer accounts.

To be able to classify overhead as either fixed or variable requires a careful study of how the particular costs are incurred. The following classification is a sample of how period costs (overhead) might be classified into variable or fixed:

Period variable cost	Period fixed cost
Plant supplies	Rent
Maintenance	Insurance
Power and light	Property taxes
Indirect labor	Depreciation
Order processing costs	General administration
Storage and shipping costs	Research and development

As the above list indicates, many costs are incurred during the period and are fixed in the sense that management has contractually agreed to incur these costs. However, often these costs can be shown to vary with activity levels, at least after some minimal level of activity has occurred. Hence, even though salaried clerks are hired to take orders, it has been shown that each order requires a specific amount of work, such as recording the customer's name and address, checking the customer's credit reference, and obtaining the customer's account number. However, the cost of processing an order for a specific quantity of a single item is less than the cost of processing a multi-item order in terms of both clerical time in processing the necessary paper work and in physically preparing the order for shipping. As discussed in Chap. 6, when the objective is to assign "full costs" to specific products, customers, or territories, then a careful analysis of how costs are incurred will permit a more logical determination of "full costs."

By applying the hour-rate method just described to classify manufacturing overhead into variable and fixed components and by using the net profit approach on marketing and distribution costs, there will be a much smaller pool of common or general costs that are not easily attributable to a product or profit segment. (See Fig. 5-1.)

In the illustration in Table 7-9, indirect manufacturing costs would be applied on the basis of the machine-hour rate basis. Direct and indirect marketing costs would be

Table 7-9   Overhead Costs Applied to Products on a Functional Basis

Cost element	Product A	Product B
Direct material	$ 6.00	$ 6.00
Conversion costs		
Direct labor	8.00	3.00
Indirect manufacturing	1.00	2.00
Direct marketing	3.00	5.00
Indirect marketing	2.00	4.00
Period variable costs	1.20	1.80
Period fixed costs	1.30	1.70
Total cost	$22.50	$23.50

applied on the basis of the net profit method discussed in Chap. 6. Hence, for product A, objectively traceable costs are $20.00 or 89 percent of the "full costs"; and for product B, the objectively traceable costs are $20.00 or 85 percent of the "full costs." Further, the direct costs for product A are $17.00 and for product B, $14.00.

For this firm, then, the minimum acceptable prices are $17.00 for A and $14.00 for B. If the market will accept a full-cost price, and the desired profit margin over full cost is 20 percent, then prices could be set at $27.00 for A, and $28.20 for B.

On the other hand, if the market is not ready to accept a full-cost price because of buyer reactions and competitive prices, management must consider less than full-cost prices. The direct costs provide the floor on prices. Finally, it is also possible that prevailing market prices for products A and B are higher, say $29 for A and $35 for B. Again, management would seriously want to consider departing from a "full cost plus standard profit margin" price.

SUMMARY

Full-cost-plus pricing is a widespread practice, mainly because it is considered fair to both buyer and seller. Seemingly, the buyer is protected against overcharging and the seller is protected against a loss. However, full-cost-plus pricing is useful only to give management a general indication of prices necessary to achieve specific profit objectives.

It is necessary for the seller to attribute the various types of costs to the products or facilities causing these costs. Direct costs that are identifiable with, and traceable to, a specific profit segment present no real difficulty. But the allocation of fixed or period costs requires using some basis for applying these costs to the different profit segments. Despite the inherent logic in some of the methods for applying overhead, they are still arbitrary. It is indefensible to believe there is one right allocation method. As shown in Table 7-10, the full-cost estimate can be quite different depending on the method used to allocate period or overhead costs. Primarily, the reason for such differences is a function of how the product is manufactured. Generally, a product that is relatively labor-intensive has a greater chance of being assigned a relatively

Table 7-10 Summary of Different Full-Cost Methods

Basis of applying overhead	Full cost	
	Product A	Product B
Direct labor	$26.00	$13.00
Direct labor and materials	21.00	13.50
Direct material	18.50	13.50
Unit of product	19.00	14.00
Conversion costs	24.00	16.00
Machine-hour rate	19.00	29.00
Functional basis	22.50	23.50

larger overhead burden despite the burden it places on the manufacturing and marketing processes.

The attempt to unitize period costs distorts prices and can actually lead to profitless prices and volume despite the relative "security" of believing the prices cover full costs. Full costing distorts the information needed to analyze the product mix and the marketing mix. Full-cost pricing fails to recognize that in multiproduct companies, the products are in different stages of their life cycles and will not be equally profitable. Finally, full-cost pricing does not recognize the benefits of low-price-induced volume, which may lead to lower per unit costs as volume increases. In the next chapter, the phenomenon of the experience curve is discussed and its impact on cost estimation illustrated.

DISCUSSION QUESTIONS

1 Discuss the role of cost in price decisions. How does the role of cost differ from that of demand?
2 Discuss the role of competition in price decisions.
3 Distinguish between full costing and direct costing for the purpose of pricing.
4 Direct costing as applied to pricing has sometimes been called marginal pricing or incremental pricing. Opponents of marginal pricing contend that this method of pricing may lead the price setter to accidently or intentionally ignore costs that do not vary with volume. If this contention is correct, or at least possible, what safeguards would you propose to make sure the firm does not price its products unprofitably?
5 Most governmental regulatory agencies require a full-cost approach to rate setting. Why do you think they stress the full-cost approach? What are some arguments against the full-cost approach for regulating price? Can you think of a way to reconcile these differences in approaches?
6 The Federal Trade Commission requires that if a firm accused of illegally discriminating on the basis of price wishes to use a cost-justification defense, full costs must be used. What do you think is the rationale for this policy?
7 You are given the following information:

Item	Estimated cost	Estimated hours	Machine-hour rate
Materials, per unit	$ 10.00		
Direct labor, per unit	2.00		
Machining, per unit	. . . . . .	5	$7.50
Finishing, per unit	. . . . . .	10	6.00
Bench work, per unit	. . . . . .	20	6.50
Direct marketing	2,000		
Indirect marketing	500		
Variable overhead	1,400		
Fixed overhead	2,500		

a   The forecasted sales volume is 1,000 units. If the firm uses the full-cost method of pricing and applies a markup, m, of 30 percent, what price should be set? (*Note*: The machine-labor rate includes manufacturing overhead.)

b   Assume that just before the firm introduces this product to the market a competitor introduces a similar product priced at $250.00. What do you advise the firm to do? What is the logic of your recommendation?

c   Assume that the competitor described in part b introduced the similar product priced at $350.00, what would your advice be? Why?

SUGGESTED READINGS

Lere, John C.: "Product Costs–Direct and Absorption," *Pricing Techniques for the Financial Executive* (New York: John Wiley, 1974), pp. 20–42.

Ostwald, Phillip F.: *Cost Estimating for Engineering and Management* (Englewood Cliffs, N.J.: Prentice-Hall, 1964).

Tucker, Spencer A.: "Cost-Estimating Methods," *Pricing for Higher Profit* (New York: McGraw-Hill, 1966), pp. 31–40.

_____: "Cost-Plus Pricing Methods," *Pricing for Higher Profit* (New York: McGraw-Hill, 1966), pp. 41–67.

Williams, Bruce R.: "Measuring Costs: Full Absorption Cost or Direct Cost?" *Management Accounting*, 58 (January 1976), 23–24, 36.

Chapter 8

Price Forecasting

In many pricing decision contexts it is vitally important to forecast the trend in market prices for a product. Since in these markets competitive prices tightly constrain the firm's pricing discretion, it is common practice to forecast prices. Price forecasts are used in decisions about marketing strategy, new investments, budgeting, and materials purchasing.[1] However, such forecasts are primarily based on management's intuition despite emerging theory and techniques of price forecasting. Moreover, even though profitability depends on prices, costs, and sales volume, much effort has been expended on forecasting costs and sales volume, but little on forecasting prices. Indeed, many corporate plans forecast period sales volume, estimate the costs to reach the forecasted sales volume, and deduce the price "necessary" to achieve the profit objective.

The purpose of this chapter is to review the methods of price forecasting and to provide a basis of moving from the problem of developing cost estimates to the problem of setting prices. From an economic perspective, if we know the appropriate demand and supply schedules for a product, service, or commodity, it should not be difficult to forecast price. Unfortunately, it is not possible to have precise demand and supply information for a product at a particular point in time. Nevertheless, some useful tools for forecasting prices help reduce the uncertainty of business planning.

[1] George B. Hegeman, "The Art of Price Forecasting," in Robert Ferber (ed.), *Handbook of Marketing Research* (New York: McGraw-Hill, 1974), pp. 4-286-4-294.

This chapter first provides an overview of the methods of forecasting price. It then develops the specific technique of forecasting using the experience curve. Recently, the strategy of increasing market share has become a focal topic in the business literature. Price is often cited as a positive way to increase market share, i.e., decreasing prices faster than competition may lead to greater market share. The experience-curve phenomenon is often cited as an explanation for this price–volume–market share relationship. Thus, for firms utilizing the experience curve there is a positive basis for developing a product's price over its life cycle. (See Chapter 9.)

METHODS OF PRICE FORECASTING

Essentially, there are three approaches to price forecasting: statistical trend analysis, judgmental, and simulation models. Often, however, a particular price forecast uses a combination of these approaches.

Statistical Trend Analysis

Statistical trend analyses rely on historical data to extrapolate from the past into the future. Among these techniques are price exclusion charts, experience or learning curves, and regression and correlation analysis. Two major cautions must be observed when using these techniques:

1 They rely on historical data that may not portray current and future trends.
2 The apparent mathematical sophistication underlying them may lull the decision maker into not considering other relevant judgmental factors affecting future prices.[2]

However, if these precautions are observed, these techniques provide a useful starting point and often are sufficiently accurate for most planning purposes.

Price Exclusion Charts[3]   Price exclusion charts provide a way of determining the range of infeasible prices for a product. Exclusion charts are totally empirical and require information on a large number of products competing in the home market.

As shown in Fig. 8-1, a price exclusion chart is constructed by plotting price versus production for each end use (market). A semilogarithmic scale is used with production volume being plotted on a logarithmic scale and price on an arithmetic scale. The purpose of the chart is to show the various price-volume combinations that competing products have experienced in the past. By then drawing a line so that nearly every price-volume point falls below and to the left, an exclusion area is determined showing what prices are infeasible.

The U.S. Tariff Commission provides such data annually for synthetic organic chemicals. Thus, price-volume exclusion charts have been successful in medicinals, flavor and perfume materials, plasticizers, surface-active agents, and pesticides. But,

---

[2]See Theodore D. Frey, "Forecasting Prices for Industrial Commodity Markets," *Journal of Marketing*, 34 (April 1970), 28–32.
[3]This section is based on George B. Hegeman, op. cit.

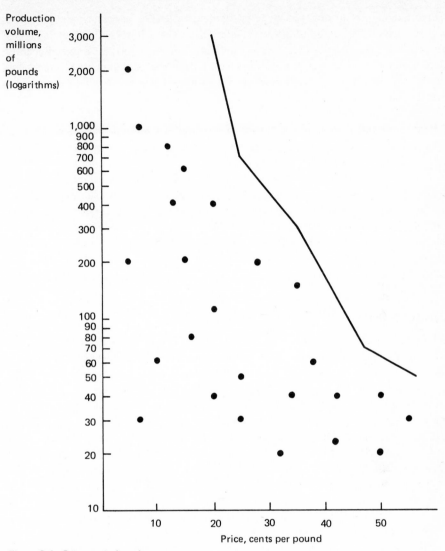

Figure 8-1 Price exclusion chart.

exclusion charts have not been successfully applied to product groups like dyes and organic pigments.[4] Clearly, a price exclusion chart will not forecast a specific price, but it seems to indicate some price-volume limits for a particular market.

Experience Curves It has been shown that costs decline by some characteristic amount each time accumulated production is doubled.[5] Accordingly, because of the

[4]See D. J. Massey and J. H. Black, "Predicting Chemical Prices," *Chemical and Engineering News*, October 20, 1969.

[5]*Perspectives on Experience* (Boston: Boston Consulting Group, 1970).

competitive nature of most products, prices tend to decline along a similar pattern as long as competitive relationships are stable. Given these long-term, predictable cost and price behavior patterns, it becomes relatively easy to forecast prices. Recently, a number of applications and approaches have been reported that make this technique a useful and practical tool for forecasting prices. Experience curves will be discussed in some detail later in the chapter.

Regression and Correlation Analysis It has been established that prices for some products follow long-term trends marked by periodic cyclical or seasonal factors. Time series analysis can be used to establish the existence of these trends and to identify the cyclical or seasonal factors affecting prices. Once the trends are established and the cyclical or seasonal patterns identified, the firm is in a position to plan both materials and finished-goods inventories by forecasting prices for such items. Furthermore, time series analysis permits the establishment of lead-lag relationships for forecasting price changes. It can also be combined with regression and correlation analysis to isolate causal relationships for price movements. Finally, these techniques permit the use of computer models for forecasting prices. For example, Weyerhauser has reported success using these models.[6]

Judgmental Methods

As indicated above, the statistical methods, because of their apparent sophistication and precision, often lull management into ignoring the value of management's experience and intuitive judgment. The proper use of judgment typically requires management to divide the forecast period into a short-range segment—1 to 3 years—and a longer-range forecast that anticipates basic changes in the industry. Generally, it takes 2 to 3 years for capital investment to become productive capacity.

In the short range, special attention must be paid to competitors and the demand-supply balance in the market. Of particular importance is the need to project any new productive capacity becoming available during the short-range period. If the demand-supply balance is loose, what are the prospects that some competitors will set their prices to cover their variable costs or make extra efforts to find export customers in other markets? Will some competitors stockpile inventories and wait for a better demand-supply situation?

If the demand-supply balance is tight, what are the costs of competitor's starting-up marginal capacity? How long will it take? As prices rise during a tight market, when will buyers begin shifting to alternative, substitute products?

In December 1976, the synthetic fiber industry had negative earnings for the second straight year. Most synthetic plants were running below the break-even points. The industry helped create this situation by expanding production capacity by 30 percent between 1973 and 1976. This additional capacity led to a decrease in prices of 10 percent on the average. Yet, at the same time, polyester staple fiber production was running at 90 percent of capacity, and a price increase was forecast for this segment of

[6]D. J. Massey and J. H. Black, op. cit.

the industry. Moreover, cotton prices were rising because of a smaller supply than expected.[7]

The long-range forecast is initially a forecast of capacity changes due to investment in plant and new technologies. Therefore, the forecaster must examine the investment policies and criteria of competitors. What competitors have inherently lower investment costs per unit of output? Do some competitors have specific tax savings or investment credits? Do some competitors have location advantages over others? What is the return on investment rate for the industry leaders?

The investment criteria and expansion economics of the industry leaders provide the basis for predicting new increments of capacity. What price would induce the leaders to expand capacity given their return criteria? What other firms would be likely to follow the lead of the leaders?

Given some estimates of available capacity over the next 3 or more years, the forecaster must also check whether this new capacity is consistent with the market's growth. Clearly, if new-capacity growth is greater than market growth, excess supply will force prices down.

Many of these judgments can be combined with statistical or other analytical models to provide a sophisticated forecasting system. In one case, linear programming models were used to develop the cost and availability of naphtha and the value of commercial aircraft.[8] In another, Bayesian decision analysis was used to combine judgment and statistical analysis for forecasting the price of the petrochemical butadiene.[9]

Simulation Models

Some firms have developed complex computer models that simulate the economy and competitors, incorporating production costs, inventory control, market share, and investment planning. Essentially, these models are an upgrading of the judgment techniques discussed earlier, but they allow for a number of "what if" questions to be answered assuming different levels of capacity expansion, market growth, and general economic activity. A major abrasives company currently uses a large simulation model to enable it to forecast market prices for its products as well as material input costs. Moreover, by including up-to-date market and company information in the model, the company also has a basis for comparing actual performance against its forecasts. Figure 8-2 shows a price forecasting model used in the plastics industry.

PRICE FORECASTING WITH THE EXPERIENCE CURVE

As mentioned above, price and cost data show that costs decline by some predictable amount each time accumulated experience is doubled. Indeed, many companies have

---

[7]See "The Losses Pile Up in Synthetic Fibers," *Business Week*, December 6, 1976, pp. 46-50; Paul C. Christopherson, "Product Pricing in the Chemical Industry," *Financial Analysts Journal*, 33 (November–December 1977), 54-62.

[8]George B. Hegeman, op. cit.

[9]Donald G. Frederick, "An Industrial Pricing Decision Using Bayesian Multivariate Analysis," *Journal of Marketing Research*, 8 (May 1971), 199-203.

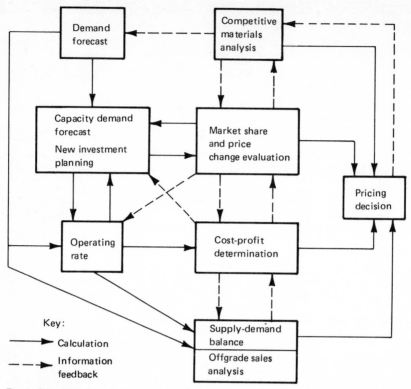

Figure 8-2 Price forecasting model—plastics. *(Source: Robert Ferber (ed.), Handbook of Marketing Research (New York: McGraw-Hill, 1974), pp. 4–292.)*

developed successful marketing and production strategies utilizing this relationship between costs, prices, and accumulated experience. From a planning viewpoint, given the experience relationship, it is clear that a firm's costs can be projected. It is also clear that competitor's costs can be estimated given some basic market information. However, this cost-price relationship to accumulated experience does not occur by accident, and there are disadvantages in a strict utilization of this phenomenon.[10]

It is important to distinguish two approaches to this volume growth and cost reduction relationship. The *learning curve* (sometimes called the startup function or progress function) shows that *manufacturing costs* (primarily labor) fall as volume increases. Typical examples include air frames, industrial chemicals, and cameras.

The *experience curve* shows that *total costs* of a product line decline over time as volume increases. Hence, the experience curve considers a broader range of costs, including material and marketing costs. Typical examples include gas ranges, facial tissues, and television receivers.

---

[10]William J. Abernathy and Kenneth Wayne, "Limits of the Learning Curve," *Harvard Business Review*, 52 (September–October 1974), 109–119.

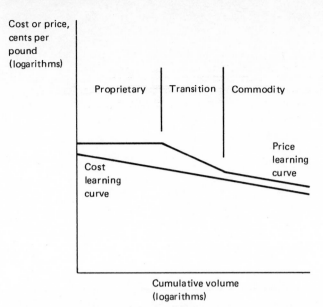

Cost or price,
cents per
pound
(logarithms)

Proprietary | Transition | Commodity

Cost
learning
curve

Price
learning
curve

Cumulative volume
(logarithms)

Figure 8-3 Price-cost pattern, industrial chemicals (89 percent cost learning). *(Source: S. A. Billon and William D. Robinson, "Price-Cost Relationships: Industrial Chemicals," Broadening the Concepts of Marketing (American Marketing Association, 1970), p. 42.)*

Figure 8-3 shows the price-cost pattern for industrial chemicals, which has three distinct phases—proprietary, transition, and commodity.[11] Empirical data show that prices and costs tend to decline when reported on a constant dollar basis. Hence, reductions in total costs for industrial chemicals should be predictable for long periods of time. The slope of the cost learning curve in Fig. 8-3 is 89 percent, which means that costs decline about 11 percent during each period when cumulative volume doubles.

Costs and Experience

As mentioned above, data show that costs decline by a predictable amount each time accumulated experience is doubled. This phenomenon makes it possible not only to forecast one's own costs, but also to forecast a competitor's. Generally, this decline in costs ranges between 10 to 30 percent, with a usual decline of between 20 and 30 percent each time accumulated volume is doubled. In constant dollars this decline goes on without limit as long as demand for a product is growing. If demand is no longer growing, then the rate of cost decline slows down and approaches zero. Figure 8-4 gives an example of a cost/price experience on a linear scale.

When accumulated units of a product are increasing at a constant percentage rate, each year of product experience produces about the same percentage effect on cost.

---

[11] S. A. Billon and William D. Robinson, "Price-Cost Relationships: Industrial Chemicals," in American Marketing Association, *Broadening the Concept of Marketing* (Chicago: American Marketing Association, 1970), p. 42.

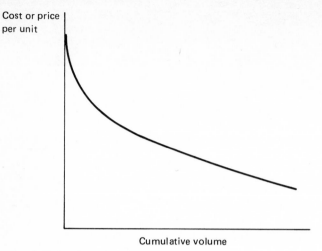

Figure 8-4 Cost/price experience relationship.

When plotted on log-log paper, percentage change is shown as a constant distance (Fig. 8-5). A straight line means that a percentage change in one factor (accumulated volume) results in a predictable corresponding change in the other factor (costs, price). The slope of the line reveals the nature of the relationship and can be read directly from the graph. Figure 8-6 shows the actual price experience curve of the Ford Model T, 1909–1923, in constant 1958 dollars.

Three key points must be understood about the cost/price experience phenomenon. First, note that we are talking about *accumulated experience* (volume) over time and not about a doubling of the production rate between two points in time. Table 8-1 provides an illustration of this point. Sometime during the second year accumulated experience doubles. It doubles again during the fourth year, the seventh year, and the

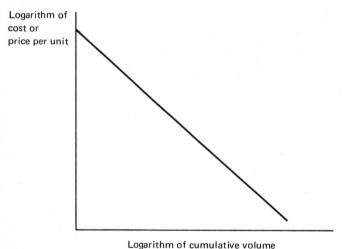

Figure 8-5 Cost/price experience relationship.

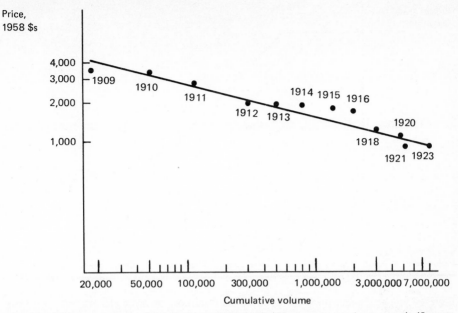

Figure 8-6 Price experience, Ford Model T, 1909–1923 (85 percent experience curve). *(Source: William J. Abernathy and Kenneth Wayne, "Limits of the Learning Curve," Harvard Business Review, 52 (September–October 1974), 111.)*

twelfth year. Thus, during the second, fourth, seventh, and twelfth years, unit costs will have declined by a constant percentage.

The second point is that costs are measured in constant dollars. Hence, cost data must be deflated through the use of an appropriate economic deflator. Because inflation primarily serves to mask the true price or cost effect of product or marketing improvements, price and cost data should always be developed on a constant dollar

Table 8-1 Accumulated Production Experience

Year	Yearly production (10.0% growth)	Accumulated experience	Periods of doubling experience, %
1	1.00	1.00	110.0
2	1.10	2.10	
3	1.21	3.31	121.0
4	1.33	4.64	
5	1.46	6.10	
6	1.61	7.71	104.3
7	1.77	9.48	
8	1.95	11.43	
9	2.14	13.57	
10	2.36	15.93	125.6
11	2.60	18.53	
12	2.86	21.39	

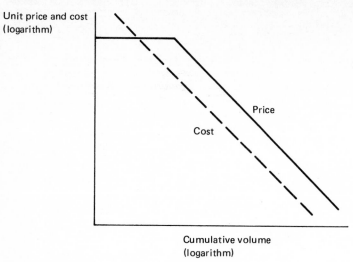

Figure 8-7 A stable cost/price experience relationship. *(Source: Perspectives on Experience (Boston, Boston Consulting Group, 1970).)*

basis to enable management to determine actual cost or price effects due to volume changes. Whenever inflation is a significant factor, as it was in the early and mid-1970s, a test of the analysis' sensitivity to the inflation corrective factor should also be made.

Third, as noted in Chaps. 4 to 7, management must be careful about what costs are included in the analysis. As much as possible, costs that vary with activity levels are the ones to be considered, since any arbitrary cost allocations will tend to hide the real changes in costs. Hence, the emphasis should be on out-of-pocket costs or cash flows. In addition, variations in accounting practice between companies, or in the same company over time, will distort the cost/price trend line, because of the distortions in reported costs.

Prices and Experience

Available data show that, in general, prices tend to decline by some given amount each time accumulated experience is doubled. In very competitive, rapid growth, technological industries prices tend to parallel costs over time, as shown in Fig. 8-7. If prices do not parallel costs in early periods, then a kink in the price pattern may result, as shown in Fig. 8-8. Initially, price may be set below cost to gain a foothold in the market (phase A). In phase B, the sellers hold a price umbrella and high-cost producers enter the market. At some point, phase C prevails, when severe price competition forces prices to decline faster than costs.[12] Finally, in phase D, stability emerges as the price-cost relationship stabilizes.

In a study of 82 petrochemicals, it was found that the experience factor was the single most important variable explaining price declines.[13] Over intervals of 5 to 7

[12]Apparently the semiconductor industry has experienced such instability. See "The Semiconductor Becomes a New Marketing Force," *Business Week,* August 24, 1974, pp. 34–42.

[13]Robert B. Stobough and Phillip L. Townsend, "Price Forecasting and Strategic Planning: The Case of Petrochemicals," *Journal of Marketing Research,* 12 (February 1975), 19–29.

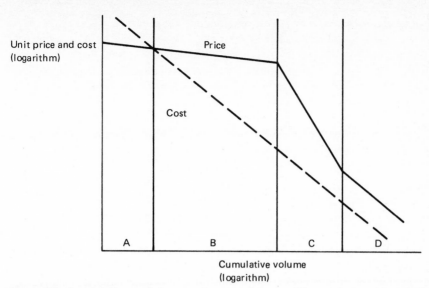

Figure 8-8 An unstable cost/price experience relationship. *(Source: Perspectives on Experience (Boston, Boston Consulting Group, 1970).)*

years, the number of competitors, product standardization, and static scale economies were also significant explanatory variables of price declines.

In December 1975, video TV games were selling for $120 to $130 each. In December 1976, these same games were selling in the $69 to $79 range. By December 1977, these video games were selling for $19 to $29. The primary reason for such a rapid decrease in price was that the electronic circuits for the game were mass-produced in such a volume that the labor, materials, and marketing costs per video game were a fraction of what they were in the fall of 1975.[14]

At the end of April 1977, Texas Instruments (TI) reduced the price of one of its most popular digital watch models to $10. This latest price cut reduced the price of a digital watch from $20, and in just over 5 years, the price of a digital watch had fallen from $2,000 to $10. William B. Heye, Jr., manager of TI's Time Products Division, explained that lower prices were possible because production costs had dropped as volume grew. He indicated that initial production costs had been reduced by 60 percent as volume increased.[15]

The reason for these greatly reduced prices lies in the incredible economies of scale realized in the manufacture of the computer chip. Every time cumulative volume doubles, the chips decline in cost by about 30 percent. This basic decline in cost leads to substantial declines in prices, and these in turn stimulate increased sales that lead to further reductions in costs. In 1971 a Sharp Electronics pocket calculator sold for $395; in 1978, a more sophisticated model sold for $10.95.[16]

---

[14]"TV's Hot New Star: The Electronic Game," *Business Week*, December 29, 1975; Peter Weaver, "Video Games Price Plummets," *Springfield Morning Union*, Springfield, Mass., March 17, 1977, p. 25.

[15]"The Great Digital Watch Shake-Out," *Business Week*, May 2, 1977, pp. 78-80.

[16]"The Age of Miracle Chips," *Time*, February 20, 1978, pp. 44-58.

The implications of such price-cost relationships are profound. The experience or learning curve provides a way to relate costs, prices, volume, and profit margins over time, providing a powerful tool for evaluating alternative price and marketing strategies. Being able to predict prices better than competition provides a major strategic advantage over the long term. Finally, the price–experience curve concept suggests the need to develop marketing plans over the product life cycle.

To be able to utilize the experience curve, it is necessary to understand how to obtain the estimates of the parameters of the curve. The Appendix to this chapter outlines an estimating procedure.

SUMMARY

This chapter has reviewed methods of price forecasting with special emphasis on applying the experience curve to cost estimating. As explained in Chaps. 4 to 7, even though costs play a limited role in price decisions, they are an important determinant of prices and profits.

The key point of this chapter is that costs, prices, volume, and profit margins are related. And if these four concepts can be objectively related to each other, a powerful tool exists for evaluating alternative pricing strategies. Moreover, being able to predict prices over time provides strategic advantages for purchasing, production planning, demand estimation, and capital planning.

The cost/price experience curve provides a method for objectively relating costs, prices, volume, and profit margins. However, simply knowing how to use this tool will not in itself allow a firm to realize its benefits. Underlying the successful application of experience curves is a management philosophy that seeks every possible way to reduce costs while recognizing that a truly profitable product is one that satisfies customers' needs. Hence, management must remain market-oriented.

Finally, cost, price, and volume analysis is a powerful conceptual and analytical tool. As has been shown in the chapters of this section, analytical techniques are not panaceas, nor do they simplify decision making. They do, however, provide a means for understanding the factors that cause certain predictable patterns to exist. Moreover, careful attention to trends and their underlying causes may help eliminate unsound pricing practices. The experience curve promises to be a useful analytical tool for forecasting costs and prices. In particular, using the experience curve to forecast the cost of a new product over its estimated life cycle can be helpful in planning the product's price during different life cycle stages. Chapter 9 discusses the pricing of products over their life cycles.

DISCUSSION QUESTIONS

1   Describe the different ways to forecast price.
2   Distinguish between a learning curve and an experience curve.
3   What is the role of cost estimating in developing a product's price?

4 Explain what is meant by the following concepts within the context of the experience curve:
   a Accumulated experience
   b Constant dollars
   c Cash flows
5 Complete Table 8-1. In what year will accumulated experience double again?
6 The experience curve is often construed to reflect economies of scale due to
   mass production. Can you provide examples of economies of scale resulting from
   marketing?

Appendix: Applying the Experience Curve

Opportunities to apply the experience curve are to be found in procurement, production, marketing, and finance. In purchasing, the experience curve may be used to
negotiate a price, or to analyze the make-or-buy decision. In cost estimation, decisions
related to bidding, pricing, and capital investment may be based on the experience
curve. Often contract negotiations are reopened after the experience of time and cost
are known for the prototype unit. Indeed, aerospace firms follow this practice with
the U.S. Air Force.

The experience curve may be defined if the total direct costs required to complete
the first unit are established and if the improvement rate due to experience is specified. Alternatively, the experience curve may be defined if direct costs for a later unit
and the experience-curve rate are estimated.

The concept of constant reduction of cost (or time) between doubled, accumulated
volumes can be expressed as

$$TC_X = KX^{1-b} \tag{8-1}$$

where TC_X = cumulative total direct cost
       X = number of units
       K = cost estimate, for the first unit
       b = slope parameter or a function of the experience (improvement) rate,
           $0 \leqslant b \leqslant 1$
The cumulative average cost, AC_X, is

$$AC_X = KX^{-b} \tag{8-2}$$

The experience curve is usually plotted on double logarithmic paper. The plot of
Eq. (8-2) will result in a straight line on log-log paper. Thus, the function can be
plotted knowing either two points or one point and the slope, e.g., cost of the first
unit and the percentage improvement.

Relationship between b and the Experience Rate

To facilitate the estimation problem, the relationship between a, the experience rate, and b is given by

$$b = \frac{\log 100 - \log a}{\log 2} \tag{8-3}$$

Table 8-2 shows this relationship for a values ranging from 50 to 100.

Cost Estimation with Cost of First Unit Known

When both the cost of the first unit, AC, and the experience rate, a, are known, the cost of X units can be calculated directly. If cost of the first unit is $1,800 and the experience rate is 80 percent, the total costs for eight units are

$$TC_8 = \$1,800 \, (8)^{1-0.322} = \$1,800 \, (8)^{0.678} = \$1,800 \, (4.095)$$

$$= \$7,371.70$$

and the average cost for the eight units is

$$AC_8 = \frac{\$7,371.70}{8} = \$921.46.$$

Alternatively, the average cost for the eight units could be calculated using

$$AC_8 = \$1,800 \, (8)^{-0.322} = \frac{\$1,800}{(8)^{0.322}} = \frac{\$1,800}{1.953}$$

$$= \$921.66 \quad \text{(the differences are due to rounding)}$$

Finding the Experience Curve from Two Points

Suppose a company audited the twentieth and fortieth production units and found that the production costs were $700 and $635, respectively. They now want to estimate the costs of producing the eightieth unit.

From Eq. (8-2), the average costs are

$$AC_{20} = K(20)^{-b} = \$700$$
$$AC_{40} = K(40)^{-b} = \$635$$

Taking logarithms,

$$\log 700 = \log K - b \log 20 \tag{A}$$
$$\log 635 = \log K - b \log 40 \tag{B}$$

Subtracting (B) from (A):

$$\log 700 - \log 635 = b (\log 40 - \log 20)$$

$$b = \frac{\log 700 - \log 635}{\log 40 - \log 20}$$

$$= \frac{2.8451 - 2.8028}{1.6021 - 1.3010} = \frac{0.0423}{0.3011} = 0.140$$

Table 8-2   Relationship between a (Percent Experience) and b

a	b	a	b
50	1.000	75	0.415
51	0.971	76	0.396
52	0.943	77	0.377
53	0.916	78	0.358
54	0.889	79	0.340
55	0.863	80	0.322
56	0.837	81	0.304
57	0.811	82	0.286
58	0.786	83	0.269
59	0.761	84	0.252
60	0.737	85	0.234
61	0.713	86	0.218
62	0.690	87	0.201
63	0.667	88	0.184
64	0.644	89	0.168
65	0.621	90	0.152
66	0.599	91	0.136
67	0.578	92	0.120
68	0.556	93	0.105
69	0.535	94	0.089
70	0.515	95	0.074
71	0.494	96	0.056
72	0.474	97	0.044
73	0.454	98	0.029
74	0.434	99	0.015
		100	0.000

Source: Adapted from C. Carl Pegels, "Start Up or Learning Curves—Some New Approaches," *Decision Sciences,* 7 (October 1976), 711.

Looking at Table 8-2, we note that a b of 0.140 lies between a = 91 percent and a = 90 percent. Interpolating, we obtain an estimated value for a of 90.8 percent.

Using the data for the twentieth unit,

$$\log 700 = \log K - 0.14 \log 20$$
$$\log K = \log \$700 + 0.14 \log 20$$
$$= 2.8451 + 0.14 (1.3010) = 3.02724$$
$$K = \$1.065$$

Therefore, the experience curve is

$$AC_X = \$1,065 \ (X)^{-0.14}$$

Finally, for the eightieth unit, average costs are

$$AC_{80} = \$1,065 \ (80)^{-0.14} = \frac{\$1,065}{(80)^{0.14}} = \frac{\$1,065}{1.845} = \$577$$

Developing Cost Estimates with a Unknown

Although a firm may be able to determine the cost of the prototype unit, it may be uncertain what experience rate will prevail. In such a situation, it may wish to determine alternative cost-experience patterns, using different values of a. In this way, the decision maker would be able to develop alternative cost schedules to assist in developing the new product's price.

Consider the situation where the cost of the first unit, AC, is $1,800, but the firm does not have a reasonable estimate of a. Assume that with previous new products the experience rate has ranged between 70 and 90 percent. Table 8-3 shows the alternative experience-cost schedules for a values of 70, 80, and 90 percent. These cost schedules

Table 8-3 Alternative Experience-Cost Schedules

Number of units	Cumulative average cost when a is		
	70%	80%	90%
1	$1,800	$1,800	$1,800
2	1,259	1,440	1,620
4	882	1,154	1,459
8	617	922	1,312
16	432	738	1,181
32	302	590	1,063
64	211	471	956
128	148	377	861
256	104	302	775
512	72	241	697

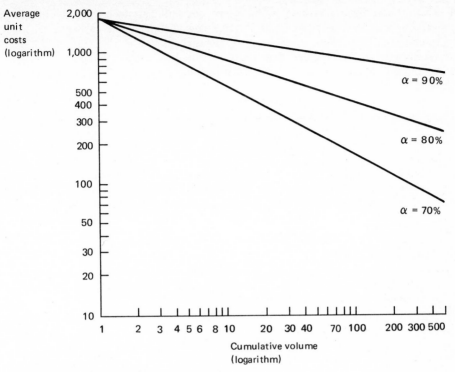

Average unit costs (logarithm)

2,000
1,000
500
400
300
200
100
50
30
20
10

$\alpha = 90\%$
$\alpha = 80\%$
$\alpha = 70\%$

1   2   3   4 5 6 8 10   20   30 40   70 100   200 300 500

Cumulative volume
(logarithm)

Figure 8-9 Alternative experience-cost schedules.

reveal the dramatic differences in feasible prices, depending on the actual experience curve that prevails. Indeed, if the 70 percent experience rate is attained, price is likely to be set lower, other things remaining the same. Figure 8-9 illustrates those same three experience curves.

DISCUSSION QUESTIONS (Appendix)

1 If costs of the first unit are $1,200 and the experience rate is 90 percent, find
   a The total costs for 10 units
   b The average costs for 10 units
   c The average costs for 100 units
2 A company audited its fiftieth and hundredth production units and determined that the production costs were $900 and $800, respectively.
   a Determine the experience curve for this firm.
   b Estimate the average costs for the 200th production unit.
3 a Develop an experience-cost schedule for the situation where the average cost for the first unit is $1,800 and the assumed experience rate is 85 percent. Develop the schedule for the first 131,072 units.
   b What conclusions do you draw about the appropriate cost to use when determining price?

4 The Springer Manufacturing Corporation is considering producing and delivering 40 units of an industrial plating machine to a new customer. The customer has indicated that the maximum feasible price for each plating machine is $5,000. The average cost of building the first unit is estimated by research and development to be $8,000. In the past, the company has usually operated along an experience rate of 85 percent.

   a Several executives believe the potential price of $5,000 is too low. Prepare an analysis that answers their concern. In your analysis show

   (1) The average and total costs for the following units: 1, 2, 4, 8, 16, 32, 40

   (2) The total revenues received for 1, 2, 4, 8, 16, 32, and 40 units

   b After the first 40 units have been delivered, the customer offers to purchase 100 more units at $2,000 each. Prepare another analysis exactly like the one in part **a**, except show the average and total costs and total revenue for 1, 2, 4, 8, 16, 32, 64, and 100 units. (*Hint:* The cost of the fortieth unit in part **a** is the beginning cost for this problem.)

SUGGESTED READINGS

Abernathy, William J., and Kenneth Wayne: "Limits of the Learning Curve," *Harvard Business Review*, 52 (September–October, 1974), 109–119.

Bump, Edwin A.: "Effects of Learning on Cost Projections," *Management Accounting*, 56 (May 1974), 19–24.

Frey, Theodore D.: "Forecasting Prices for Industrial Commodity Markets," *Journal of Marketing*, 34 (April 1970), 28–32.

Hegeman, George B.: "The Art of Price Forecasting," in Robert Ferber (ed.), *Handbook of Marketing Research* (New York: McGraw-Hill, 1974), pp. 4-286–4-294.

McIntyre, Edward B.: "Cost-Volume-Profit Analysis Adjusted for Learning," *Management Science*, 24 (October 1977), 149–160.

Pegels, C. Carl: "Start Up of Learning Curves—Some New Approaches," *Decision Sciences*, 7 (October 1976), 705–713.

Perspectives on Experience (Boston: Boston Consulting Group, 1970).

Section Four

Pricing Decisions and Price Administration

Chapters 9 through 12 use the concepts and analyses presented in Chaps. 2 through 8 to discuss positive approaches to determining prices. A strong focus will be to integrate both demand analysis and cost analysis for each decision. Chapter 9 focuses on the different pricing problems and solution approaches as the product matures through the life cycle. The emphasis of the chapter is on analysis and planning pricing strategy. Behavioral and market implications are discussed, and costing and price forecasting techniques applied.

Most firms produce and sell multiple products that often are demand-related and sometimes also cost-related. From a market perspective, many firms have discovered that there are specific price-market segments for their products and that determining prices that differentiate these products is a complex process. Whether to add a middle-priced product or reduce or increase the number of price offerings depends not only on the potential number of price-market segments, but also on clearly differentiating the products in the minds of buyers. Chapter 10 develops a behavioral approach to determine ways to position products in a line according to price. The chapter will also apply costing principles developed in earlier chapters to analyze the sales-volume mix and will suggest ways that pricing may be used to profitably change the sales-volume mix.

Chapters 11 and 12 review the problem of administering the pricing decisions. While Chaps. 9 and 10 were concerned with developing the basic or list price, such a price is rarely the actual price received. The decisions to discount from list for volume purchases or for early payment, to extend credit, or to charge for transportation effectively change the list price. In Chap. 11, such decisions are discussed and an analytical framework is presented for handling discount decisions.

Pricing decisions and the policies that are derived have impact on dealer cooperation and motivation as well as on salespeople's morale and effort. While it is legally difficult to control prices through the distribution channel, it is nevertheless possible to elicit cooperation and provide motivation to adhere to company-determined pricing policies. Since price directly affects revenues of the trade and commissions of salespeople, it can be used to foster desired behaviors by channel members and salespeople. Finally, feedback is essential for a firm in today's dynamic economy. Chapter 12 discusses these management problems and offers approaches to solving them.

Chapter 9

Pricing over the Product Life Cycle

Of all the marketing variables that influence demand, price is the one that has received the least amount of attention from marketing professionals. Essentially, pricing practice remains largely intuitive and routine. Further, the pricing literature has produced few new approaches that would stimulate the practitioner to change the way prices are set. Despite its obvious lack of realism, the economist's theory of price has dominated the conceptual framework. And until recently, the seller was primarily concerned with stimulating demand.

However, as noted in Chap. 1, recent environmental changes in the market for goods and services have stimulated new interest in pricing. Yet many of the changes in pricing practices lack a clear-cut conceptual framework and often lead to unanticipated consequences. The previous chapters have outlined cost and demand approaches to obtaining relevant information for pricing decisions. The next four chapters explore the many types of pricing decisions that must be made and offer ways to utilize the analytical framework developed earlier.

It is the thesis of this book that the management of a multiproduct firm should be concerned with managing products over their products' life cycles. As will be developed below, management, therefore, must develop plans that consider the life cycles of sales, total contribution, separable fixed costs, and separable assets employed with the different products. Moreover, management must control production and marketing costs as well as the level of common costs and common assets employed.

Indeed, the experience-curve evidence suggests that, as product sales grow, costs and price decline, although this is not automatic. There is also a tendency for the level of common costs and common assets employed to increase with growth in product sales. Hence, common costs, if uncontrolled, can seriously erode direct-cost reduction due to accumulated experience.

The purposes of this chapter are to review the conceptual product life cycle model, and to present methods for developing pricing strategies during different stages of the product life cycle.

PRODUCT LIFE CYCLES—THE CONCEPTUAL MODEL

Although it is popular to convey the product life cycle primarily in terms of a sales trend, there are several relevant life cycles as indicated in Fig. 9-1. Further, as Fig. 9-2 shows, the cash flow life cycle has direct relevance to payback and profitability. Indeed, Fig. 9-2 indicates that an earlier life cycle stage—development—has relevance to the pricing decision.

Development Stage

In the development stage, the product concept is engineered from the idea to the actual design. During this stage no revenues are generated, only costs represented by direct cash outflows. Once the product idea is engineered, market tests are conducted to determine market acceptance, and preparations are made for producing the product. Thus, the accumulated investment grows to a substantial amount before the product is introduced for sale.

Introduction

Once the product is introduced, initial market awareness is minimal and market acceptance slow. If the firm is the only seller of the product, even though there may be functional substitutes, competition is also minimal. The firm's marketing efforts are geared to stimulating primary demand—demand for the product itself—and there may be some difficulty in gaining widespread distribution. The introduction stage is the period of initial success or failure.

Growth

The product begins to make rapid sales gains as the rate of market acceptance accelerates. It becomes easier to obtain distributors, and competition increases as imitators introduce their versions of the product. Competitors' marketing strategies focus on stimulating secondary demand with emphasis on product differentiation. Market volume expands and new market segments are opened up. Unit costs decline as sales volume grows, facilitating still lower prices.

Maturity

Eventually the rate of market acceptance decreases as the number of new potential customers diminishes. Pressures of excess capacity lead to some price competition,

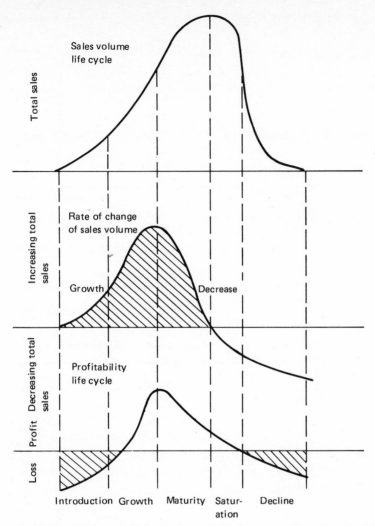

Figure 9-1 Product life cycles. *(Adapted from John Sizer, "Accountants, Product Managers and Selling Price Decisions in Multi-Consumer Product Firms," Journal of Business Finance, 4 (Spring 1972), 73.)*

and further price competition comes from private-label versions. Replacement sales constitute an increasing proportion of demand. Marketing strategies are designed to create customer preference and loyalty, and continued growth requires an increase in market share.

Saturation

At this stage, products and production methods have become standardized, and buyers generally are well aware of similarities and differences between products. The market is crowded by competitors, and competition for market share is very tough. Replace-

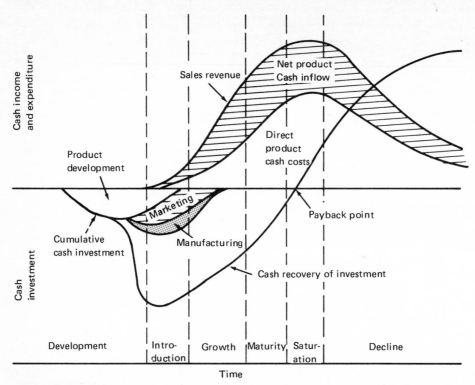

Figure 9-2 Investment life cycle. *(Adapted from John Sizer, "Accountants, Product Managers and Selling Price Decisions in Multi-Consumer Product Firms," Journal of Business Finance, 4 (Spring 1972), 76.)*

ment demand is the major source of demand and there is extensive private labeling. Brand switching takes place, encouraged by pricing strategies that involve offering specials, better credit terms, more services, and increased discounts. Inefficient producers begin to leave the market.

Decline

Sales begin to diminish as customers turn to new or better products. Private labels take an increasing share of the market and profits tend to be minimal.

Strategy Implications

The intuitive appeal of the product life cycle, its theoretical foundation in the adoption process, and empirical verification suggest the model's validity.[1] Yet, there is no fixed time length for a cycle, nor for the lengths of the various stages within the cycle. If anything, advances in technology have led to a shortening of the typical life cycle.[2]

---

[1]See, for example, William E. Cox Jr., "Product Life Cycles as Marketing Models," *Journal of Business*, 40 (October 1967), 375–84 and Rolando Polli and Victor J. Cook, "Validity of the Product Life Cycle," *Journal of Business*, 42 (October 1969), 385–400.

[2]"New Products: The Push Is on Marketing," *Business Week*, March 4, 1972, 72–77.

And as shown in Figs. 9-1 and 9-2, the profitability life cycle is even shorter. Thus, it is important to recognize that

1 Products have a limited life.
2 Under accelerating technological growth, a product's life span is likely to be shorter than previously.
3 Sales and profits tend to follow a predictable trend.
4 Products require different marketing strategies at each stage of the life cycle.
5 Pricing strategy is vitally important at each stage of the life cycle, but particularly at the introduction stage.

BASIC PRICING DECISIONS

The pricing decisions for a modern business organization are complex and important. Today, business firms are encountering competitors who have more efficient methods of production and generally lower labor costs. Thus, foreign firms are able to set prices that are lower than comparable prices set by American businesses. Also, the federal government has taken an increasing and active interest in the prices established. As a result, more and more firms are rediscovering price as an active determinant of demand and are actively making pricing decisions.

As shown in Table 9-1 there are many kinds of pricing decisions that a firm must make. There is the decision on what specific price to charge for each product or service marketed. But, the specific price to charge depends on the type of customer to whom the product or service is sold. If different customers purchase in varying quantities, should the seller offer volume discounts? If the firm markets through a mixed distribution channel, what prices should be charged to wholesalers who in turn distribute the products to their retail customers, and what prices should be charged to retailers who buy direct from the manufacturer?

The firm must also decide whether to offer discounts for early payment. If the firm decides on a cash discount policy it must then determine when a customer is eligible for a cash discount and how much to allow for early payment. Should the firm attempt to suggest retail prices or should it only price to the immediate customer?

Normally, the firm sells multiple products and the pricing questions just posed must be answered for each product. Additionally, the need to determine the number of

Table 9-1 Basic Pricing Decisions

1. What to charge for the different products and services produced by the firm
2. What to charge different types of customers
3. Whether to charge different types of distributors the same price
4. Whether to give discounts for cash and how quickly payment should be required to earn them
5. Whether to suggest resale prices or only set the price charged one's own customers
6. Whether to price all items in the product line as if they were separate or to price them as a "team"
7. How many different price offerings to have of each item
8. Whether to base prices on the geographical location of buyers (i.e., whether to charge for transportation)

price offerings per product and the price relationships between the products offered make the pricing problem more complex. For example, should a camera manufacturer produce and sell only one camera model or should several models be sold? Usually, the decision to sell several models of a product means the seller is attempting to appeal to several market segments. Once it is decided to offer a number of differently priced models, the seller must decide on the price of the lowest model and on price differentials between each alternative offering.

Today's pricing decisions are difficult and complex and are deserving of careful managerial thought. Since the traditional practice of pricing has been to imitate the pricing practices of others, it is likely that many managers will seek to follow the pricing prescriptions found in the contemporary literature. However, each firm should carefully analyze its markets, competitors, and costs before developing a pricing strategy.

NEW-PRODUCT PRICING

One of the most interesting and challenging decision problems is that of determining the price of a new product. New-product pricing decisions are usually made with very little information on demand, costs, competition, and other variables that may affect the chances of success. Given the rate of new-product introductions and the rate of failures, the importance of the new-product price decision is apparent.

Many new products fail because they do not possess the features desired by buyers, or because they are not available at the right time and place. Others fail because they have been wrongly priced, and the error can as easily be in pricing the product too low as in pricing it too high. One reason for new-product pricing errors is the lack of knowledge on how pricing decisions should be made. Thus the decision maker often relies on intuition, and experience does not appear to measurably improve chances of success.

When the first home permanent kit was marketed, it was priced to sell slightly below $1.00. However, many women were suspicious of a product priced so low when permanents in the beauty parlors were priced between $10 and $15. When the manufacturer of the home permanent kit discovered that the new product was priced too low, the price was raised by a dollar to slightly under $2.00. Today, home permanent kits are accepted and well-established in the market.

The difficulty in pricing a new product depends on the relative "newness" of the product. Some products are new in the sense that a product which already exists in the market is offered by a company that is new to the market. For example, the introduction of Cycle brand canned dog food in the mid-1970s signaled the entry of a new company into the canned dog food market. Generally, the price of such functionally identical products is determined by existing prices of competing products. The new product's price is likely to be similar to existing products' prices.

Other new products are new both to the company and to the market, but they are functionally competitive with established products. For example, Maxim competed directly with regular and instant coffees, although it was the first freeze-dried coffee on the market. Pricing new products is more difficult but the prices of similar products influence the decision. Perhaps the critical question is how much buyers will be willing to pay for perceived differences in function, utility, or appearance.

The most difficult new-product pricing problem occurs when the product is unique, i.e., functionally dissimilar to any other product. If the product is a major innovation in the market, there is much uncertainty surrounding the pricing decision. Essentially, the market is undefined, i.e., demand is unknown, and not all potential uses of the product are known. There are no comparable market experiences, e.g., channels of distribution, markups, or production and marketing costs. Potential customers will be uncertain about the product in terms of its functioning, reliability, or durability. They may be concerned about whether improvements will be made later and what the effects of these improvements will be on the product. Customers may also wonder whether prices will be reduced later when more sellers are distributing the product and when mass production techniques lower production costs. The first black-and-white television set and the trash compactor are good examples of this type of new product.

Approaches to New-Product Pricing

There are several approaches to determining a new product's price: intuitive, systematic, or simulation. The intuitive approach involves the decision maker in subjectively assessing the information available and, more by instinct than design, setting a price. Crude as this approach seems, it is probably the most common one. It is not at all uncommon for a marketing research project for a new product to be designed with price already determined. The purpose of such a research project might be to investigate how to effectively design a communication campaign for the new product.

Several authors have suggested pursuing a more systematic approach to new-product pricing. As Table 9-2 indicates, these approaches vary. Welsh's approach

Table 9-2 Systematic Approaches to New-Product Pricing

Step	Dean*	Oxenfeldt†	Welsh‡
1	Estimate demand	Select market target	Estimate demand
2	Select market target	Choose brand image	Determine marketing requirements over product's life cycle
3	Design promotional strategy	Compose marketing mix	Plot product's expected life cycle
4	Choose distribution channels	Select a pricing policy	Estimate costs over life cycle
5		Determine a pricing strategy	Estimate competitor's entry capabilities
6		Select a specific price	Estimate competitor's probable entry dates
7			Select a specific price

*Joel Dean, "Pricing Policies for New Products," *Harvard Business Review*, 28 (November–December 1950), 28–36; "Pricing a New Product," *The Controller*, April 1955, pp. 163–165.

†Alfred R. Oxenfeldt, "Multi-Stage Approach to Pricing," *Harvard Business Review*, 38 (July–August 1960), 125–133.

‡Stephen J. Welsh, "A Planned Approach to New Product Pricing," *Pricing: The Critical Decision*, AMA Management Report No. 66 (New York: American Management Association, 1961), pp. 45–57.

specifically takes a long-range view in that the three major determinants of price—demand, cost, and competition—are specifically estimated over the product's estimated life cycle. Although less apparent in their case, both Dean's and Oxenfeldt's approaches also suggest a long-range view in that they emphasize the development of a marketing plan.

Thus, these three systematic approaches emphasize the development of a "true" marketing plan. Instead of viewing pricing as an isolated problem, the systematic planning approach considers price as only one of the variables that interacts to determine product success. The pricing decision, therefore, is only one of several interrelated decisions to be made.

The most sophisticated approach to new-product pricing decisions is the development of a mathematical model to help determine the new price. Although this approach also considers price and the other marketing mix variables concurrently, it is more sophisticated in that the interrelationships between the variables are specified mathematically. By programming this model on a computer and inputting the necessary information, it is then possible to experiment with values for different decision variables, under several environmental assumptions over a simulated time period. The value of such an approach is that the decision maker can assess the relative implications of different assumptions and decision alternatives prior to making specific assumptions. Unfortunately, few workable new-product pricing models exist.[3]

Estimating Demand for a New Product

Each of the three systematic approaches outlined in Table 9-2 suggests that the first step in new-product pricing is to estimate demand in the selected market targets. But, how can demand for new products be estimated? How can the range of prices that people will consider acceptable for a new product be estimated?

The demand estimation problem can be separated into a series of research problems. The first problem is concerned with whether the product itself will fill a need or want and, therefore, will sell if the price is right. The second problem is to determine the range of prices that will make the product economically acceptable to potential buyers. Next, at feasible price points in the acceptable price range, expected sales volumes must be estimated. Finally, potential competitive reaction must be determined.

Gabor and Granger[4] suggest a method for determining estimates of the range of acceptable prices for a new product. Their method is based on the price threshold concept and the adaptation-level theory discussed in Chap. 3. Two basic kinds of information must be generated from potential users of the product: (1) the highest and lowest prices they would consider paying for the product and (2) the price last paid for the nearest comparable product or service. The first piece of information provides estimates of the acceptable price range and can be translated into a probability

[3] Kent B. Monroe and Albert J. Della Bitta, "Models for Pricing Decisions," *Journal of Marketing Research*, 15 (August 1978), 413–428.
[4] Andre Gabor and C. W. J. Granger, "The Pricing of New Products," *Scientific Business*, 3 (August 1965), 141–150.

distribution called a *buy-response function.* The midpoint price of the buy-response curve provides an estimate of the price likely to be judged most acceptable by potential buyers, as well as an estimate of the proportion of buyers likely to consider buying the product at that price.

The second piece of information indicates a reference point buyers may use when contemplating the purchase of the new product. A comparison of the midpoint of the buy-response curve with the midpoint of the price-last-paid curve will indicate the degree of discretion available in pricing the new product. For example, if the midpoint of the buy-response curve is at a higher price than the midpoint of the price-last-paid curve, then a price higher than the price last paid may have a degree of buyer acceptance. A limitation to this research approach occurs if the product is such a major innovation that buyers have no concept either of the product or of comparable alternatives.

Alternative Strategies for Pricing a New Product

It has been generally presumed that there are two alternatives in pricing a new product: "skimming" pricing calling for a relatively high price, and "penetration" pricing calling for a relatively low price. A skimming price may be appropriate for new products if

1 Demand is likely to be price inelastic.
2 There are likely to be different price-market segments, thereby appealing to those buyers first who have a higher range of acceptable prices.
3 Little is known about the costs of producing and marketing the product.

A penetration price may be appropriate if

1 Demand is likely to be price elastic.
2 Competitors are likely to enter the market quickly.
3 There are no distinct and separate price-market segments.
4 There is the possibility of large savings in production and marketing costs if a large sales volume can be generated (the experience factor).

Caution is suggested in any selection of a skimming or penetration pricing strategy. Generally there may be at least one current product that will serve as a frame of reference for potential buyers, and they are likely to use this product to form their opinions of the value and price of the new product. Where such a reference product exists, the price setter must determine the price differential (higher or lower price than the reference product) and fit the new product into the established population of existing products.

The factors mentioned above may suggest an overall pricing strategy for a new product. However, *these two alternative strategies should not be viewed as either/or alternatives.* Rather, they merely reflect two opposite strategy extremes. Considerable latitude, therefore, exists in choosing the specific price level for a new product. Attention is now turned to the decision problem of selecting the actual price level.

CONTRIBUTION ANALYSIS FOR LIFE-CYCLE PRICING

Ideally, the analysis and planning for pricing a product over its life cycle begins at the start of the development stage. One of the primary considerations for accepting a new-product proposal and initiating the developmental investment is the rate of return on investment expected during the product's life. But, the investment analysis requires an estimate of revenues and expenditures over time for each alternative under consideration. And, as previous chapters have demonstrated, there is an explicit price-volume-cost relationship that influences both revenues and expenditures. As Fig. 9-2 indicates, the analysis must project estimated cash flows over the entire investment life cycle. Therefore, it is necessary at the outset to have some preliminary price-volume estimates for the different stages of the product life cycle. The operational approach developed in Chap. 3 is well-suited for this task.[5]

New-Product Pricing

Perhaps the most common error management makes in pricing new products is to attempt to recover its investment in a new product as quickly as possible. A reasonable price for a new product is one that will attract both resellers and ultimate users. A high price requiring substantial selling effort to overcome buyer resistance will not receive enthusiastic support from distributors.

Further, a high price with an introductory discount designed to stimulate initial trial may, as suggested in Chap. 3, lead to a lower adaptation price level. And later when the product is marketed at its "regular" price, the perception of an increase in price may forever dwarf the sales growth of the product. In addition, an introductory discount might be considered a deceptive pricing practice according to Federal Trade Commission guidelines. (See Chap. 12.)

A second common error made in pricing new products is to base initial prices on the wrong cost data. Including development costs and high initial unit production costs in the new product's costs is likely to result in a price that will repel both distributors and final customers and effectively kill the product. Development costs must be considered as an investment to be recovered over the life of the product. The appropriate unit direct costs are those costs expected when the product reaches its growth stage, or when steady production and sales rates are achieved. The value of the experience curve discussed in Chap. 8 becomes readily apparent for forecasting these relevant direct costs.

Much of the analysis relevant to the pricing of a new product involves contribution analyses similar to those developed in Chap. 5. For alternative, feasible prices and expected, reasonable costs, a profit-volume break-even chart can be constructed as shown in Fig. 9-3. The data are shown in Table 9-3. While the break-even chart of Fig. 9-3 reveals different break-even points for prices P_1 through P_6, it provides no information on price-demand-cost-profit relationships. It simply confirms that, for a given cost structure, a lower price results in a higher break-even point. What is needed is a way to incorporate demand into the chart.

[5]See also James J. Finerty, "Product Pricing and Investment Analysis," *Management Accounting*, 53 (December 1971), 15–18.

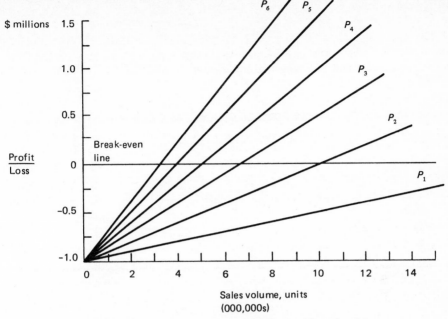

Figure 9-3 PV break-even chart: Price-volume combinations for life-cycle pricing.

However, it is first necessary to develop price-volume estimates for the alternative prices. Again, the operational approach outlined in Chap. 3 would be useful. At this point in the analysis, it would be more realistic to develop several demand (volume) estimates for each alternative price. To simplify the presentation, assume only the most likely volume estimate for each price.

Then, for each price-volume estimate, direct production and marketing costs must be estimated. Again, it is important to emphasize the need to consider realistic costs (i.e., costs that are comparable to costs to be incurred during the product's growth stage). It is also important to avoid the temptation to apportion common costs to the product since, as shown in Chap. 7, any apportionment is essentially arbitrary. Full cost estimates would be inappropriate because

Table 9-3 Price-Volume Data for Life-Cycle Pricing
Introductory Stage

Unit selling price	$6.50	$7.00	$7.50	$8.00	$8.50	$9.00
Unit variable cost	6.00	6.00	6.00	6.00	6.00	6.00
Unit contribution	$0.50	$1.00	$1.50	$2.00	$2.50	$3.00
PV	0.077	0.143	0.200	0.250	0.294	0.333
Volume (units)	1,500,000	1,400,000	1,300,000	1,225,000	1,000,000	800,000
Revenue	$9,750,000	$9,800,000	$9,750,000	$9,800,000	$8,500,000	$7,200,000
Fixed expenses	$1,000,000	$1,000,000	$1,000,000	$1,000,000	$1,000,000	$1,000,000
Variable costs	$9,000,000	$8,400,000	$7,800,000	$7,350,000	$6,000,000	$4,800,000
Profit (Loss)	$ (250,000)	$ 400,000	$ 950,000	$1,450,000	$1,500,000	$1,400,000

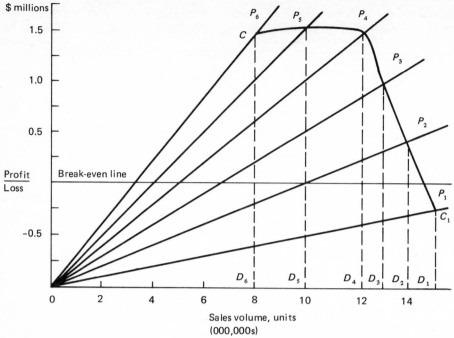

Figure 9-4 PV break-even chart: Price-volume combinations for life-cycle pricing.

Full costs include past costs which are not relevant to the pricing decision.

Overhead absorption rates are poor measures of the opportunity costs of using scarce resources.

Full costs may lead to cost-plus pricing which does not consider demand or competition.

Table 9-3 shows the type of data that needs to be generated. Note that the highest price, $9.00 ($P_6$), is not necessarily the most profitable choice. When the profit and volume data of Table 9-3 are plotted on the PV break-even chart for each price, the result is as shown in Fig. 9-4. In Fig. 9-4, CC_1 is the contribution curve for the new product. The contribution curve shows the relationship between demand (D_1 to D_6), direct product profit, total contribution, and break-even points for alternative prices. Thus, the analysis has considered the estimated demand function and the relevant costs for the pricing decision.[6]

As the data in Table 9-3 and Fig. 9-4 show, the most profitable price is $8.50 with a most likely volume estimate of 1,000,000 units. Frequently, during the introductory stage the firm does not have full production capacity, since the firm may wish to wait until the product has been successfully introduced before making additional investments in productive capacity. Indeed, assume during the introductory period the firm has productive capacity for only 900,000 units. As the data in Table 9-3 show, not

[6] This analysis has been adopted from John Sizer, "Accountants, Product Managers and Selling Price Decisions in Multi-Consumer Product Firms," *Journal of Business Finance*, 4 (Spring 1972), 70–84.

until price is above $8.50 does estimated volume go below a million units. Therefore, the firm may wish to set the initial price around $9.00. Later, price may be reduced when (1) additional productive capacity becomes available, (2) competitors begin to enter the market, or (3) price elasticity increases. Figure 9-5 shows the break-even chart with the capacity constraint.

The advantage of the product profit-volume analysis is that it allows the manager to trace the implications of different introductory pricing strategies. For example, if the product is easily imitated by competitors, the firm may wish to pursue a penetration pricing policy to build early high volume and maintain a relatively higher market share in a growing market. In the example given in Table 9-3, a penetration price of $7.00 yields a short-term profit of $1,000,000 less than the skimming price of $9.00. This million dollars represents a short-term opportunity cost that should be balanced by expected gains due to a higher market share during the growth stage of the product.

Another factor that might influence a penetration pricing policy would be the rate at which the experience factor reduces direct production and marketing costs per unit. For example, if experience could reduce the variable costs to $5.00 per unit for production of 1,400,000 units or more, then estimated profits for prices $7.00 and $6.50 would be $1,800,000 and $1,250,000 respectively.

Pricing during Growth

If the new product survives the introductory period, as demand grows both the *position* and *shape* of the contribution curve change. Usually, a number of competitors

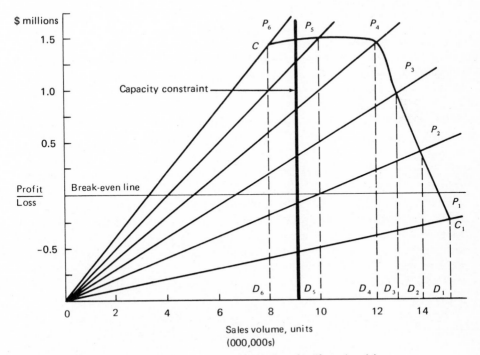

Figure 9-5 PV break-even chart: Price-volume combinations for life-cycle pricing.

Table 9-4   Price-Volume Data for Life-Cycle Pricing
Growth Stage

Unit selling price	$6.00	$6.50	$7.00	$7.50
Unit variable cost	5.00	5.00	5.00	5.00
Unit contribution	$1.00	$1.50	$2.00	$2.50
PV	0.167	0.231	0.286	0.333
Volume (units)	2,800,000	2,500,000	2,000,000	1,400,000
Revenue	$16,800,000	$16,250,000	$14,000,000	$10,500,000
Fixed expenses	$ 2,500,000	$ 2,500,000	$ 2,500,000	$ 2,500,000
Variable costs	$14,000,000	$12,500,000	$10,000,000	$ 7,000,000
Profit	$ 300,000	$ 1,250,000	$ 1,500,000	$ 1,000,000

are producing and selling a similar product, and a market price emerges. Normally, there is a relatively wide range of market prices early in the growth stage, but this market price range narrows as the product approaches maturity.

Table 9-4 and Fig. 9-6 provide illustrative data for pricing during the growth stage. Three essential points should be noted: (1) the range of feasible prices has narrowed since the introductory stage; (2) unit variable costs have decreased due to economies of scale (experience factor); and (3) fixed expenses have increased because of increased capitalization and period marketing costs. The pricing decision during the growth stage is to select a price that, subject to competitive conditions, will help generate a sales volume that enables the firm to realize its target contribution.

Pricing a Mature Product

As a product moves into the maturity and saturation stages, it is necessary to review past pricing decisions and to determine the desirability of a price change. As the description of the product life cycle indicated, replacement sales constitute the major demand, and manufacturers also incur competition from private labeled products. Market conditions do not appear to warrant a price increase, hence the pricing decision usually is to reduce price or stand pat.

When is a price reduction profitable? We know that when demand is price elastic it is profitable to reduce prices if costs do not rise above the increase in revenues. But since it can be expected that any price decrease will be followed by competitors, it is also necessary that the market demand curve be elastic within the range of the price reduction.

Because of the number of close substitutes, a firm's demand curve will probably be elastic. But if all sellers match the price reduction, the firm's market share will remain relatively constant, and any increase in the firm's demand will result from an increase in market demand. Therefore, to reduce price for a mature product, market demand must be elastic, the firm's demand must be elastic, and the marginal revenues associated with the increased volume must be greater than the marginal costs of producing and selling the additional volume.

As an example, assume that a firm is selling 3,000,000 units at $6.00 per unit.[7] Further, assume that both the market and the firm's demand is price elastic with an

---

[7]This example is adapted from Clare E. Griffin, "When Is Price Reduction Profitable?" *Harvard Business Review*, 38 (September–October 1960), 125 ff.

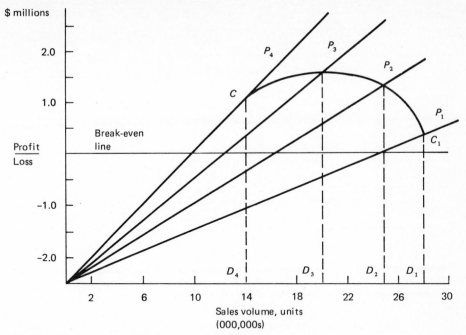

Figure 9-6 PV break-even chart: Price-volume combinations, growth stage.

elasticity value of -1.43. Assume also that a price reduction by the firm is exactly matched by competitors, such that relative market shares remain constant. This means that a marketwide price reduction will increase market demand, but that each firm's demand increases only in direct proportion to its market share. The firm is considering reducing its price to $5.75, or 4.2 percent. Because demand price elasticity is -1.43, a 4.2 percent price reduction will increase demand by 6 percent (-4.2% × -1.43 = +6%). The comparative effect of the price reduction on the firm's revenues is shown in Table 9-5A. With a price of $5.75 revenues will increase by an amount of $285,000.

However, although revenues have increased, it is possible that profits have not increased. To determine the effect of the price decrease on profits, assume that variable costs per unit are $4.80, and that the product has fixed costs of $2,500,000. Table 9-5B shows the effect of a 6 percent increase in volume on costs and Table 9-5C shows the comparative effect on profits. Thus, while the price reduction produced an increase in revenue of $285,000, profits were reduced by $579,000. As Table 5-6 and Fig. 5-6 indicated, for a product with a PV of 0.20 [($6.00 - $4.80)/$6.00], a price reduction of 4.2 percent must be accompanied by a volume increase of better than 26 percent if profits are to remain unchanged.

At the maturity stage of the life cycle, the firm probably should attempt to maximize short-run direct product contribution to profits. Hence, the pricing objective is to choose the price alternative leading to maximum contribution. If competition reduces prices, the firm may, however reluctantly, match the price reduction. On the other hand, it may try to reduce costs by using cheaper materials, eliminating several labor operations, or reducing period marketing costs. All or any of these actions may

Table 9-5

	Before	After
A Effect on revenues of a 4.2% price reduction		
Demand, units (Q)	3,000,000	3,180,000
Price (P)	$6.00	$5.75
Revenues (P × Q)	$18,000,000	$18,285,000
B Effect on costs of a 4.2% price reduction		
Fixed expenses	$ 2,500,000	$ 2,500,000
Variable costs ($4.80 × Q)	14,400,000	15,264,000
Total costs	$16,900,000	$17,764,000
C Effect on profits of a 4.2% price reduction		
Total revenues	$18,000,000	$18,285,000
Total costs	16,900,000	17,764,000
Profits	$ 1,100,000	$ 521,000

allow the firm to match competitively lower prices and still maintain target contributions to profit.

For example, assume a competitor has reduced price to $5.75. Since the firm wishes to meet that $5.75 price, it attempts to maintain profitability by modifying production procedures and reducing marketing period expenditures. The effects on costs are shown in Table 9-6A and the profit effect is shown in Table 9-6B.

Pricing a Declining Product

During the declining phase of a product's life, direct costs are very important to the pricing decision. Normally, competition has driven the price down close to direct costs. Only those sellers who were able to maintain or reduce direct costs during the saturation stage are likely to have remained. If the decline is not due to an overall

Table 9-6

	Before	After
A Change in cost structure		
Fixed expenses	$ 2,500,000	$ 2,250,000
Variable costs per unit	4.80	4.60
B Effect on profits of a 4.2% price reduction and change in cost structure		
Total revenues	$18,000,000	$18,285,000
Total costs	16,900,000	16,878,000
Profits	$ 1,100,000	$ 1,407,000

cyclical decline in business but to shifts in buyer preferences, then the primary objective is to obtain as much contribution to profits as possible.

So long as the firm has excess capacity and revenues exceed all direct costs, the firm probably should consider remaining in the market. Generally, most firms eliminate all period marketing costs (or as many of these costs as possible) and remain in the market as long as price exceeds direct variable costs. As noted in Chaps. 4 and 5, the direct variable costs are the minimally acceptable prices to the seller. Thus, with excess capacity, any market price above direct variable costs would generate contributions to profit.

SUMMARY

This chapter has developed techniques for establishing prices over a product's life cycle. Contribution analysis has been extended to show its adaptability and usefulness for pricing over the life cycle. Since it is advocated that a pricing plan be developed during the development stage, both price *and* cost forecasting are important to the analysis.

To avoid the common mistake of basing a new product's price on unrealistic introductory production and marketing costs, the experience curve can be utilized to obtain more realistic cost estimates. Furthermore, developing an experience curve for a product permits knowing when volume increases due to price reductions will also lead to unit cost decreases.

Finally, it is important for the price setter to be provided proper accounting and financial data. Accountants who prepare data for pricing administrators should tailor their analyses to the life-cycle stage for each product. Product profit-volume charts can be used to provide a good understanding of the implications of each pricing alternative.

DISCUSSION QUESTIONS

1 Describe the pricing environment for each stage of the product life cycle.
   a What are the possible pricing objectives?
   b What are the general pricing strategies for each of these objectives?
   c As a product progresses through the different life-cycle stages, how do these objectives and general pricing strategies change? Why?
   d Carefully discuss the role of competition on the objectives and strategies you have developed in parts **a** and **b**.
2 During Fall 1977, the TV-set tape recorder caught on in the United States consumer market. Prior to this time Sony had priced its Betamax model at $1,295. In August 1977, RCA set a suggested price for its model at $1,000. In November 1977, Zenith reduced its price to $995 from $1,295.
   a What do you anticipate will be the pricing reaction of Sony? Why?
   b What do you anticipate will happen to prices of TV-set tape recorders in 1978? Why?
3 In November 1977, Sony reduced the price of its Betamax TV-set recorder from $1,295 to $1,095 in response to the competitive price moves by Zenith and RCA described in Question 2. What is your evaluation of the price change?

4 The Scientific Corporation is in the final stages of developing a new product. Preliminary market tests show that potential customers like the product. Based on these market tests and customer surveys, the market research staff has provided the following sales estimates for the first 3 years of the product's life:

Price	Year 1	Year 2	Year 3
$12	20,000 units	40,000 units	60,000 units
$14	15,000 units	25,000 units	45,000 units
$16	12,000 units	22,000 units	40,000 units
$18	10,000 units	20,000 units	35,000 units
$20	8,500 units	18,000 units	30,000 units

After reviewing the marketing, production, and financial plans for the new product, the controller estimates that direct variable costs will average $8.00 for the first 25,000 units produced, $7.00 after the first 25,000 units produced, $6.50 after the first 50,000 units produced, and $5.00 after the first 100,000 units produced. Period fixed costs are expected to be $50,000, $100,000, $150,000 for the first 3 years, respectively. Further, it is expected that the Malloy Corporation will be able to market a similar product by the beginning of the second year and that they will have a cost experience similar to that of the Scientific Corporation.

Develop a pricing strategy for the first 3 years of the product for the Scientific Corporation. Support your strategy with the necessary exhibits and analyses. What is the rationale of your strategy?

SUGGESTED READINGS

Böer, Germain B.: "Additional Applications of Direct Cost Information to Pricing Decisions," in *Direct Cost and Contribution Accounting* (New York: John Wiley, 1974), pp. 164–183.

Dean, Joel: "Pricing Policies for New Products," *Harvard Business Review*, 54 (November–December 1976), 141–153.

Gabor, Andre, and C. W. J. Granger: "The Pricing of New Products," *Scientific Business*, 3 (August 1965), 141–150.

Griffin, Clare E.: "When Is Price Reduction Profitable?" *Harvard Business Review*, 38 (September–October 1960), 125ff.

Monroe, Kent B., and Albert J. Della Bitta: "Models for Pricing Decisions," *Journal of Marketing Research*, 15 (August 1978), 413–428.

Oxenfeldt, Alfred R.: *Pricing Strategies* (New York: American Management Association, 1975).

Robinson, Bruce, and Chet Lakhani: "Dynamic Price Models for New-Product Planning," *Management Science*, 21 (June 1975), 1113–1122.

Sizer, John: "Accountants, Product Managers, and Selling Price Decisions in Multi-Consumer Product Firms," *Journal of Business Finance*, 4 (Spring 1972), pp. 70–84.

Chapter 10

Product-Line
Pricing Decisions

A fundamental marketing decision problem is the determination of price for a product or service. Many factors complicate pricing decisions, such as cost per unit, competitor and buyer sensitivity to price, objectives of the firm, legal constraints, potential entry or exit of competing sellers, and the total product-service offering of the firm. The pricing literature has discussed in some detail each of these factors, with the exception of the total product-service offering of the firm. Exclusion of the product-service offering as a factor is the result of the attention given the problem of determining price for a single product or service. However, today most firms sell multiple products. Hence, there is a need to consider the effect that total product-service offering has on pricing decisions.

From a market perspective, many firms have discovered that there are specific price-market segments for their products and that determining prices to differentiate these products is a complex process. Whether to add a middle-priced product or change the number of price offerings depends not only on the number of price-market segments, but also on clearly differentiating the products in the minds of buyers. This chapter develops a behavioral approach to determine ways to position products in a product line according to price. In addition, costing principles developed in Chaps. 4 through 8 are used to analyze the sales-volume mix.

NATURE OF THE DECISION PROBLEM

Generally, a firm has several product lines—a group of products that are closely related because they are used together, they satisfy the same general needs, or they are marketed together. Within a product line there are usually some products that are functional substitutes for each other, and some that are functionally complementary. For example, a photographic product line would include cameras, film, flashbulbs, projectors, screens, and other accessories. Different camera models are functional substitutes, whereas films, flashbulbs, and accessories are functionally complementary products. Because of the demand interrelationships inherent within such a product line, as well as the cost interrelationships, and because there are usually several price market targets, the product-line pricing problem is one of the major challenges that faces a marketing executive.

Although an organization may wish to pursue a pricing policy of high prices only (or low prices only), it still must decide how high (or low) its prices should be and the differentials between different products in the line. In addition, it must decide on the lowest (or highest) price that helps to maintain a consistent price policy. Thus, three types of pricing decisions are required.

1 Determining the lowest priced product and its price
2 Determining the highest priced product and its price
3 Setting the price differentials for all intermediate products

Compounding the pricing problem is that complementarity may exist even if the products are functionally substitutable. For example, one researcher discovered that a substitute relationship existed for the product-line brand vs. competitors' brands, but that a complementarity relationship existed between brands within the product line.[1] In addition, by adding new items or reducing certain prices, a firm may increase demand for already existing products. Finally, it is known that the lowest and highest priced products are more frequently remembered and perceived, implying a further complementarity.[2]

The low-end price usually is the most frequently remembered one and probably has considerable influence on the marginal buyer (the buyer doubtful about buying, but still seriously considering making the purchase). Hence, the lowest priced product is often used as a traffic-builder. On the other hand, the highest priced product is also quite visible and, through quality connotations, may also stimulate demand.

Some of the recent behavioral pricing research holds the promise of providing the price setter with information for solving these complex pricing problems. Price threshold research may not only help the firm establish the boundary of different price-market segments but also provide information on where the lowest and highest priced products should be slotted to enhance the salability of the entire product line.

[1]Glen Urban, "A Mathematical Modeling Approach to Product Line Decisions," *Journal of Marketing Research*, 6 (February 1969), 40–47.
[2]Alfred Oxenfeldt, "Product Line Pricing," *Harvard Business Review*, 44 (July–August 1966), 135–143.

In addition to the inherent complementary relationships within a product line, products that are functionally complementary present a pricing problem. For example, the pricing of cameras and film, or the pricing of razors and razor blades, introduces further problems. Clearly, demand for film or razor blades is enhanced by the sale of cameras or razors. Should the firm intentionally set the price of razors and cameras low in order to increase demand for blades and film?

Conceptual Framework

Generally, a firm produces and distributes multiple products either because (1) the demands for the various products are interrelated, (2) the costs of production and distribution are interrelated, (3) both costs and demands are interrelated, or (4) multiple products enable the firm to appeal simultaneously to several diverse market segments (i.e., the products are neither demand- nor cost-related, but instead permit the firm to pursue expansion or diversification objectives).

Products are demand-related if a change in the price of a product, Q_1, induces the buyer to change the quantity of his or her purchases of other products $(Q_2, \ldots, Q_n)$, along with changing purchases of Q_1.

Similarly, products are related by production and distribution if a change in the quantity produced and distributed of a product, Q_1, results in a change in the unit costs of other products, $Q_2, \ldots, Q_n$.

Thus, if the firm's products are related by both demand and costs, the quantity produced and sold of any particular product affects both the revenues and costs of the other products a firm may sell. Hence, an adjustment in the price of a particular product to increase net profit for that product may or may not increase profits for the entire firm. In such situations, if the firm is interested in *maximizing profits*, it must consider not only the effect on revenues and costs of the particular product for which price is being adjusted, but also the changes in revenues and costs for all other related products.

Theoretically, the optimal solution for a firm producing multiple products is to equate the marginal revenues for each product with the firm's total marginal costs. Such a solution assumes that demand for any product is a function only of its own price. That is, if the firm sells more than one product, each product is sold in a separate market under separate demand conditions. Hence it is relatively easy to specify the equating of marginal revenues as an optimum solution.

In contrast, of course, today's multiproduct firm sells its products in markets that are not completely separable, and it becomes intuitively obvious that the level of sales of any one item in a product line may be influenced by the price of other items in the line. Thus, the variation of price for any given product may or may not produce the desired result unless prices of the other products in the line are also varied.

Moreover, recent research and observation of buyer reactions to price indicates that the lowest priced product in the product line may affect the quantity sold of all products in the line to a greater degree than the price of any other product.[3] These reac-

---

[3] Kent B. Monroe, "The Information Content of Prices: A Preliminary Model for Estimating Buyer Response," *Management Science*, 17 (April 1971), B519-B532.

tions appear to be related to the Gestalt principle of *outstandingness*—some objects have certain special qualities that make one's perception of them easier and more lasting than a perception based merely on their physical attributes. Applying this principle and these observations, it can be suggested that the price of the lowest priced product is the most perceived price and the one most frequently remembered. To complete the use of the principle of outstandingness, it is also suggested that the price of the highest priced product in a product line also is relatively more visible to potential buyers than prices spaced between the lowest and highest prices (end prices).

If the end prices of a product line are relatively more visible to buyers than other prices in the line, then these end prices may influence sales of all products in the line. That is, end prices may have information content for potential buyers, and these buyers may then transfer their interpretation of this information to the entire product line, e.g., a bargain vs. a quality interpretation. Recognizing that end prices may affect demand for products within a product line introduces the problem of determining the optimum end prices which will enhance the sale of products in the product line, in addition to determining the optimum price for each individual product.

Product-Line Examples

The discussion above has illustrated the concept of a product line with reference to cameras and photographic accessories, and razors and razor blades. In both examples one type of product is a complement to the other type. Sometimes, however, it is convenient to consider only a line of cameras, or a line of hand razors.

In the camera example, the manufacturer may have several models each with different features appealing to different types of camera uses. The simplest camera may appeal to the young photographer or infrequent picture taker who wants a simple "aim and shoot" camera. The next camera in the line may have a telescopic lens, while other models may feature 12 or 20 exposures, 35 mm, adjustable focus, or range finder. As the manufacturer expands the line of cameras from the simplest camera to the sophisticated camera used by professionals, each camera appeals to a different market segment, and each differential feature is valued differently by these segments. The pricing problem is to decide on a set of prices that corresponds to what each market segment is willing to pay. Table 10-1 shows the Polaroid camera line as of November 1977.

Moreover, the price differentials between camera models must correspond to perceived differences in the separate cameras. For example, if the simplest camera model A is priced at $25 and model B, which includes a telescopic lens, is priced at $29, buyers may perceive that $4 is or is not too much to pay for this added feature. But if buyers would be willing to pay up to $35 for model B, then a pricing error has been made *unless* it is the seller's intent to "trade buyers up" to model B. When Chevrolet introduced Corvair in the early 1960s, the Corvair was priced close to the regular-sized models to facilitate the selling of the regular models. On the other hand, Ford priced its compact Falcon to differentiate it from the larger models. Thus, the Falcon outsold the Corvair, but the larger and more profitable Chevrolet models outsold the larger Ford models.

Table 10-1 Polaroid Camera Product Line, Fall 1977

Model	Price, $	Description
Electric Zip	25.00	Takes color pictures in a minute or black and white in seconds. Comes in three colors: red, white, blue.
Minute Maker	24.95	Exposures are fully automatic. Takes both rectangular and square format film to deliver color shots in 60 s.
Minute Maker Plus	31.95	Takes five different types of instant film: rectangular, square, color, black and white, printable negative.
One Step ·	39.95	Aim and press one button; the motor hands you an SX-70 picture; 14½ oz, fits in the palm of your hand.
The Reporter	57.00	A folding camera, fits into a briefcase; takes five kinds of instant film; can shoot black-and-white pictures indoors without a flash.
Pronto! B	59.00	Set the distance, frame, and shoot. Pictures are automatically ejected by a motor drive. You can shoot every 1.5 s.
Pronto! Extra	70.00	A self-timer lets you get into the picture. The battery is built into the film pack.
Pronto! RF	88.00	Built-in range finder for focusing. Self-timer. Motor drive. SX-70 electronics prevent you from shooting if either the flash or film is used up.
SX-70 Alpha Model 2	180.00	Same optics and electronics as SX-70 Alpha 1; more modest wrappings.
SX-70 Alpha 1	233.00	World's only folding single-lens reflex camera. You can get as close as 10.4 in. without attachments. Automatic time exposures, fine leather and brushed chrome.

Source: Advertisement in *The Washington Post*, Thursday, November 24, 1977, p. D8.

The pricing of hotel or motel rooms is a product-line pricing problem. Most motels or hotels have different-sized rooms and some rooms face a desirable location such as a pool or park, while others face a less desirable location such as a back alley or a busy highway. Moreover, management must determine a single and a double rate for each type of room. And if suites are available, an additional pricing decision must be made.

Product lines are also prevalent in the industrial sector of our economy. For example, a company selling in the communications copy markets normally sells platemakers, offset duplicators, plate materials, chemicals, parts, and has service/maintenance contracts. Moreover, the company may have several models of platemakers and several models of offset duplicators, each with different features.

THE PROBLEM OF MULTIPLE PRODUCTS

In a multiple-product business, different products produce different profit volumes.[4] Even the shirt store in the example of Chap. 5 could have a product mix. The retailer could sell ties at a PV of 0.10, shirts at a PV of 0.20, sweaters at a PV of 0.40, and

[4]Material in this section is adapted from Spencer A. Tucker, *Pricing for Higher Profit* (New York: McGraw-Hill, 1966).

pants at a PV of 0.30. With a PV for ties of 0.10, the retailer would have to sell twice as many ties as shirts to gross the same contribution as shirts alone. But, he or she would only have to sell one-half as many sweaters as shirts to generate the same original contribution. Therefore, depending on the relative product mix, it would be possible to generate greater profits on fewer sales or smaller profits on more sales.

Within a multiproduct firm, each product generates a different amount of volume, a different cost structure, including variable and fixed costs, different unit prices, and, of course, different revenues. Not only are these important factors different, but they are changing. And as developed in Chap. 5, the conventional break-even chart is not dynamic and assumes a single-product situation.

However, multiple lines, each corresponding to a product or decision alternative, can be drawn on a PV chart. It is then possible to show variations in profit with volume and the effect of changes in prices on PV and profit. Figure 10-1 shows a PV break-even chart for the retail shirt store. On this chart we can contrast the profit at any volume for shirts with a PV of 0.20 to pants with a PV of 0.30. At this point, the chart is drawn as though the retailer faces the alternative of either sell shirts or sell pants. Now we will show how to combine the products in the analysis.

DEVELOPING PRICES FOR THE PRODUCT LINE

The PV break-even chart can be used to analyze the relative profit contributions of each product in a product line. The analysis as developed above must now be modified to consider relative differences in cost structure, volume generated, and profit contribution by each product in the line. To illustrate how we can adapt the PV analysis to the multiproduct firm, consider the data given in Table 10-2.

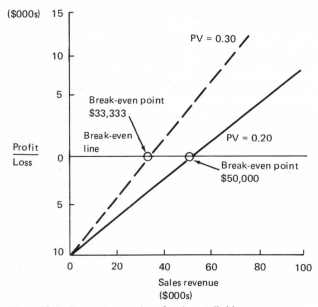

Figure 10-1　PV break-even chart for the retail shirt store.

Table 10-2

Product	PV	Percent of total volume
A	0.40	40
B	0.20	30
C	0.10	30

Annual common fixed costs: $500,000

As the data show, each product has a different PV value and different planned volumes as a percent of the firm's total volume. The problem now is to integrate these PVs and planned volumes to determine the appropriate PV for the analysis. In multiple-product problems the PV is determined by weighting the PV of each product by the percentage of the total volume for all products. For this example, the appropriate calculations are shown in Table 10-3.

The composite PV is used to determine the break-even point.

$$\text{BES} = \frac{\text{fixed costs}}{\text{PV}} = \frac{\$500,000}{0.25}$$

$$= \$2,000,000$$

For a total sales volume of $4,000,000, profits are

$$\text{Profit} = (\text{sales} \times \text{PV}) - \text{fixed costs} = (\$4,000,000 \times 0.25) - \$500,000$$

$$= \$500,000$$

Figure 10-2 illustrates this example. Note that because there are common fixed costs, we cannot determine the unique break-even point for each product. Rather, we can only determine the break-even point assuming the products are simultaneously sold.

What happens if the volume mix of the three products changes? To illustrate, assume the data of Table 10-2 changes to the relationships given in Table 10-4. Table

Table 10-3

(1)	(2)	(3)	(4)
			Weighted
		Proportion of total	PV
Product	PV	volume	(2) × (3)
A	0.40	0.40	0.16
B	0.20	0.30	0.06
C	0.10	0.30	0.03
Composite PV			0.25

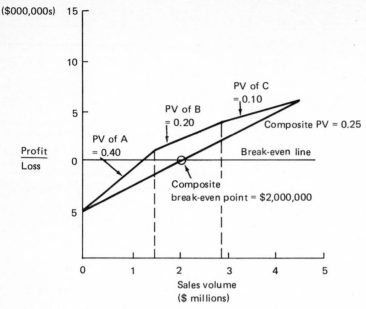

Figure 10-2 The composite PV break-even chart.

10-5 shows the development of the composite PV. For a composite PV of 0.21, the new break-even point is

$$\text{BES} = \frac{\$500,000}{0.21}$$

$$= \$2,380,950$$

For a total sales volume of $4,000,000, profits are

$$\text{Profit} = (\$4,000,000 \times 0.21) - \$500,000$$

$$= \$340,000$$

Thus, profits now are 68 percent of the original profit level. To determine the new total sales volume required to return profits to $500,000, we compute

$$\text{Sales} = \frac{\text{desired profit} + \text{fixed costs}}{\text{PV}} = \frac{\$500,000 + \$500,000}{0.21}$$

$$= \$4,761,905$$

Or, total sales must increase by 19 percent to regain the original profit level if the sales volume mix shifts as indicated in Table 10-4.

Often, when a shift in product mix results in a poorer PV, management attempts to recover the profit level by an across-the-board increase in prices. While the effect of

Table 10-4

Product	PV	Percent of total volume
A	0.40	20
B	0.20	50
C	0.10	30

this increase in prices helps to restore the original PV, this pricing reaction can lead to a further decline in profits. This further deterioration of profits may occur because management has attempted to force the external factors of competition and demand to support the internal need for profit. When an across-the-board increase in prices leads to a substantial decrease in sales volume, it is quite possible that the remedy has aggravated the problem.

When there are differences in the PVs among products in a line, a revision in the product selling mix may be more effective than an increase in prices. That is, a firm, by shifting emphasis to those products with relatively higher PVs, has a good opportunity to recover some or all of its profit position. For example, assume that a firm with common fixed costs of $100,000 sells two products: A with a PV of 0.60 and B with a PV of 0.20. Figure 10-3 illustrates the effects of changing the proportion of the product selling mix. It should be clear that the slope of the PV line depends on the relative proportion of the product selling mix. Hence, profit at any sales level is a function of prices, volume, and the product selling mix.

PRODUCT-LINE PRICING MODELS

Little attention has been given to the formulation of product-line pricing models. As the conceptual framework developed earlier in this chapter suggests, this decision problem is complex not only because of the demand interrelationships of substitutability and complementarity, but also because the buyer's perceptions of product-line prices do not necessarily conform to the economist's notions of demand interdependence. Within the published literature there are some attempts to handle this pricing problem as a part of the more familiar product-mix problem. However, the three product-line pricing decisions discussed above are not explicitly covered in the

Table 10-5

(1) Product	(2) PV	(3) Proportion of total volume	(4) Weighted PV (2) × (3)
A	0.40	0.20	0.08
B	0.20	0.50	0.10
C	0.10	0.30	0.03
Composite PV			0.21

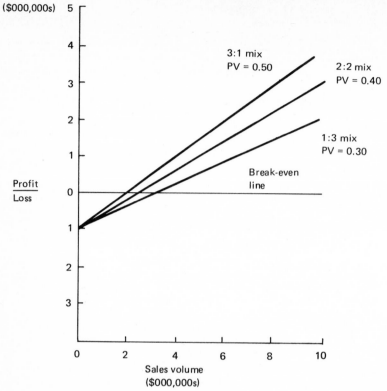

Figure 10-3 The effect of changing the product mix.

product-mix models. Here we will only sketch the nature of the product-line models. The Appendix to this chapter gives a more detailed description of the models.

Related-Products Model

In one approach to developing product-line pricing models, Urban[5] developed a mathematical model of the interactions between products for marketing strategy recommendations. The entire model considers several factors affecting product-line profitability.

The first part of the model develops a mechanism for determining total industry demand as a function of the total industry's efforts relative to price, distribution, and advertising. The model then considers the interdependencies of demand for product group j by introducing the notion of cross elasticities for products j and another product m for each of these three marketing strategy variables. For the ith firm in industry j, its market share is determined by the product of the sensitivity of industry demand to the marketing effort of the firm, the demand interdependencies of demand for product class j with demand for product class m, and the ratio of relative effectiveness of firm i's marketing effort to the total effectiveness of industry j's marketing

[5]Glen Urban, "A Mathematical Modeling Approach to Product Line Decisions," *Journal of Marketing Research*, 6 (February 1969), 40–47.

efforts. Finally, the firm's cost function explicitly recognizes the production inter-dependencies for products j and m by using the concept of cross-cost elasticity.

Although this normative model conceptualizes the product-line pricing model when there are both demand and cost interdependencies, it does not enhance the decision maker's ability to decide on an appropriate product-line price structure. Further, it is inconceivable that the necessary information to estimate the model's parameters would be accessible without relatively high cost.

However, Urban did estimate a demand function similar to Eq. (10-7) for three related products in a frequently purchased food product class. The estimated demand function obtained for the first product was

$$X_1 = a_1 P_1^{-3.52} F_1^{-0.07} P_2^{-1.33} F_2^{0.94} P_3^{-0.22} F_3^{-0.30} s_i \qquad (10\text{-}1)$$

where F_i is the industry total number of package facings on the store shelf for product i and the exponents are the measured elasticities. After analyzing the elasticities and cross elasticities, it was apparent that the company's brands were *substitutes* for competing brands but *complements* to each other. This particular finding reinforces the observation made at the beginning of this chapter that items within a product line, even though functionally substitutable, may actually serve as demand complements to other items in the product line.

Product-Line Change Models

One important product-line pricing decision involves the addition and/or deletion of products to the line and the subsequent price changes necessary to maintain a consistent pricing policy. Hess[6] has developed two models related to this particular pricing problem. The first involves a consumer product. The manufacturer had just introduced a modified, lower-priced version of its existing product, Ancient. Modern was expected eventually to replace Ancient and it was expected that distributors would seek to return substantial quantities of the higher-priced Ancient for credit. The company wished to develop a pricing and credit return policy to minimize the impact of returns on profits. A model was developed to investigate three possible courses of action.

1 Reduce Ancient's price to Modern's at some future time T and compensate the distributors for losses on inventory value with *free* quantities of Ancient.

2 Recall all quantities of Ancient remaining with distributors at some future time T and replace these quantities with *free* quantities of Modern.

3 Do nothing except to accept returns of Ancient and to credit distributors at the wholesale price.

Hess's analysis of the problem led to a recommendation not to cut Ancient's price until 10 months after Modern's introduction. The firm, upon implementing this recommendation, discovered that promotion of Modern stimulated demand for

Ancient and returns never occurred. Thus, although the products were functionally substitutable and differentially priced, their presence in the product line led to a complementary demand interdependence.

The second model involves an industrial product. In this case, a new product, Cheap, was replacing an old product, Dear. The lower-priced Cheap performed equally as well as Dear, but customers had to undergo a one-time fixed cost to convert to Cheap. However, Cheap was less profitable per unit than Dear and the firm wondered whether a price change for Dear would lead to increased short-term profits. Specifically, would a price reduction for Dear slow down the penetration of Cheap? Or would a price increase for Dear be more profitable in spite of an increase in market penetration by Cheap? Therefore, *the key analytical problem was to determine the optimum price differential between the two products.*

Historical data for six periods suggested that the conversion rate of Dear buyers to Cheap was similar to the Weber-Fechner law of Chap. 3.

$$R = k(\log T) + a \tag{10-2}$$

where R = proportion of Dear customers remaining
     T = time in equal intervals
  a, k = parameters

To determine the appropriate price change, Hess estimated response under the assumption that the slope of the conversion rate curve was proportional either to ΔP, $(\Delta P)^2$, or $(\Delta P)^3$, where ΔP is the price differential. In all three cases a higher price yielded higher total profits.

Models with Interdependent Demand

Recall that the definition of demand interdependence is based upon the change in prices of the products. Price is the determining variable in the case of demand interdependence because this model assumes other demand stimulation devices to be constant, i.e., advertising and sales promotion and the product service offering to the firm. Hence, it is only through variation in the price of the products in the line that demand for the product line can be influenced.

Conceptually, then, demand for the ith product can be represented as

$$q_i = f_i(p_1, p_2, \ldots, p_n) \tag{10-3}$$

where q_i = quantity demanded for the ith product, $i = 1, 2, \ldots, n$
    p_i = price of the ith product, $i = 1, 2, \ldots, n$

Intuitively, Eq. (10-3) can be interpreted as meaning the demand for product i may increase or decrease given a *change* in price of any other product j.

Assume for each possible set of prices, demand for any given product k is known, and that the demand and cost interrelationships are linear for all product relationships. That is, given the assumption of linear demand and cost interrelationships, profits for any ith product depend upon the profit margins of *all* products and the demand interrelationships for all products.

Given the need or desire to change price of the kth product, the optimum prices of all other products can be derived. The solution indicates the price of the nth product depends upon the sum of the product of the interdependent costs assigned to the ith product from each product and the effect the price of the kth product has upon demand of each product.

Reflecting upon the meaning of this relationship, one can see the logic of the solution. For example, assume the price change of the kth product has the effect of increasing demand for another product, j. Recall also, the model assumes cost interdependency among products. Thus, if demand for product j increases, there will be a direct change in the cost of producing and distributing product j. Now given a relationship of cost interdependency between, say, products j and i, the change in the costs of product j will result in a change in the assignable costs from j to i.

Summary

These three product-line models specifically indicate that a product line cannot be priced as though each product were produced and marketed as a separate entity. Both the models by Urban and Hess have shown that products that seem to be strictly substitutes do complement each other's sale. The main reason for this complementary relationship is that each product caters to a specific price-market segment with different ranges of acceptable prices. Moreover, where there are also cost interdependencies, a price change for one product may influence not only the sales volume of another product in the line, but also the costs of producing and marketing that second product. Hence, the profitability of the second product will also be affected by a price change in the first product. Again, to find an optimum set of product-line prices is a complex task.

DETERMINING END PRICES AND PRICE DIFFERENTIALS

End-Price Concept

The concept of end prices was briefly developed at the beginning of this chapter. It was suggested that buyers are likely to have a range of acceptable prices for a product, and that, if the desired product is priced within this price range, the buyer may be favorably disposed to complete the purchase. Also, extending the concept of a price range to a product line provides the concept of an acceptable range of product-line prices.

In effect, then, the existence of high and low price limits represents a price-decision constraint. That is, if a product is priced too low or too high for a particular buyer, there is small probability that he or she will purchase the item unless the parameters of the buyer's decision change. Similarly, if some products are priced outside the acceptable price range and others are priced within this range, there would seem to be a smaller probability that a buyer would buy any product than if all the products in the line were priced within the acceptable price range. In such a situation, the price setter seemingly would want to constrain his or her pricing flexibility to those prices lying within the price range with highest probability of being accepted.

Extending the analysis to include all potential buyers within a market segment necessitates allowing for expected variation among individual buyers since all buyers are not expected to have identical threshold prices. Thus, a given market target would have a distribution of high and low threshold prices. A procedure has been developed for determining the mean and variance of this distribution when the decision objective is to determine the end prices of the product line.[7] Knowing the mean and variance of the distribution enables one to determine precisely the particular distribution of either the low end price or the high end price, depending upon whether relatively low or high prices were used to stimulate the market responses.

Determining Price Differentials

Chapter 3 presented the concept of the Weber-Fechner law representing the relation between the measured magnitude of a stimulus and the measured magnitude of response.

$$R = k (\log S) + a \tag{10-4}$$

This law has been used to justify the use of the logarithmic relationship between a price and a market response as well as the use of the lognormal distribution when the market response is probabilistic.[8] Of interest when determining price differentials is the concept of a constant proportion between just noticeably different (JND) stimuli. Or, stating the situation in reverse, the prices of two products should not be different unless the products themselves are perceived as different by buyers.

Beginning with the lowest price in the product line, P_{min}, the price of the next product would be determined by adding a constant rate, k, to the P_{min}. Continuing in this manner by adding a constant rate, k, to the previously determined price until each product has been priced results in a set of prices reflecting noticeable differences among products.

The basic assumption of this approach is that the subjective price scale of the buyer resembles a ratio (logarithmic) scale rather than a natural scale. *That is, the differences in prices between products should reflect relative differences rather than absolute differences.* For example, it is often the practice of clothing retailers to carry three price lines of merchandise, with the price difference between lines being a constant amount of dollars. But, if the low line is priced at $10.00 and the medium line is priced at $15.00, the high line should be priced at $22.50, not $20.00, so as to represent a 50 percent difference in price at each level.

Assuming the products in the product line have been ranked in ascending order (i.e., the product designated the lowest priced product is ranked one, the product designated as the next-to-lowest-priced product is ranked two, and so on until the

[7]Kent B. Monroe, "The Information Content of Prices: A Preliminary Model for Estimating Buyer Response," *Management Science*, 17 (April 1971), B519–B532.
[8]Ibid.

highest priced product is ranked n), then any product can be priced once the P_{min} has been set. The price of the jth ordered product is given as

$$P_j = P_{min}k^{j-1} \tag{10-5}$$

where k is the constant rate, $k > 1$, and j is the jth ordered product.

Since it is assumed that there are a given number of products in the line, and that the low and high end prices have been determined, the constant rate k is easily determined using the relationship

$$\log k = \frac{1}{n-1} (\log P_{max} - \log P_{min}) \tag{10-6}$$

$$\text{or } k = \left[\frac{P_{max}}{P_{min}} \right]^{[1/(n-1)]}$$

Knowing P_{min} and k, the price of any product in the line can be set, thereby determining the price differentials among products. Specific application of this procedure to pricing hotel rooms follows.

Summary

It has been the purpose of these two sections to review models for determining the prices for a product line and the price differentials between products. Previously published sources provide evidence of the complementary demand relations inherent within a product line even when the products are functionally substitutable. Hence, the pricing of the product line may enhance this complementarity relationship among a "family" of substitutable products.

Because of the uncertain nature of demand (market response) to price, it is suggested that realism forces consideration of a probabalistic model to handle the product-line pricing problem. Observing empirical evidence of the logarithmic relationship between price and behavioral response, it has been suggested that previously developed methodology can be used to obtain the required response estimate for a set of alternative product-line prices. Further, using an extension of this methodology, end prices (lowest and highest prices in the product line) can be determined.

Determining the two end prices provides a range of prices for the product line. Given the price range and the number of products in the line, price differences among the products may be obtained by adding a constant proportion to the previously determined price to get the next price in the line.

The correct pricing of a product line should follow three principles:

1 Each product should be priced correctly in relation to all other products in the line. Specifically, perceptibly noticeable differences in the products should be equivalent to perceived value differences.

2 The highest and lowest prices in the product line have a special complementary relation to other products in the line and should be priced so as to facilitate desired buyer perceptions.

3 Price differentials between products in the product line should get wider as price increases over the product line. This principle follows the behavioral finding that price perception follows a logarithmic scale rather than an arithmetic or linear scale.

To clarify these principles and the conceptual framework developed previously, we will now develop a detailed application of product-line pricing.

PRICING HOTEL ROOMS—A SPECIFIC APPLICATION

As mentioned at the beginning of this chapter, a hotel or motel may be viewed as offering a product line consisting of different types of rooms and different types of occupancy—usually single or double. Most hotels derive a large part of their room business from repeat transients. However, repeat transient business comes from satisfied guests. Most hotel guests are willing to pay a reasonable room rate provided they perceive that they have received a fair value for that rate. For example, if a guest is given a $20 room when he or she has expected to pay $15, that individual will probably not be dissatisfied if the $20 room is *noticeably worth $5 more than the $15 room of a previous visit.* Thus, the pricing problem is to price each room correctly in relation to other rooms, *and* to match the number of rooms at each rate to the demand for rooms at each rate. Table 10-6 provides the pricing policy statement of a major hotel chain in the United States that reflects these points.

To price hotel rooms, four analytical steps should be taken

1 Analyze demand for rooms.
2 Compare the supply of rooms with room demand.
3 Rank the rooms according to noticeable, physical attributes.
4 Establish the room prices.

Each of these steps will be illustrated with an actual pricing problem.

Analyze Room Demand

The hotel used in this example had 600 rooms and 21 different single-room rates.[9] To analyze demand, two groups of 10 days each were sampled. The two samples were chosen to be representative in terms of the usual transient occupancy rate—75 percent. On each sample day, the actual number of persons paying each single rate was recorded. These data were converted into the average percentage of persons paying each rate (Table 10-7). From Table 10-7 a demand characteristic curve was developed that showed the cumulative percentage of persons vs. the rate actually paid (Fig. 10-4).

[9]This example is developed from Elmer Roth, "How to Increase Room Revenue," *Hotel Management,* 67 (March 1955), 52ff.

Table 10-6 Guest Room Pricing

Base rack pricing of hotel guest rooms must consider and evaluate at least the following several interrelated factors:

The property
    Market and location
    Competition
    Image and position
    Type, quality, facilities, services
    Costs
    Profit objectives

The rooms
    Type, furnishings, quality
    Size
    Facilities
    Location

The essential elements toward objective consideration and evaluation of these factors are: assure verified current information; involvement of at least a key, relevant, top management member of the hotel and an "outside" Rooms or Marketing specialist (although ultimate pricing should be reviewed by both functions) who must arrive at consensual evaluation of each factor by visiting and testing the competition and analyzing their hotel's market position and price/value relationship to competition; evaluation of each guest room, or type, in the hotel, considering all factors and recognizing the advantages/disadvantages of the relative hotel product in the market. Appropriately positioned price ranges are the limits for pricing of specific rooms and types. *Each price in the structure must be associated with a readily distinguishable physical attribute of the room or type.*

The initial base prices thus determined must then be analyzed relative to rate and revenue potentials (considering the number of rooms at each price and relationships of room-types and prices) and then tested relative to cost/profit factors and objectives, which may necessitate certain adjustments ... but which must be done consistently and realistically relative to the market, and associated with tailored selling strategies. All special prices and rate packages should be directly derived from a percentage of the then determined base rack prices utilizing a consistent discount concept.

Compare Room Supply with Room Demand

From the demand characteristic curve and the data of Table 10-7, the demand for each room price was determined. It was reasoned that if 5 percent of the guests occupied a $16 dollar room, then 5 percent of 600, or 30 rooms, was the relative demand for a $16 room (Table 10-8). The room data of Table 10-7 were compared to Table 10-8 using Fig. 10-5. As Fig. 10-5 indicates, the actual supply of rooms, particularly at $17, did not match the determined demand for rooms. Indeed, there were too many rooms at $17, an insufficient number of rooms in the $18 to $24 range, and too many rooms over $24. In addition, the data indicate that the spacing of room prices was too close, especially at the higher prices.

Rank the Rooms

All the rooms in the hotel were evaluated and factors of "noticeable differences" were established. As suggested in Table 10-6, the noticeable difference attributes are

Table 10-7   Sample Occupancy Data

Room price, $	Number of rooms	Average percentage paying price	Cumulative percentage
16.00	20	5.0	5.0
16.50	20	4.0	9.0
17.00	285	3.0	12.0
17.50	55	8.0	20.0
18.00	20	10.0	30.0
18.50	40	10.0	40.0
19.00	15	20.0	60.0
19.50	10	10.0	70.0
20.00	20	8.0	78.0
21.00	10	7.0	85.0
22.00	10	5.0	90.0
24.00	25	3.0	93.0
26.00	5	1.0	94.0
27.00	10	1.0	95.0
27.50	5	0.5	95.5
28.00	5	0.5	96.0
29.00	10	1.0	97.0
29.50	5	1.0	98.0
30.00	5	0.5	98.5
32.00	15	1.0	99.5
35.00	10	0.5	100.0

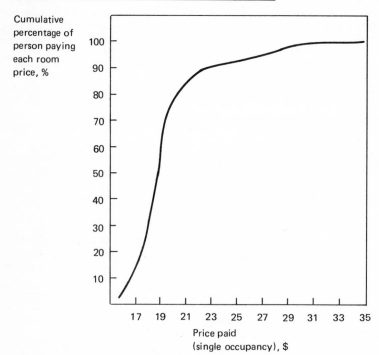

Cumulative percentage of person paying each room price, %

Price paid (single occupancy), $

Figure 10-4   Demand characteristic curve.

Table 10-8 Room Demand

Room price, $	Average percentage paying price	Number of rooms to meet demand*
16.00	5.0	30
16.50	4.0	24
17.00	3.0	18
17.50	8.0	48
18.00	10.0	60
18.50	10.0	60
19.00	20.0	120
19.50	10.0	60
20.00	8.0	48
21.00	7.0	42
22.00	5.0	30
24.00	3.0	18
26.00	1.0	6
27.00	1.0	6
27.50	0.5	3
28.00	0.5	3
29.00	1.0	6
29.50	1.0	6
30.00	0.5	3
32.00	1.0	6
35.00	0.5	3

*The number of rooms .needed was determined by applying the average percentage paying price to the total of 600 rooms, e.g., 5% of 600 = 30 rooms.

room size, location in terms of height (floor number) and view, and facilities available such as TV, air conditioning, refrigerator, storage space, size and type of bedding, and accessory furniture. Each room was coded according to its number of noticeably different factors and assigned a room classification in rank order. It was determined that the hotel had nine noticeably different types of rooms. Hence, it was concluded that there was a greater number of different prices than there were classes of rooms of noticeably different value.

Establish the Room Prices

Using the nine room classifications, the rooms were ranked according to the number of noticeably different factors. The lowest ranked room class was to be the lowest priced room, and each higher ranked room class would be assigned a higher price.

The lowest ranked and highest ranked room classes were priced first. The lowest price, P_{min}, was established at the traditional minimum rate of \$16.00, and the highest price, P_{max}, was set at the traditional high price of \$35.00.

Once the minimum and maximum single-occupancy prices were set, Eq. (10-6) was applied.

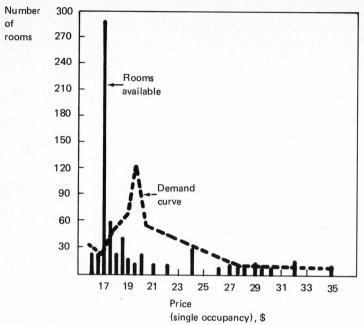

Figure 10-5 Room demand at original prices.

$$\log k = \frac{\log 35 - \log 16}{n - 1} = \frac{1.54401 - 1.20412}{8}$$

$$= 0.042486$$

Taking the antilog of 0.042486 provided the solution $k = 1.103$.

According to the Weber-Fechner law, and given the maximum and minimum price constraints, and the number of room classifications, multiplying the minimum price of $16 by 1.103 would produce the correct price for the next room classification, or $17.65 ($16 × 1.103 = $17.65). The next price was determined by multiplying $17.65 by the constant k, 1.103, to obtain $19.47. Successive application of the constant 1.103 produced the theoretical price structure found in Table 10-9. Management decided to round the theoretical prices to the nearest multiple of $0.25, producing the actual single-occupancy price schedule shown in Table 10-9.

To set double-occupancy prices, management desired to have one room price below $20 and all room prices below $40. Moreover, management had traditionally priced a twin bed, double occupancy more than a double bed, double occupancy, and wanted to continue this policy. Thus it was decided to differentiate the different types of double occupancy by a constant $0.50. The double bed double-occupancy prices were set at $3.50 more than single-occupancy prices, and the twin bed double-occupancy prices were set at $4.00 more than single-occupancy prices.

The number of rooms to provide at each price was determined by considering the demand characteristic curve of Fig. 10-5. As nearly as possible, the number of rooms were chosen to match the cumulative percentages shown in Fig. 10-5 and Table 10-7.

Table 10-9   Revised Room Price Structure

Number of rooms	Single occupancy		Double occupancy	
	Theoretical price, $	Actual price, $	Double bed price, $	Twin bed price, $
55	16.00	16.00	19.50	20.00
125	17.65	17.75	21.25	21.75
150	19.47	19.50	23.00	23.50
120	21.47	21.50	25.00	25.50
90	23.68	23.75	27.25	27.75
30	26.12	26.00	29.50	30.00
15	28.81	28.75	32.25	32.75
10	31.78	31.75	35.25	35.75
5	35.05	35.00	38.50	39.00

The hotel was constrained by the fact that not enough rooms contained sufficiently different physical attributes to justify a closer alignment of rooms to previous sample data. However, it was felt that by pricing according to perceived room differences, the room and price schedule would receive a high rate of guest satisfaction. Figure 10-6 compares the revised room and price schedule with the estimated demand curve for hotel rooms.

A comparison of Fig. 10-6 with Fig. 10-5 reveals improvements in the new price schedule according to the pricing principles given in the previous section.

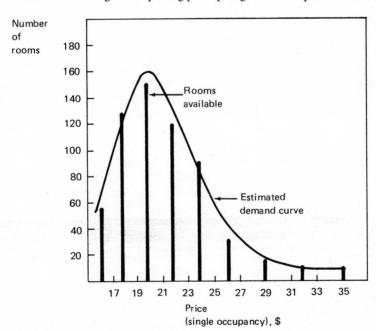

Figure 10-6   Room demand at revised prices.

1 The different prices correspond to noticeably different classes of rooms.

2 The highest and lowest priced rooms correspond to previous experience about the acceptability of these prices.

3 Price differentials between classes of rooms get wider as price increases over room classes. The spacing of prices at the higher prices is greater than at the lower price levels. Price differentials range from $1.75 at the lower-priced room classes to $3.25 at the higher-priced rooms.

4 The number of rooms at each new price more closely approximates the estimated demand at each price.

SUMMARY

The purpose of this chapter has been to extend the costing principles developed in Chaps. 4 through 8 and the behavioral concepts developed in Chap. 3 to pricing a product line. The chapter first extended profit-volume analysis to the dynamics of considering price changes and analyzing the sales-volume mix of a multiple-product firm. Then, after reviewing previous attempts to conceptualize models of the product line, a number of behaviorally oriented pricing principles were developed. Finally, the application of these behavioral pricing principles was illustrated by an actual problem of pricing hotel rooms.

Chapter 10 has also placed more emphasis on the noncost aspects of price determination. A firm that produces multiple products sells products that are distinguishable in terms of the products' life cycles, extent of competition, and buyer acceptance of the products and their prices. Hence, as shown in Chap. 7, basing prices on a full-costing formula is arbitrary and does not consider market factors. As shown in this chapter, a changing sales mix due to nonprice changes in the market can affect a product line's profitability. Attempting to correct a decline in profits by across-the-board price increases can exacerbate an erosion in profits. Finally, a more careful consideration of how price affects buyers' perceptions of a firm's product offerings can isolate new pricing alternatives. To develop pricing alternatives based on buyer and market considerations is more difficult than using a cost-oriented approach. But the reward is an opportunity to profitably improve buyer acceptance and satisfaction.

Little has been written previously about product-line pricing except to distinguish between complementary and substitutable items. However, we do know that the pricing structure for a product line can enhance demand for all items in the line even when some or all of the items are functionally substitutable. Such complementary relationships are behaviorally based phenomena and the emerging interest in price perception research has begun to provide a better conceptual basis for solving product-line pricing problems.

DISCUSSION QUESTIONS

1 Explain and provide examples of the following concepts:
   a Functional substitute
   b Functional complement
   c Product line

2 Explain the product-line pricing problem. What are some of the complexities affecting the pricing of a product line?

3 If you have recently eaten in a restaurant what do you remember about the prices of the entrees? Can you explain why you remember some of the prices? In general, how would you characterize the prices of this restaurant?

4 Critically evaluate the prices of the product line in Table 10-1.

   a Can you identify possible price-market segments?

   b What do you consider to be the distinguishing features of Pronto! Extra as compared to the Pronto! B? Does the price difference between these two models reflect these noticeable differences? What is your reasoning?

   c What do you consider to be the differences between the Electric Zip and the Minute Maker? Does the price difference between these two models reflect these noticeable differences?

   d Compare the Minute Maker, the Minute Maker Plus, and the One Step. Do the price differences between these three models reflect noticeable differences in the models?

5 The Justso Manufacturing Company produces and sells five models of an electric drill. The data provided below are for 1978.

	Model				
	A	**B**	**C**	**D**	**E**
Price per unit	$20.00	$22.50	$25.00	$30.00	$35.00
Variable costs per unit	$14.00	$15.00	$16.00	$18.00	$20.00
Sales (units)	15,000	20,000	40,000	30,000	20,000

Common fixed costs were $100,000.

   a Calculate the composite PV for the electric drill product line. Explain the meaning of the composite PV.

   b Assume that prices and variable costs remain the same, but sales for 1979 are A, 20,000 units; B, 40,000 units; C, 30,000 units; D, 20,000 units; and E, 15,000 units. Compute a new composite PV ratio.

   c Compare the composite PV ratio for 1978 to the composite PV ratio for 1979. What is the reason for the change? What might be some underlying causes for the situation at the end of 1979?

   d The marketing research director has submitted a report to the Vice-President of Marketing that competitive prices for similar electric drill product lines range from $25.00 to $75.00. The report also indicates that customers perceive the Justso product line as lower quality when compared to competitive drills. The Vice-President is perplexed because he knows that engineering and performance tests indicate that the Justso line is more durable and performs as well as competitive drills. Can you offer any possible explanation for the customers' perceptions?

   e Design a new pricing schedule for the electric drill product line. What factors influenced your solution? If the product-selling mix returns to the 1978 relationship, what would be the composite PV for the product line? Explain the reasoning you used to set the price differentials between models in the line.

APPENDIX: The Structure of the Product-Line Models

The purpose of this appendix is to provide more detail about the structure of the product-line models described in Chap. 10. The organization of the appendix will be the same as the models section in the chapter.

Related-Products Model

This model considers the interactions of several factors affecting product-line profitability. Looking at the factors separately, this model is

$$X_{jI} = aP_{jI}^{EPI} \, A_{jI}^{EAI} \, D_{jI}^{EDI} \tag{10-7}$$

where X_{jI} = industry sales of product j

$\quad\quad a$ = scale constant

$\quad\quad P_{jI}$ = average price of all brands in product group j

$\quad\quad D_{jI}$ = total distribution level for all brands in product group j

$\quad\quad A_{jI}$ = total advertising of all brands in project group j

$\quad\quad$ EPI = industry elasticity for price

$\quad\quad$ EAI = industry elasticity for advertising

$\quad\quad$ EDI = industry elasticity for distribution

Thus, the first part of the model develops a mechanism for determining total industry demand as a function of the total industry's efforts relative to price, distribution, and advertising.

Next the model considers the interdependencies of demand for product group j by introducing the notion of cross elasticities for products j and another product m for each of these three marketing strategy variables.

$$b = P_{IM}^{cP_{jm}} \, A_{IM}^{cA_{jm}} \, D_{Im}^{cD_{jm}} \tag{10-8}$$

where $\quad\quad\quad b$ = scale constant

$\quad\quad\quad\quad P_{Im}$ = average price of product group m

$\quad\quad\quad\quad A_{Im}$ = total advertising for product group m

$\quad\quad\quad\quad D_{Im}$ = total distribution for product group m

$cP_{jm}, cA_{jm}, cD_{jm}$ = cross elasticities for products j and m

For the ith firm in industry j, its market share is determined by the product of the sensitivity of industry demand to the marketing effort of the firm, the demand interdependencies of demand for product class j with demand for product class m, and the ratio of relative effectiveness of firm i's marketing effort to the total effectiveness of industry j's marketing efforts.

The firm's cost function explicitly recognizes the interdependent nature of production interdependencies for products j and m:

$$\text{TVC}_j = \text{AVC}_j(x_j)\Pi_m(x_m)^{cc_jm} \tag{10-9}$$

where TVC_j = total variable cost of producing the firm's brand of product j

AVC_j = separable average variable costs for the firm's brand of product j

x_j = quantity produced of product j

x_m = quantity produced of product m

cc_{jm} = cross cost elasticity of the firm's brands of products j and m.

Π_m = mathematical symbol for multiplying over all m.

The results of empirically testing the part of the model shown in Eq. (10-7) are given in the chapter's commentary on page 151.

Product-Line Change Model

To evaluate the alternative of reducing Ancient's price to Modern's at some future time T and compensate the distributors for losses on inventory value with free quantities of Ancient, a single-equation model was developed consisting of three parts.

1 The profit from time 0 to time T is the profit of selling Modern less the costs of returned Ancient:

$$Z_{0T} = \int_0^T (P' - C_v' - C_f')S_{mw}' \, dt - \int_0^T (P + C_f - C_s) S_{wm} \, dt \tag{10-10}$$

where P = price of Ancient to wholesaler

P' = price of Modern to wholesaler

C_v = variable production costs of Ancient

C_v' = variable production costs of Modern

C_s = salvage value for returned Ancient

C_f = freight on Ancient

C_f' = freight on Modern

S_{wm} = quantity of Ancient returned per month at time T

S_{mw}' = sales per month of Modern to wholesalers at time T

Z_{0T} = profit from time 0 to time T

2 The profit after the price cut at time T is profit on net sales achievable without free goods, less those sales lost because of the injection of free goods:

$$Z_T = (P' - C_v' - C_f')\left\{\int_T^\infty S'_{mw'} dt - \beta a\left[I_w(T) + I_r(T)\right]\right\} \qquad (10\text{-}11)$$

where $I_w(T)$ = inventory of Ancient at wholesale at time T

$I_r(T)$ = inventories of Ancient at retail at time T

β = fraction of free goods given to distributors that "take away" future sales of Modern

a = units of free modern to be given per unit of Ancient to compensate distributors for inventory value change

Z_T = profit from time T and beyond

3 The cost of free goods to compensate distributors after a decrease in Ancient's price at time T is

$$CFG = (C_v' + C_f')\, a\, [I_r(T) + I_w(T)] \qquad (10\text{-}12)$$

where CFG is cost of free goods.

Since the first term in the profit expression (10.10) represents the profits associated directly with the sale of Modern, it is independent of the decision variable, T, i.e., when to reduce the price of Ancient. Hence, total profits will be maximized when the cost of returns plus the cost of free goods is minimized.

The empirical results of using this model are given in the chapter on pages 151–152.

Models with Interdependent Demand

The interdependent demand model assumes that demand for any product in the line is known. Further, the model assumes that the demand and cost interrelationships are linear for all product relationships. The structure of the model follows:

C_j = total cost of the jth product after allocation of all joint and common costs, $j = 1, 2, \ldots, n$

q_j = quantity demanded of the jth product

p_j = price of the jth product

R_j = total revenue of the jth product

π_j = profits of the jth product

a_{ij} = proportion of interdependent costs assigned to product i resulting from a variation in quantity sold of product j, $0 \leqslant a_{ij} \leqslant 1$

b_j = separable costs assigned to product j; these costs are assumed to be noninterdependent; $b_j \leqslant 0$

d_{ij} = effect of other demand stimulating factors, other than price, on demand for product i resulting from direct application to product j; $-\infty \leqslant d_{ij} \leqslant \infty$

v_{ij} = demand coefficient; indicates the effect of price of the jth product on demand for the ith product, $-\infty \leqslant v_{ij} \leqslant \infty$

The parameter d_{ij} considers the possible effect of all other demand stimulating factors except price. For example, promotion for product i will directly affect the quantity of the ith product demanded. But this promotion also helps to promote demand for any other product line. Implied is the assumption that some brand loyalty (or disloyalty) is created by the firm's other demand stimulating endeavors.

Demand for the ith product is a linear function of all products in the line:

$$q_i = \Sigma_{j=1}^{n} d_{ij} + \Sigma_{j=1}^{n} v_{ij} p_j \qquad (10\text{-}13)$$

Total cost of producing and distributing the ith product is a linear function of demand for all products in the line:

$$C_i = \Sigma_{j=1}^{n} a_{ij} q_j + b_i \qquad (10\text{-}14)$$

To solve for the optimal set of prices given the basic equation structure of (10-13) and (10-14) requires the development of a set of simultaneous equations. The solution to this system of equations is given by

$$P_{ii} = \frac{B_i}{v_{ik}}$$

$$P_{kk} = \left(\frac{1}{v_{kk} \pi_{i=1}^{n} v_{ik}} \right) \left(2B_k - \frac{\Sigma_{i=1}^{n} B_i v_{ki}}{v_{ik}} \right) \qquad (10\text{-}15)$$

where $B_i = \Sigma_j a_{ij} v_{jk}$
$B_k = \Sigma_j a_{kj} v_{jk} - \Sigma_j d_{kj}$

The interpretation of this solution is given in the chapter on pages 152-153.

SUGGESTED READINGS

Anderson, Lane K.: "Expanded Breakeven Analysis for a Multi-Product Company," *Management Accounting*, 57 (July 1975), 30–32.

Grinnell, D. Jacque: "Product Mix Decisions: Direct Costing vs. Absorption Costing," *Management Accounting*, 58 (August 1976), 36–42, 53.

Hess, Sidney: "The Use of Models in Marketing Timing Decisions," *Operation Research*, 15 (July–August 1967), 17–34.

Oxenfeldt, Alfred: "Product Line Pricing," *Harvard Business Review*, 44 (July–August 1966), 135–143.

Roth, Elmer: "How to Increase Room Revenue," *Hotel Management*, 67 (March 1955), 52ff.

Tucker, Spencer A.: "Pricing and Product-Mix Decisions," *Pricing for Higher Profit* (New York: McGraw-Hill, 1966), pp. 113–117.

Urban, Glen: "A Mathematical Modeling Approach to Product Line Decisions," *Journal of Marketing Research*, 6 (February 1969), pp. 40–47.

Chapter 11

Developing a Price Structure

We now turn to consider the problem of administering base prices throughout the channels of distribution and the markets in which the products are sold. Price administration deals with price adjustments for sales made under different conditions, such as

1 Sales made in different quantities
2 Sales made to different types of middlemen performing different functions
3 Sales made to buyers in different geographic locations
4 Sales made with different credit and collection policies

The discussion on pricing so far has been oriented toward determining what may be called a base or list price. It is this price, or some reasonable deviation therefrom, that buyers normally encounter. However, there is another vital dimension to prices called price structure. Price structure involves determining

1 The time and conditions of payment
2 The nature of discounts to be allowed the buyer
3 Where and when title is to be taken by the buyer

In establishing a price structure there are many possibilities of antagonizing distributors and even incurring legal liability. Thus, it is necessary to avoid these dangers while at the same time using the price structure to achieve the desired profit objective.

Chapter 11 begins by providing an overview of the different types of discount decisions. Two types of discounts—functional and promotional—will be discussed in greater detail in Chap. 12. After reviewing the different types of discounts, this chapter will discuss the problems of determining quantity discounts, cash discounts and credit policies, and geographical pricing.

AN OVERVIEW OF DISCOUNT DECISIONS

Trade or Functional Discounts

Functional discounts are based on a distributor's place in the distributive sequence and represent payment for performing certain marketing functions. Although we are accustomed to think of price as a single number, price is usually quoted to distributors as a series of numbers, for example: "30, 10, 5, and 2/10, net 30" or "30, 20, 5, and 2/10, net EOM (end of month)." The first three numbers represent successive discounts from the list or base price. The list price usually designates the approximate or suggested final selling price of a product and is the price usually referred to when discussing the methods of price determination. However, the list price is used to quote and figure the discounts.

In the first example above, if the list price was $10.00, then the price the dealer pays is $10.00 - .30($10.00) = $7.00; then $7.00 - .10($7.00) = $6.30; and $6.30 - .05($6.30) = $5.98. The 2/10, net 30 part of the quotation reveals that a 2 percent discount is further allowed if payment is made within 10 days, and in any event the full $5.98 is due within 30 days. If the "30, 10, 5" part of the quotation is for a specific dealer, the 30 will refer to the trade discount for the position the dealer occupies within the distribution channel; the 10 and 5 then refer to discounts allowed for promotional expenses the dealer might incur or other functions performed for the manufacturer.

The justification for trade discounts is that different distributors perform different functions within the distribution channel and should be compensated accordingly. For example, some wholesalers provide storage facilities for the manufacturer, help the retailer set up displays, extend credit to the retailer, as well as perform personal selling services for the manufacturer. Often it is difficult to fully identify the various functions the middlemen perform, and therefore hard to determine a trade discount structure that reflects the services performed. Much of this difficulty is due to the fact that some distributors combine the functions of wholesalers and retailers. It is also due to the existence of so many different kinds of wholesalers and retailers.

Promotional Discounts

A *promotional discount* is given to distributors as an allowance for the distributors' efforts to promote the manufacturer's product through local advertising, special displays, or other promotions. These allowances may take the form of a percentage reduction in the price paid or they may be an outright cash payment either to the distributor or to the promotional vehicle, e.g., a local newspaper.

Cash Discounts

A *cash discount* is a reward for the payment of an invoice or account within a specified period of time. In the example on page 169, the terms 2/10, net 30 refer to the cash discount, 2 percent, that may be taken if payment is made within 10 days. The net 30 provides the information concerning the length of the credit period the seller is willing to grant; that is, if the cash discount is not taken because payment did not take place within 10 days, then the entire invoice or account must be paid in full within 30 days.

The cash discount is intimately tied to credit policy and is both a financial and a marketing decision. From the financial viewpoint, the extension of credit incurs costs from two basic sources: (1) the risk of bad-debt losses and (2) resources embedded in accounts receivable that forego alternative uses. The gains from extending credit revolve around the increase in demand because of this pseudo reduction in price.

Quantity Discounts

Perhaps the most common type of discount is the *quantity discount*. Such a discount is granted for volume purchases (measured in dollars or units), either in a single purchase (noncumulative) or over a specified period of time (cumulative, deferred, or patronage discount). The discount schedule may specify a single product or a limited number of products, or the discount may allow for a complete mix of products ordered in a single purchase or over a period of time.

For example, the *Harvard Business Review* provides reprints of all articles published, and the following price schedule applies to "total quantity of reprints ordered at one time, whether for the same or assorted articles, and shipped to one address:[1]

	English ($US)	Translation ($US)
1 reprint	$ 1.00	$ 1.25
2 reprints	1.30	1.65
3 reprints	1.50	1.90
4 to 99, each	.40	.50
First 100	39.70	49.65
Additional 100's up to 1,000, each	20.00	25.00
First 1,000	215.00	268.75
Additional 100's over 1,000, each	15.00	18.75

Noncumulative quantity discounts such as the example above serve to encourage large orders, which leads to fewer orders over a given time period. This ordering policy benefits the seller in that he has fewer orders to process, ship, and invoice, thereby reducing total costs for these activities. Cumulative discounts do not have these benefits, but they do tend to tie a buyer to a seller over the discount period, if the buyer is anxious to obtain the discount. However, sometimes the nature of the product makes it advantageous to place small orders, for example, perishable products and large con-

[1]"Nineteen Seventy Two Series Index," *Harvard Business Review*, 1972.

sumer durables or heavy equipment and machinery. For these kinds of products, buying in small quantities is practical and a cumulative discount schedule is beneficial to both parties.

To illustrate the nature of these discounts assume that the Stepup Ladder Company produces and sells a line of ladders for commercial and household use. The company produces five different types of ladders that vary in the materials used and ladder length. The suggested list prices of these ladders are $30, $50, $90, $120, and $150. These ladders are sold through hardware distributors to discount department stores and hardware stores. Typical trade discounts are 40, 10, 5. Further, the company quotes a cash discount of 3/10, net 30, and allows an additional 5 percent discount to distributors for orders of $1,000 or more at list prices.

The Hardware Distributing Company places an order as given in Table 11-1. As Table 11-1 shows, the total order amounted to $2,700 using list prices. Since the order exceeds $1,000, the quantity discount of 5 percent applied, making the net amount of the order $2,565. The trade discounts are then applied successively in the order shown in Table 11-1C. The total amount of the trade discounts is $1,249.16 ($1,026 +

Table 11-1 Applying Discounts

A. The Hardware Distributing Company order

10 ladders @ $30	$ 300
6 ladders @ $50	300
10 ladders @ $90	900
5 ladders @ $120	600
4 ladders @ $150	600
Total	$2,700

B. Applying the quantity discounts

Total order amount	$2,700
Discounts, $2,700 × 0.05	135
Net order amount	$2,565

C. Applying the trade discounts

Net order amount	$2,565.00
Less: 40% discount	1,026.00
	$1,539.00
Less: 10% discount	153.90
	$1,385.10
Less: 5% discount	69.26
Amount due manufacturer	$1,315.84

D. Applying the cash discount

Amount due manufacturer	$1,315.84
Less: 3% discount	39.48
Net remittance	$1,276.36

153.90 + 69.26). Finally, if the order is paid within 10 days of delivery, an additional discount of 3 percent is allowed. Thus, if all discounts are applied, the manufacturer receives $1,276.36 from an order that amounted to $2,700 at list prices.

QUANTITY DISCOUNTS

There are four decisions required when setting up a quantity discount schedule.

1 The minimum quantity to be purchased before any discount is applied
2 The number of breaks or additional discounts for larger purchases
3 The maximum quantity qualifying for any additional discount
4 The amount of discount to offer at each quantity level

These decisions have largely been made on the basis of intuition, and the results of such a nonanalytical approach are exemplified by the price structures of four manufacturers selling similar products shown in Table 11-2. Ignoring possible list price differences, the only price advantage in buying from manufacturer A occurs when purchasing 5 to 9 items, because thereafter it becomes more economical to buy from another seller. Further, the relative inconsistency across manufacturers on the price breaks and discounts offered suggests an intuitive decision process and an unclear conception of the role of a quantity discount schedule.

A Simple Quantity Discount Model

The basic purpose of a quantity discount schedule is to enhance demand while reducing the costs of meeting that level of demand. Viewing the discount as a price reduction suggests that the elasticity of demand with respect to the percentage discount

Table 11-2 Pricing Structure of Four Competing Manufacturers

Price	Volume (units)			
	Manufacturer A	Manufacturer B	Manufacturer C	Manufacturer D
List price	1–4	1–9	1–24	1–49
List price less 5.4%	5 or more			
List price less 7.0%			25–29	
List price less 7.5%		10–24		
List price less 15%				50–99
List price less 16.7%		25–49		
List price less 21.7%		50–99		
List price less 24%				100 or more
List price less 25%		100–249		
List price less 29%		250 or more		
List price less 40%			100–499	
List price less 50%			500–999	
List price less 55%			1,000 or more	

Source: Adopted from John F. Crowther, "Rationale for Quantity Discounts," *Harvard Business Review*, 42 (March–April 1964), 121–127.

should be a decision consideration. However, this demand elasticity depends on the relative costs to buyers of balancing their ordering costs with their inventory carrying costs. That is, increasing the size of their orders results in fewer orders being placed within a given time period, but also results in buyers carrying a higher level of average inventory over the same time period. Hence, a quantity discount schedule should recognize the potential change in buyers' inventory costs if they change the size of their orders. The seller must consider the cost of obtaining an order as a function of order size. For example, if customers were to place their entire set of orders on the first day of the planning period, then because of the seller's ability to reinvest these revenues, this represents a gain to the seller. Further, the seller's total cost of filling orders decreases as the number of orders decreases, that is, as the volume per order increases.

Crowther[2] offers a simple model for determining these two costs, i.e., *the change in buyers' inventory costs as quantity purchased increases, and changes in the seller's costs as the purchase order size increases.* The buyers' cost function is given as

$$\text{TEK}_B = \frac{Ad}{q} + \frac{qki}{2} \tag{11-1}$$

where TEK = total expected inventory costs
A = the cost of placing a single order
d = number of units required during the planning period
q = number of units ordered at one time
k = price of one unit
i = cost of carrying one unit of inventory per period expressed as a fraction of the unit's value

Using differential calculus to find the minimum value for TEK_B as q varies and then solving for q produces the equation for the economic purchase quantity:

$$q_0 = \left(\frac{2Ad}{ki}\right)^{\frac{1}{2}} \tag{11-2}$$

The seller's cost function is

$$\text{TEK}_S = \frac{Ad}{q} - \frac{pkiq}{2} \tag{11-3}$$

where p is the percent gross margin on an item.

Now both the seller's and buyer's optimal annual ordering and inventory costs can be determined before any discount is offered. Then for any larger quantity ordered, it would be possible to determine

1 The increased cost to the buyer
2 The decreased cost to the seller
3 The net decrease in total cost to both parties

[2]John F. Crowther, "Rationale for Quantity Discounts," *Harvard Business Review*, 42 (March–April 1964), 121–127.

By splitting the decrease in cost to the seller, between both parties the amount of the possible discount can be determined. The exact proportional split can be determined according to the seller's perceived relative worth of inducing the buyer to purchase in larger quantities.

To be nondiscriminatory, the seller must offer the discount structure to all buyers. Therefore, customers must be classified according to historical average order size, and then the seller may select the order classification to develop the above analysis. The seller then can determine whether more or fewer price breaks would allow a broader appeal to other order-size buyer classifications. The primary advantage of such an approach is that the seller is forced to consider customers and their needs, and to balance these needs against the seller's own pecuniary objectives.

An Example[3]

A chemical company offered a product in 55-gallon drums using the following price schedule:

Number of drums	Price per gallon
1–4	$2.57
5–9	2.50
10–19	2.44
20 or more	2.38

The total purchase cost for five drums purchased singly is $706.75 whereas the total purchase cost for five drums purchased in quantity is $687.50. The discount for a quantity purchase is $19.25 or a discount of 2.72 percent. Similarly, the discount allowed for 10 drums is 5.06 percent and is 7.39 percent for 20 drums. The company's comptroller estimates that it costs the firm $10 to process an order (A), and that an effective interest rate, i, for carrying the product in inventory is 20 percent.

After examining sales records, the data in Table 11-3 were developed. Table 11-3 indicates that the price break at five drums does not stimulate additional volume per order. Otherwise, customers buying three or four drums would be fewer in number than those purchasing five drums per order. The sales records also indicate that the average customer ordering one or two drums per order purchases four to five drums per year. Thus, if the small buyers' economic purchase quantity is assumed to be 1.25 drums (q_0) and if their yearly demand (d) is 4.5 drums, then from Eq. (11-2)

$$1.25 = \left[\frac{2A\,(4.5)}{\$140(i)}\right]^{1/2}$$

(The actual purchase cost of a drum is $141.35, but it is rounded to $140 for simplicity.)

<hr>

[3]This example is adopted from John F. Crowther, "Rationale for Quantity Discounts," *Harvard Business Review*, 42 (March–April 1964), 121–127.

Table 11-3 Frequency Distribution of Order Size

Number of drums per order	Number of shipments in sample period
1	3,073
2	910
3	336
4	271
5	254
6	183
7	38
8	89
9	68
10	158
11 or more (usually more than 20)	6,630
Total	12,010

Solving Eq. (11-2) produces

$$\frac{A}{i} = \$24.31$$

which would result if a small customer's ordering cost were about \$3.00, with an interest rate of about 12.5 percent. Using Eq. (11-1) it is possible to determine the small buyers' costs as a function of order size, q:

$$TEK_B = \frac{\$3(4.5)}{q} + \frac{\$140(0.125)q}{2}$$

$$= \frac{\$13.5}{q} + \$8.75q$$

For an order size, q, of 1 to 4 drums the total cost, TEK_B, would be

q	TEK_B
1	\$22.25
2	24.25
3	30.75
4	38.38
5	45.67

And for an order size of five drums, the cost is \$45.67 despite the price per drum falling to \$137.50. Thus, the small buyer would pay \$23.42 more in inventory costs to place one order for five drums as opposed to placing five orders for one drum each.

The seller's cost of serving the small buyer can be computed using Eq. (11-3) where $p = 40$ percent margin:

$$TEK_S = \frac{\$10(4.5)}{q} - \frac{0.4(\$140)(0.2)q}{2}$$

$$= \frac{\$45}{q} - \$5.60q$$

For an order size, q, of 1 to 3 drums, the seller's cost, TEK, would be

q	TEK_S
1	$39.40
2	11.30
3	-1.80

Thus, for an order size of three drums, the seller's savings is $41.20 [$39.40 - (-1.80)], whereas the buyer's added costs are $8.50 ($30.75 - 22.25). Now, if the average yearly demand for the small buyer is 4.5 drums, then the yearly purchase cost is $636. If the small buyer can be persuaded to purchase three drums at a time then the seller saves $41.20/$636 or 6.48 percent, but the buyer incurs an additional cost of $8.50/$636 or 1.34 percent. Thus, with a discount of 3.5 percent for quantity purchases of three drums, the seller gains about 3 percent and the buyer gains about 2.15 percent.

However, the seller recognized that buyers of four drums per order will also receive a discount of 3.5 percent, reducing the seller's savings. But, on the other hand, the data of Table 11-3 revealed little to be gained by offering an additional discount for purchases of 10 to 19 drums per order. Hence, the seller's new price schedule was

Number of drums	Price per gallon
1-2	$2.57
3-19	2.48
20 or more	2.38

It is important to remember that if the seller offers a quantity discount to induce the buyer to increase the size of the purchase order, then the lower price obtained for taking the quantity discount may lead to lower total inventory costs by reducing the quantity $qki/2$ in Eq. (11-1). Further, if the seller reduces price to induce greater order quantities but does not increase total demand over the planning period, then the savings, in Eq. (11-3), $pkiq/2$, will diminish since price k will have decreased and the profit margin p must also fall. Hence, the seller's cost function will jump at the quantity break point. Figures 11-1 and 11-2 illustrate these points.[4]

[4] For a model developing the solution technique to this problem see Kent B. Monroe and Albert J. Della Bitta, "Models for Pricing Decisions," *Journal of Marketing Research*, 15 (August 1978), 413-428.

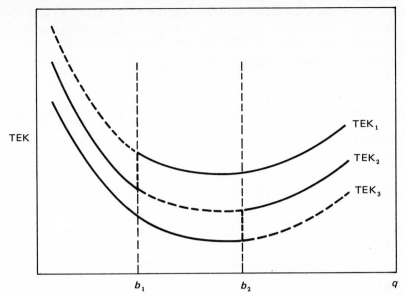

Figure 11-1 Economic order-size curves—two price breaks (buyer).

Legal Considerations

Quantity discounts have been regularly scrutinized by the Federal Trade Commission for possible Robinson-Patman Act violations. It is the responsibility of the seller to prove that the noncumulative discount schedule has been offered to all competing buyers on the same basis and can be justified because of demonstrable cost savings. However, in the past, primarily due to inadequate cost data, the cost defense has had

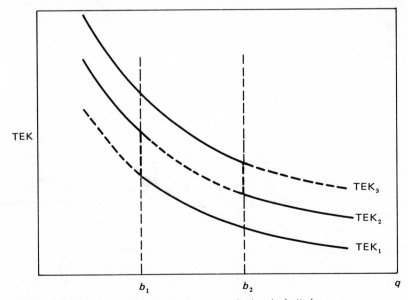

Figure 11-2 Economic order-size curves—two price breaks (seller).

little success. Hence, there are strong reasons for removing intuition and arbitrary decisions rules from such pricing decisions. The more rational approach to developing quantity discount decisions illustrated above would provide a stronger economic defense of a discount schedule. Chapter 16 discusses the problem of justifying price differences in detail.

Cumulative quantity discounts are quite difficult to justify because they invariably favor large-volume purchasers and, therefore, are discriminatory to small purchasers. However, this price discrimination is unlawful only if potential or real injury to competition can be shown (providing there are measurable cost savings involved).

CASH DISCOUNTS AND CREDIT DECISIONS

As observed above, a cash discount is a reward for the payment of an invoice or account within a specified amount of time. For example, assume that after the trade and promotional discounts have been applied, the invoice indicates the amount due is $456. Further, the invoice indicates the credit policy of the seller is 2/10, net 30. If the buyer pays within 10 days, the correct remittance is $446.88 (98 percent of $456). If the cash discount is not taken because payment did not take place within 10 days, then the full amount, $456, must be paid within 30 days. From a decision perspective, the seller must decide on

1 The amount of cash discount (2 percent in the above example)
2 The length of the credit period (the total time the bill is outstanding which equals 30 days in the above example)
3 The amount to spend on attempting to collect overdue accounts
4 The customers to whom to offer credit terms
5 The magnitude of the line of credit

Cash discounts and credit decisions have traditionally been considered the purview of finance, and this viewpoint has persisted because of the practice of making these decisions in the light of industry practice and historical practice. Closer analysis of the elements of credit policy decisions suggests that demand is affected by these decisions and therefore that a more active decision approach can have positive effects on a firm's demand.

To take an active approach to determining credit policy requires analyzing the relationship between demand and (1) the credit period, (2) the amount of the cash discount, and (3) collection expenditures. Other things remaining the same, we would expect demand to increase with a lengthening of the credit period. That is, for a given list price, a movement away from an "all sales cash" policy to allowing purchases on account would result in an increase in demand which would grow with the number of days an account is allowed to be outstanding. In addition, increasing the amount of the cash discount or lengthening the time period that the discount applies will normally result in increases in demand. In either decision the key information is to know the elasticity of demand with respect to changes in these variables.

Reasons for Cash Discounts

Among the reasons cited for using cash discounts are

1 To encourage prompt payment of invoices, thereby keeping the seller's cash flow in a more rapid turnover condition. As will be discussed in Chap. 13, cash is an asset and the more times it is turned over (used successively), the better the firm's pricing flexibility.

2 To reduce credit risks and the cost of collecting overdue accounts. Since buyers are rewarded for prompt payment, in theory there will be fewer overdue invoices.

3 To follow industry practice. One manufacturer in the clothing industry recently was puzzled over the custom of offering a cash discount of 8/10, net EOM. An examination of sales records revealed that the firm had granted about $500,000 in cash discounts on $7,000,000 sales.

Problems with Cash Discounts

Cash discounts tend to be taken regularly by buyers because of the amounts of savings involved. In the example of the clothing manufacturer mentioned above, if we assume that the cash discount is taken by the tenth day of the month, then the seller has the use of the money 20 days sooner than if payment was made by the end of the month. In essence, the clothing manufacturer was willing to pay the retail buyers an interest rate of 144 percent on an annual basis for the privilege of using the money 20 days earlier. [In a 360-day year, there are 18 periods of 20 days. Thus, $(\frac{360}{20})8 = 144$.] Clearly, it may be more economical for a firm to borrow money on a short-term basis than to offer cash discounts.

A second problem occurs when large buyers take the cash discount as a matter of routine, even though payment is not made within the discount period. In such circumstances, many sellers are reluctant to press the issue and the effective interest rate they are granting these buyers is even higher. Hence, the problem of equitably policing the discount policy is often a difficult one. Further, permitting such variances in the cash discount policy is unlawful. Cash discounts are legal under the Robinson-Patman Act so long as they are offered under the same terms to all competing buyers.

Cash Discount Models

The extension of credit involves two costs: The first stems from the risk of bad-debt loss. The second results from leaving resources in accounts receivable which are foregoing returns from alternative uses. But the gains from extending credit revolve around the increase in the long-run sales rate. Therefore, an appropriate credit and cash discount policy requires the balancing of the sacrifice in alternative returns and potential bad-debt losses against the loss in profits because of lost sales.

Conceptualization of the Problem[5] To develop insights into the decision problems, we will analyze the relationship between the rate of demand and (1) the credit

[5]Much of the material developed in this section is adapted from William Beranek, *Analysis for Financial Decisions* (Homewood, Ill.: Richard D. Irwin, 1963).

period and (2) the cash discount. If we can initially hypothesize some of the characteristics of these relationships, it will be easier to make intuitive decisions. To do so,
other factors affecting the demand for the firm's products will be considered constant.
Finally, to simplify, we will assume all sales are credit sales.

Other things being equal, we would expect demand to increase with a lengthening
of the credit period. That is, as the firm moves from an "all sales cash" policy to an
extension of sales on credit, demand would increase up to a limit. As illustrated in Fig.
11-3, demand would increase to T_0. It should be emphasized, though, that a credit
period equal to T_0 does not imply a profit-maximizing credit period. Although it is
unlikely that the elasticity of demand with respect to changes in the credit period will
be known, the relationship shown in Fig. 11-3 would seem to be reasonable.

To analyze the relationship between the size of the cash discount and the demand,
it is important to recognize that offering a cash discount is equivalent to reducing the
price of a product. Thus, an increase in the cash discount (cd) should result in an
increase in the rate of demand. Figure 11-4 illustrates the relationship between
demand and cash discount. Clearly, as the cash discount approaches 100 percent, the
price approaches zero.

A second aspect of the cash discount decision is determining the length of the discount period. Generally, it would be expected that, for a given cash discount, a lengthening of the cash discount period would lead to an increase in the rate of demand.

Some Simple Models[6]   A number of models have been developed that deal with
the problem of developing an optimal cash discount and credit policy structure. As a
point of departure, denote profits as

$$PR = p_0 Q - VC(Q) \qquad (11\text{-}4)$$

where PR = profits
  p_0 = unit price
  Q = rate of demand and output
  VC = unit variable costs

Assume that price, the cash discount, the credit period, and the rate of expenditures
on collections are given, that is, $p = p_0$, cd = cd_0, $T = T_0$, and $E = E_0$. Assume that
credit terms allow for a cash discount if payment is made by the 10th day of the
month following the month the sales were made. Using Eq. (11-4) the adjusted profit
function is

$$PR_1 = (1 - cd_0)p_0 Q - VC(Q) \qquad (11\text{-}5)$$

Thus, the adjusted profit is lower by the amount $cd_0 p_0$. The effect of an increase in
cd is virtually equivalent to a lower price for the firm's output. Therefore, demand will
increase depending on the price elasticity of demand. The effect on profits depends on
whether the marginal revenue due to this "price reduction" is greater than the mar-

---

[6] This section is adapted from Kent B. Monroe and Albert J. Della Bitta, "Models for Pricing
Decisions," *Journal of Marketing Research*, 15 (August 1978), 413–428. See also William Beranek,
Analysis for Financial Decisions (Homewood, Ill.: Richard D. Irwin, 1963).

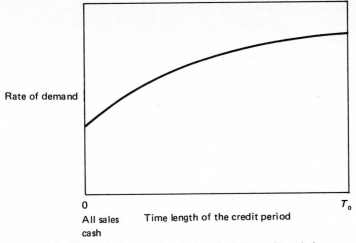

Rate of demand

0
All sales   Time length of the credit period T_0
cash

Figure 11-3 Relations of demand to the length of the credit period.

ginal costs of the greater volume of output. As noted above, the net price $(1 - cd_0)p_0$ is less, due to the discount, making adjusted profits less. Thus, for a cash discount to be profitable, the elasticity of demand to the cash discount must lead to a demand rate that is sufficiently greater to overcome the lower per unit profit. (See pages 69 to 74, Chap. 5.)

Now consider a situation where a given proportion of total sales volume does not take the cash discount, but instead pays in full at the end of the month. This situation means that some receivables will be outstanding between the 10th and 30th of each month, thereby requiring additional resources and foregoing the returns that these resources could obtain if allocated to the next best opportunity. Denote this alternative rate of return as i per dollar per month. If ΔA are the resources required to carry nondiscounting customers from the 10th to the 30th, then the firm foregoes the amount $\frac{2}{3} i \Delta A$ each month by permitting nondiscounting. Since these customers do

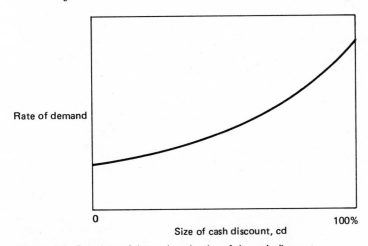

Rate of demand

0   100%
Size of cash discount, cd

Figure 11-4 Relations of demand to the size of the cash discount.

not receive the discount cd_0 profits serving these customers will be larger than in Eq. (11-5). But allowing a 30-day credit policy means there is the opportunity cost as given above. Hence, profits are

$$PR_2 = p_0 Q - VC(Q) - \frac{2}{3} i\Delta A \tag{11-6}$$

As before, it is again obvious that the only way greater profits can result from this policy is for the credit policy to generate an increase in the demand to offset the additional costs of credit extension. Further, if the firm permits a credit period that is longer than the discount period, then optimal nondiscounting requires

$$PR_2 - PR_1 \geqslant 0 \tag{11-7}$$

These basic models can be extended to include analysis for determining the optimal length of the nondiscount credit period, as well as deciding on optimum level of collection expenditures. However, it should be quite apparent that to offer either a cash discount or extended credit terms is optimal only as long as demand is sufficiently elastic to these decision variables to offset additional costs (or reductions in unit profitability). Thus, the problem again becomes one of demand estimation, not an easily resolvable problem.

The primary advantage of the above models is they force us to reconsider the influence of decision variables on demand, and to turn away from tradition as a means of making basic pricing decisions. Furthermore, recognition of the effects on demand of these decisions suggests the need for greater involvement by marketing personnel in these heretofore financial decisions. Further, these models indicate that traditional cash discounts of a given magnitude, for example, 2 percent, are not necessarily optimal policy. Thus, existing policies of cash discount and credit extension should be reexamined as economic and demand conditions change.

A Behavioral Note

If it is assumed that the motive for extending a cash discount is to increase the number of buyers making prompt payments, consideration should be given as to how to state the policy to customers. Recent research suggests that people seek out positive alternatives; choosing among negatives seems like no choice at all.[7] Consider one way the cash discount and credit policy may be stated on an invoice:

Terms: 2/10; net 30. Invoices outstanding more than 30 days will be assessed a service charge of 10%.

On a bill for $100, the buyer is faced with paying $98 in 10 days, $100 within 30 days or $110 later. That is, the buyer is offered a *reward* for early payment and threatened with a *penalty* for late payment.

---

[7]See Jerald M. Jellison and John H. Harvey, "Determinants of Perceived Choice and the Relationship between Perceived Choice and Perceived Competence," *Journal of Personality and Social Psychology*, 28 (1973), 376-382; Jerald M. Jellison and John H. Harvey, "Why We Like Hard, Positive Choices," *Psychology Today*, 9 (March 1976), 47-49.

Now suppose the invoice states the bill is $110, but offers the buyer a $12 reward if payment is made in 10 days, or a $10 reward if payment is made between the tenth and thirtieth days. In this case, the buyer is offered a choice between two positive alternatives—paying early and saving $12 or paying a little later and saving $10. In the original statement, the buyer was offered a choice between a positive alternative—save $2 if paying early, a neutral alternative—paying within 30 days, or a negative alternative—paying a penalty of $10 if paying late.

Apart from the economic reason for making early payment—savings—the idea of presenting a cash discount and credit policy to the buyer in terms of positive choices seems likely to increase the chance of early payments. Developing positive feelings on the part of buyers will increase their desire or willingness to respond favorably to the cash discount and credit policy. Early payment is the behavioral objective of a cash discount.

GEOGRAPHICAL PRICING DECISIONS

One of the most significant costs in marketing arises from the transportation of goods from points of origin to points of destination. We normally think of marketing as primarily related to the stimulation of demand. However, a necessary corollary activity is to supply the various markets with the demanded products. The costs of performing this supply activity range well into billions of dollars annually for transportation alone. The way that sellers solve the transportation problem affects their marketing programs by influencing the range of geographic market areas they serve, the degree to which they may be vulnerable to price competition in some markets, their profit margins, their ability to control resale prices, and the effectiveness of their personal salespeople.

From a pricing perspective, the decision problem revolves around whether sellers wish to account for their shipping costs in their price structure. If they do, there are two general methods they can use: the f.o.b. origin pricing method and the delivered pricing method.

F.O.B. Origin Pricing

F.o.b. origin pricing means the seller quotes prices from the point of shipment. *Free on board* (f.o.b.) means it is the buyer's responsibility to select the mode of transportation, choose the specific carrier, handle any damage claims, and pay all shipping charges. Thus, the net return to the seller is the same for all buyers purchasing in the same quantities and with the same trade status, regardless of their locations. Freeing the seller of responsibility for the transportation and providing the same net return for every similar sale are the primary advantages of the f.o.b. origin method.

However, unless all sellers are located in geographical proximities, product demand is relatively inelastic, and there is a degree of product differentiation, it becomes more difficult to sell a product the further away a market is located. Also, because the cost to distributors varies with their distance from the seller it becomes more difficult to control and maintain resale prices. Finally, the seller's salespeople will find it more difficult to quote an accurate cost to distributors since the costs will vary with distance and with the transportation method(s) selected by the buyer.

Delivered Pricing

In *delivered pricing*, the price quoted by the manufacturer includes both the list price and the transportation costs. In such cases, the prices are quoted as f.o.b. destination, meaning the manufacturer bears the responsibility of selecting and paying for the method of transporting the product.

Single-Zone Pricing   In *single-zone pricing*, the seller receives a different net return (delivered price minus transportation costs) when transportation costs for different customers vary. That is, the seller quotes one list price plus transportation costs to all buyers regardless of their location. On the other hand, buyers pay a uniform delivered price regardless of their location relative to the seller. In essence then, all buyers pay the same "average transportation cost."

Multiple-Zone Pricing   In a *multiple-zone pricing* system, delivered prices are uniform within two or more zones. Most retail mail order catalogs use a multiple-zone pricing system. That is, buyers must determine which concentric circle (zone) around the catalog's distribution center they are in to determine the shipping costs per pound for their order. The differences in price between zones depend on distance from the shipping point, competition, and demand in geographic market segments.

Zone systems, in general, make it easier to sell in distant markets, since prices are determined by "average" transportation costs. Within any zone, therefore, it is easier to control resale prices and increase the ability of salespeople to quote prices. Using multiple zones enables the seller to geographically segment markets if there are varying price elasticities, and, therefore, to be able to determine several satisfactory prices. Multiple-zone systems also make it easier to deal with variations in strength and type of competition.

But, the seller does not receive the same net return per sale since the net return varies with the actual shipping costs. Another difficulty arises if the demand center(s) for the firm shifts geographically, leading to, for example, more shipments going to more distant buyers than before. However, a properly designed information system can monitor these market shifts and alert the firm to change its pricing methods. Within any zone, some buyers are actually paying more for transportation than the actual cost and some buyers are paying less because of the average transportation charge for any zone. Moreover, buyers located on the boundaries of zones may pay more than nearby buyers because they have arbitrarily been positioned in a different price zone. Finally, zone pricing methods require the seller to choose the mode of transportation, select the carrier, handle the damage claims, and pay the freight bills. Each of these responsibilities may become an increased burden to the selling firm.

F.O.B. with Freight Allowed   Another form of delivered pricing is *f.o.b. with freight allowed*. Under this arrangement the buyer arranges and pays for the transportation, but deducts these transportation costs from the invoice total and remits the net amount. Thus, by arranging cheaper transportation methods, for example, using a private fleet of trucks, the buyer pays a lower total price. However, the seller receives varying net returns and the resale prices may also vary.

Basing-Point Pricing In another variation of delivered pricing, the delivered price is the product's list price plus transportation costs from a basing point to the buyer. The *basing point* is a designated city where the product is produced. But, in basing-point pricing the product may actually be shipped from a city other than the basing point. Firms or plants at the basing points receive the same net returns, whereas firms or plants not at a basing point receive different net returns from different sales. This variation in net returns is due to the difference between actual shipping costs and the transportation factor used in the price quotation.

Figure 11-5 illustrates the principle of basing-point pricing. All three mills, X, Y, and Z, quote the same delivered price to customer A, $120, which is determined by adding the $100 base price at mill X to the freight charge of $20 from mill X to customer A. In order to quote the $120 delivered price, mill Y must absorb $10 of freight charges, whereas mill Z collects $10 of phantom freight.

One or more basing points can be used for any transaction, depending on whether the pricing method used is a *single basing-point system* or a *multiple basing-point system*. Further, the system may be a company system used by a firm with several geographically dispersed production plants, or an industrywide system used by most firms in the industry. An industrywide system may develop as a result of industry tradition in which traditional basing points are used, or it may evolve from a practice of price leadership where firms follow the basing-point pricing practices of the price leader. An industrywide system may also be the result of collusion by the firms involved.

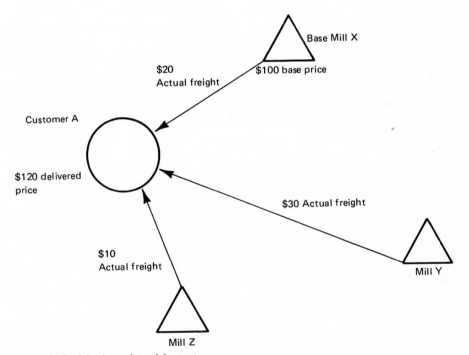

Figure 11-5 A basing-point pricing system.

In a multiple basing-point system several locations are designated as basing points. On a particular sale, the choice of a basing point is the point that yields the lowest delivered cost to the buyer. With a multiple basing-point system, both the basing-point plant or firm and the plants or firms not located at a basing point receive varying net returns from different sales.

There are a number of advantages and disadvantages in both types of multiple basing-point systems. The advantages of a companywide basing-point pricing system are:

1 It eliminates price competition between the firm's different production facilities. The buyer pays the same price no matter where he or she is located or what the origin of the shipment is.

2 It allows the firm to balance shipments from the different plants, and thus ensure that plants receive enough shipments to keep them operating at a desirable level of capacity.

3 It simplifies price quotations in that a schedule of delivered prices need be prepared only for the basing points and not for every production facility.

The disadvantages of a companywide basing-point system are:

1 Customers who discover they pay more for transportation than the actual costs will be unhappy. This unhappiness will be more pronounced when they discover that other customers pay less for transportation than the actual costs.

2 It may result in a large amount of freight absorption.

3 The return to the seller varies on each sale.

4 The price discrimination features of companywide basing-point pricing may produce legal difficulties.

The advantages of an industrywide basing-point pricing system are:

1 Price competition based on differences in transportation costs is eliminated.

2 It permits a firm to secure greater volume since large transportation costs do not prevent the firm from expanding its geographic market area.

3 Any firm or plant can sell in a larger geographic area since transportation costs are not a factor in buyers' purchasing decisions.

Among the disadvantages of an industrywide basing-point system are:

1 It creates buyer unhappiness when they find they are paying for transportation costs from producing plants that do not originate the shipment.

2 Buyers may object to the lack of price competition as far as transportation costs are concerned.

3 Since the delivered price is the same regardless of shipping point, there is less incentive to obtain the least costly transportation mode.

4 The reduced basis for price competition may lead to higher and more inflexible prices.

5 It may lead to excessive freight absorption for a seller, varying sales returns to the seller, and may lead to legal difficulties.

Legal Issues of Geographical Pricing

There is a long history of legal questions surrounding geographical pricing practices. F.o.b. origin pricing is legal. But in zone pricing systems, there is an inherent element of price discrimination since some buyers pay more than the cost of transportation while other buyers pay less. Sellers who practice single-zone pricing have not been prevented from maintaining a uniform delivered price. Apparently, since there are no price differences at the point of *destination* with this system, the Federal Trade Commission and the federal courts have not viewed the system as discriminatory.

Multiple-zone systems have had difficulty only when all firms have had similar zone pricing systems. Indeed, the Federal Trade Commission has taken the position that when competing firms establish zone systems with identical boundaries and identical price differentials, collusion is likely to be present.

Basing-point pricing has had considerable difficulty under the Robinson-Patman Act and the Federal Trade Commission Act. These difficulties stem primarily from the fact that different firms or plants receive varying net returns from different sales under similar circumstances without real cost justifications. Generally, such sales are held to be price discriminatory. However, unless there appears to be clear-cut evidence of conspiracy, it is relatively unlikely that the Federal Trade Commission will initiate proceedings against delivered pricing systems.

Despite the position of the Federal Trade Commission, basing-point pricing is patently unfair to at least some customers. The unfairness of the system can eventually lead to customer dissatisfaction. In a competitive environment, dissatisfied customers will seek out alternative sources of supply from domestic or foreign sellers.

SUMMARY

This chapter has introduced the problem of administering the prices of products and services. Usually, determining the price to offer to buyers is the beginning of the problem of price administration. The price setter must also consider adjusting prices for sales made in different quantities, sales made to different types of buyers in different geographic markets, and sales made with different credit and collection terms.

Chapter 11 has considered the decision problems connected with developing a quantity discount schedule and with setting cash discount and credit policies. Generally, quantity and cash discount decisions have been made on the basis of convenience and tradition. One consequence of such nonanalytical decision making has been the inability to defend such pricing decisions when faced with legal or buyer scrutiny.

However, if the motive for offering quantity and cash discounts is to influence the behavior of buyers, that is, to order more at a time, or to pay early, then analysis underlying these decisions must begin with the buyers. For both types of decisions, the problem is determining what "price breaks" will motivate buyers to behave in a manner favorable to the firm. The seller must then balance these price breaks against the costs of providing them. When a firm sells to many different types of buyers, it must set the price breaks or rewards so as not to discriminate on the basis of price to buyers who are in competition with each other. Hence, the problems of price administration are also fraught with legal complications.

Geographical pricing involves large dollar amounts and there is a lack of understanding of its difficulties and importance. As with quantity and cash discounts, the determination of a geographical pricing policy should begin with a consideration of the buyers. Transportation charges vary with many factors including weight and distance. Geographical pricing practices are primarily concerned with the effect shipping distances have on delivered prices. Again, developing a geographical pricing policy solely on the basis of convenience and tradition will ignore real differences in buyers and in the costs of serving them. Dissatisfied customers are not the proper basis for long-run profitability.

DISCUSSION QUESTIONS

1 Briefly discuss the different types of decision problems in price administration.
2 Explain what is meant by
  a Price structure
  b Base or list price
  c Functional discount
3 Explain the difference between a cumulative quantity discount and a noncumulative quantity discount.
4 Explain and illustrate the decision problems encountered when developing a quantity discount schedule.
5 Explain and illustrate the decision problems encountered when establishing a cash discount and credit policy.
6 What are the behavioral objectives involved in establishing trade discount, quantity discount, and cash discount policies? What can a price administrator do to reach these behavioral objectives?
7 Explain and illustrate the decision problems encountered when establishing a geographical pricing policy.
8 Explain what is meant by
  a Free on board origin
  b Free on board destination
  c Delivered pricing
  d Zone pricing
  e Basing-point pricing
  f Phantom freight
  g Free on board with freight allowed
9 If the list price is $600, and the seller quotes a chain discount of 30, 10, 5, with a cash discount of 3/10, net 30, what is
  a The total trade and promotional discount amount?
  b The cash discount amount?
  c The correct remittance if all discounts are taken?
10 Discuss the legal implications of determining a geographical pricing policy.
11 In the mid-1970s, the United States economy was beset with a relatively high rate of inflation. Manufacturers were faced with the problem of frequently increasing their prices to compensate for increased labor and material costs. Manufacturers also incurred the expense and the problem of informing customers and salespeople of these price changes. One West Coast manufacturer handled this pricing problem by establishing what was believed to be the price that should be charged about a

year later. Customers were then offered relatively large discounts, so that the actual price paid reflected what the firm believed the current price should be. Then, as production costs increased, the firm reduced the amount of the discounts available to customers, until it was time to increase the list price again. What do you believe to be the advantages and disadvantages of such a pricing policy? What do you think would be competitor and buyer reaction?

SUGGESTED READINGS

Crowther, John F.: "Rationale for Quantity Discounts," *Harvard Business Review*, 42 (March–April 1964), 121–127.

Monroe, Kent B., and Albert J. Della Bitta: "Models for Pricing Decisions," *Journal of Marketing Research*, 15 (August 1978), 413–428.

Chapter 12

Pricing to and through the Channel

In our previous discussions of variables to consider and pricing methods to follow, it was implicitly assumed that the price setter could control the prices paid by the ultimate buyers. Such an assumption is valid only when the manufacturer sells directly to the final user. Although this assumption predominates the thinking in economic price theory, in practice it is clearly the exception rather than the rule. When the manufacturer sells products through several independent businesses before the final purchase by a user, control over the way the products are ultimately marketed is usually relinquished. However, because of the importance of the marketing methods used, the manufacturer has a vested interest in the way the products are sold as they move through the channels of distribution. Thus, the manufacturer seeks ways to influence the way distributors market the products, including the setting of the resale prices.

In Chap. 3 we discussed how price structure influences buyers' perceptions of product prices. It was suggested that certain prices serve to anchor buyers' responses, e.g., the end prices of a product line, the price of the brand last purchased, and the price of the leading brand. It was also pointed out that the price differentials between products in a product line, as well as between national and private brands and between different national or private brands, serve to influence buyers' perceptions. In addition, for some products and under certain conditions a positive price-quality relationship may exist. Thus, since price structure may affect perceptions and, possibly, behavior by ultimate buyers, the manufacturer is naturally concerned that prices should be optimal.

Suppose a manufacturer has determined what is believed to be an optimal pricing strategy. Can he or she then ensure that the price to the ultimate buyer is the price decided upon? The possibility that the product may be sold through several channel levels before the point of final resale makes this more difficult, and if the common resale pricing practice is to apply a percent markup over cost, any pricing deviations during the product's flow through the channel will not produce the desired final selling price.

Basically, the problem of controlling price through the channel lies in the setting of discount policy for distributors. Warshaw suggests several principles for handling this problem.[1] Where there is competition from rival sellers for distributor support, the price paid for distributor cooperation must reflect not only the marketing functions distributors perform but also the competitive environment. That is, the manufacturer must consider not only competition from other manufacturers but also the competition the distributors face at each level in the channel. For example, if competition at the distributors' level has pared the distributors' margins, then to gain the distributors' support for the manufacturer's policies, it may be necessary to increase the trade or functional discount.

Pricing decisions and the policies that are derived from them have impact on dealer cooperation and motivation as well as on sales force morale and effort. While legally difficult to control prices through the distribution channel, it is nevertheless possible to motivate people to adhere to company-determined pricing policies. Since price directly affects the revenues of the trade and salespeoples' commissions, it can be used to foster desired behaviors by channel members and salespeople.

To use price as a means of influencing channel members, the seller may offer trade discounts or special price promotions and deals. As defined in Chap. 11, a trade or functional discount is offered to members of the distribution channel because they provide certain marketing services (functions) for the seller. Although the offering of a functional discount may seem easy, in fact this discount decision is fraught with many managerial and legal difficulties. Similarly, the strategy of price promotions and short-term price deals is more complex than is apparent. Judging by both the number of legal cases and complaints by distributors, there is much to be concerned about in making trade discount and price promotion decisions. This chapter discusses these managerial problems and suggests some approaches for their solutions.

TRADE OR FUNCTIONAL DISCOUNTS

Trade or functional discounts are based on a distributor's place in the distributive sequence and represent payment for performing certain marketing functions. The justification for trade discounts is that different distributors perform different functions within the distribution channel and should be compensated accordingly. For example, some wholesalers provide storage facilities for the manufacturer, help the retailer set up displays, extend credit to the retailers, as well as perform personal selling services for the manufacturer. Often it is difficult to fully identify the various

---

[1]Martin R. Warshaw, "Pricing to Gain Wholesalers' Selling Support," *Journal of Marketing*, 26 (July 1962), 50-54.

functions the middlemen perform and therefore it is difficult to determine a trade discount structure that reflects the services performed. Much of this difficulty is due to some distributors being combinations of wholesalers and retailers, and is also due to the many different kinds of wholesalers and retailers that exist.

Legal Status of Functional Discounts

Since functional discounts are not specifically mentioned in the Robinson-Patman Act, their legality has not been completely resolved. However, the general interpretation is that these discounts are lawful so long as they are offered to all competing buyers of the same distribution class on the same terms, and so long as the discounts accurately reflect cost savings to the seller.

The Validity of Functional Discounts[2] Primarily, the legal question is whether a particular discount is valid for particular kinds of buyers. Since the Robinson-Patman Act fails to specifically mention functional discounts, the validity of these discounts is determined by case law under Section 2(a), wherein it is unlawful to discriminate in price when the effect may be to lessen competition or to injure competition. The legal test is whether the price difference due to a functional discount has an adverse competitive effect. Thus, *the validity of a functional discount derives solely from the doctrines and facts of competitive effect, not from any general principles governing functional discounts.*

If the purchasers do not compete with each other, then there is no probable adverse competitive effect. Thus, a functional discount to an original equipment manufacturer can probably be justified since the item becomes a part of a larger and distinct product. A functional discount to auto manufacturers when buying automobile tires for new cars generally can be justified. However, if the automobile manufacturer buys the tires for resale to car dealers as replacement parts, then the automobile manufacturer may be in competition with the tire manufacturer's own distributors. In this latter situation, the functional discount to the automobile manufacturer would no longer be valid.

Traditionally, wholesalers are given larger discounts than retailers because it is recognized that these two types of distributors are on different functional levels. Economically, distributors positioned higher up the distribution channel, such as wholesalers, have a need to buy at lower prices than direct-buying retailers in order to survive. This traditional discount is valid if it does not lessen the ability of the direct-buying retailers to compete with the wholesalers' retail customers. Although direct-buying retailers are, in effect, performing all or most of the wholesaler's function, it would probably be construed that competition might be harmed if they set lower prices because of a more favorable discount afforded them.

Parenthetically, it should be clear that there is no requirement that wholesalers and retailers be priced differently. Wholesalers and retailers may be offered the same

---

[2]The material on valid functional discounts is adapted from William E. Beringer, "The Validity of Discounts Granted to Dual Function Buyers under the Robinson-Patman Act," *The Business Lawyer*, 31 (January 1976), 783–800.

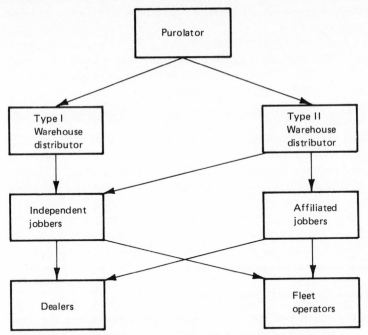

Figure 12-1 Purolator's distribution system for automotive filters.

prices. When there are no price differences, there is no price discrimination, even though there may be adverse competitive effects. (This point is discussed in greater detail in Chap. 16.)

Dual-Function Discounts The above observations refer to *single-function buyers*, i.e., buyers who perform essentially the same marketing services irrespective of the level or position in the distribution channel. However, there is a question of the validity of a functional discount for a particular service (function) performed by one buyer, when that buyer and the competitors of that buyer perform other functions for which no one receives a discount. Buyers who perform more functions than their competitors and who receive a discount for these additional functions are referred to as *dual-function buyers*.

To illustrate the nature of a dual-function discount system, consider the Purolator case.[3] Figure 12-1 provides a flow chart of the distribution system used by Purolator, a manufacturer of automotive filters in the replacement parts market. Purolator sold only to warehouse distributors. However, there were two types of warehouse distributors: type I distributors, who had only a single warehouse location; and type II distributors, who had either branch warehouse locations or affiliated jobbers. The type II distributors sold either to independent jobbers or to their affiliated jobbers. Type I

---

[3]Purolator Products, Inc., 65 F.T.C. 8, CCH Trade Reg. Rep. ¶ 16, 877 (1964), *affirmed,* 352 F.2d 874 (7th Circuit, 1965).

distributors sold only to independent jobbers. All jobbers sold to dealers and fleet operators.

The amount of functional discount Purolator gave to its warehouse distributors depended on (1) whether or not the distributor had either branch locations or affiliated jobbers and (2) the type of customer, dealer or fleet operator to whom the filters were resold. Purolator offered a 4 percent discount to the type II distributors. The type II distributors performed an additional distribution function that the type I distributors did not perform.

The Federal Trade Commission held that the additional 4 percent discount to the type II distributors injured competition because it subsidized their internal operation. Purolator had offered evidence that the reshipping operations of the type II distributors (from their central warehouse to the affiliated branches) increased the operational costs of these distributors, and the discount was granted to offset these costs. The commission noted that the affiliated warehouse distributors had selected their method of operation and that customers' internal costs could not justify a price difference. As with single-function discounts, dual-function discounts are valid only if there are no probable adverse competitive effects.

Guidelines for Setting Functional Discount Policy

As the above discussion on the legal status of functional discounts indicates, the policy of offering price concessions to members of the distribution channel can be cumbersome and legally involved. It should be quite clear that traditional policy is no excuse or defense for a discount policy that is legally challenged. Today, with the additional complexities of vertically integrated distribution systems, it is encumbent on sellers to carefully analyze functional discount policies.

When establishing a functional discount pricing structure, the seller should determine

1   The functions the distributors should perform for the seller.
2   The costs to the distributors for performing these functions.
3   The relative costs of selling to different types of distributors.
4   The trade status of each buyer, i.e., the buyer's position in the distribution sequence.
5   The extent of competition among buyers at all levels in the distribution sequence.
6   For combination wholesaler-retailer buyers, the sales that are wholesale and the sales that are retail. (By segregating the wholesaler-retailer's purchases between the wholesale and retail function and allowing a wholesale discount only on legitimate wholesale purchases, the seller is demonstrating compliance with Section 2(a) of the Robinson-Patman Act.)
7   The savings in cost of serving the various distributors (see Chap. 16).

Above all, "any supplier who extends a functional discount—whether to a dual- or a single-function buyer—needs to get and keep reasonable proof that the functional classification is lawful and that all the purchases for which the functional discount was given do in fact fit the classification."[4]

PRICE PROMOTIONS AND DEALS

Advertising and personal selling have received considerable attention as methods of stimulating demand for products and services. However, the activities of sales promotion are not as well studied, yet they represent an important aspect of the marketing scene. Major forms of sales promotion include cents-off deals, two-for-one offers, sampling, coupons, refunds, rebates, premiums, and contests. "According to new thinking, couponing should be thought of as primarily a price promotion. 'Couponing is the best way to deliver a short-term price incentive directly to the consumer'... according to Don Pratt, president, Newspaper Co-op Couponing."[5] Temporary price reductions may be used to

1   Generate new interest in an old product.
2   Accelerate demand for products or to flush out old merchandise to make room for new merchandise.
3   Introduce a new product. Kodak offered cash rebates to retailers and customers when introducing the instant camera.
4   Meet specific competitive situations in different geographic locations, for limited time periods, for specific products or services.

Presumably, one of the advantages of price dealing is that the results are directly observable in terms of market share. The basic attractiveness of the price deal is that it can stimulate sales by appealing to the bargain-mindedness of buyers. However, although price deals have been widely used by manufacturers and retailers, there is little evidence available on the characteristics of deal-prone buyers or their reasons for using these deals.

Who Redeems Coupons

Coupons are documents that entitle the holder to a reduced price, or to "x" cents off the actual purchase price of a product or service. In a national telephone sample, the A. C. Nielsen Company found that the main appeal of a coupon is its money-saving feature, followed closely by the consumer's inclination to use a coupon to try a new product at a "reduced" price. Further, it was shown that the households which reported the highest levels of coupon usage were those with higher incomes, larger families, and larger weekly expenditures for groceries.[6]

[4]William E. Beringer, op. cit., p. 794.
[5]Louis J. Haugh, "Record Couponing Reflects New Price Promo Philosophy," *Advertising Age*, October 17, 1977, pp. 62–63.
[6]"What Consumers Think of Coupons," *The Nielsen Researcher*, vol. 30, no. 6 (1972), pp. 3–10.

Three panel studies have investigated the characteristics of consumers who are responsive to "deals." Webster determined that only the age of the housewife was significantly related to deal-proneness; deal-proneness tended to increase as the housewife's age increased.[7] Montgomery found that a housewife's brand loyalty was inversely related to dealing activity; that venturesomeness, media exposure, and gregariousness were directly related to dealing activity; and that opinion leadership, interest scores on health, raising children, and food buying, and presence of children did not seem to relate to dealing activity.[8] Frank and Massy found that households responsive to deals were characterized by higher housewife educational attainment, but neither housewife employment/unemployment, household income or size, nor age of housewife were significantly related to deal responsiveness.[9]

Schiffman and Neiverth reaffirmed earlier findings that demographic characteristics are weak indicators of consumer dealing behavior.[10] They also found support for the inverse relationship between deal-proneness and brand loyalty in that a significantly greater portion of the coupon users were either multibrand users or loyal users of the deal brand. In a more recent study, the *Ladies Home Journal* reported that 60 percent of the women surveyed regularly take advantage of cents-off coupons, with 80 percent being interested in them.[11]

The Strategy of Price Deals

Price deals have been popular since the late 1800s, when C. W. Post offered a box of Grapenuts, a new product, for one cent. In 1977, 62.2 billion cents-off coupons were distributed, 36 percent more than in 1976.[12] The popularity of price deals has led to questions of when is it best to offer a price deal, how many price deals a product should have in a given time period, and what the optimum duration of a price deal is. Consumer advocates have also noticed the increased use of price deals and have expressed some alarm at the possible and sometimes fraudulent use of price deals. However, temporary price reductions remain a legitimate price decision.

A study by Hinkle revealed a number of strengths and shortcomings of price deals:[13]

1   Off-season price reductions are more profitable.
2   Too frequent price promotions make the consumers more price conscious.
3   Deals are not very effective in countering new competitive brands nor are they necessarily more effective when accompanied by product or package innovations.

[7]Frederick E. Webster, "The 'Deal-Prone' Consumer," *Journal of Marketing Research*, 2 (May 1965), 186-189.
[8]David B. Montgomery, "Consumer Characteristics Associated with Dealing: An Empirical Example," *Journal of Marketing Research*, 8 (February 1971), 118-120.
[9]William F. Massy and Ronald E. Frank, "Short Term Price and Dealing Effects in Selected Market Segments," *Journal of Marketing Research*, 2 (May 1965), 171-185.
[10]Leon G. Schiffman and Clifford J. Neiverth, "Measuring the Impact of Promotional Offers: An Analytic Approach," in Thomas V. Greer (ed.), *Increasing Marketing Productivity* and *Conceptual and Methodological Foundations of Marketing*, Combined Spring and Fall, 1973 Conference Proceedings, (Chicago: American Marketing Association), pp. 256-60.
[11]Louis J. Haugh, "Women Cool to Promotions, 'LHJ' Tells Premium Executives," *Advertising Age*, October 10, 1977, pp. 10, 102.
[12]"Marketing Briefs," *Marketing News*, 11 (February 24, 1978), p. 3.
[13]Charles Hinkle, "The Strategy of Price Deals," *Harvard Business Review*, 43 (July–August 1965), 75-85.

4 Price deals are more effective for new brands.

5 Price deals are not cures for generally "sick" products.

A price deal may be offered to consumers only, with appropriate dealer compensation for participating, or to dealers, presumably leading to expanded distribution, better product displays, or other conditions favorable to greater consumer purchasing. Often, however, the consumer or trade deals fail to realize the objective of greater sales volume because the retailer may not or cannot fully comply with the special deal.

The meager evidence on price deals suggests that many sellers misuse this pricing strategy. Some sellers run price deals during the peak selling season, thereby providing a price discount at a time *when demand is heavy* and relatively less elastic. Other sellers run frequent price deals and find it is most difficult to sell the product at its "regular" price because the buyers have either stocked up or are waiting for the next deal.

Other problems in developing a price deal strategy include:

1 One in four coupons are redeemed without a corresponding purchase, costing manufacturers approximately $80 million per year.[14] Fraudulent claims by grocers for supermarket coupons are estimated at 15 percent of all claims.[15]

2 Refunding and coupon clipping have become a hobby. Today, there are approximately 50 bulletins published that alert members to all the new offers currently available, and exchange coupons, labels, and information on the latest trends. In addition, four refunders' conventions were planned for 1977. According to a representative of The Nestle Co., Inc., these couponers and their newsletters are "the bane of our existence." And a spokesperson for a major soup company indicated that coupons meant to be used in one part of the country show up in other areas and ruin test markets.

3 Competitors often react quickly to counter an offer or even offer a more attractive deal.

4 Many deals require changing the retail prices. At one chain store, price deals required the changing of prices on 44 different brands of products on the same day.

5 The distributor often is offered an insufficient allowance to justify price changes or special promotional efforts. One deal offered the retailer $0.60 per case on a slow-moving item if each retailer would set up a special display and reflect the allowance in a lower retail price. The retailers did not believe the $0.05 per item was a sufficient inducement and the deal allowance failed.

6 Many offers create utter confusion to retailers and distributors. One instant coffee producer offered an allowance of $2.40 per case, encouraging retailers to change the retail price from $3.35 to $3.15. However, before this deal expired, the producer offered 2 oz of coffee free at the regular retail price of $3.35. Distributors did not know whether to reprice the original deal back to $3.35 or continue to offer the regular jar at $3.15 and simultaneously the "2 oz free" jar at $3.35.

7 In the past few years, a number of regulations have come into force to counter potential and actual deception in the use of price deals. Often, a price deal has been used to camouflage a price increase. For example, a box of 125 paper tissues had been

[14]"The Marketing Observer," *Business Week*, August 11, 1974, p. 54.

[15]Louis J. Haugh, "Record Couponing Reflects New Price Promo Philosophy," *Advertising Age*, October 17, 1977, p. 63.

Figure 12-2   Using a bonus offer to conceal a price increase.

retailed at $0.33. The manufacturer then offered a box of 150 paper tissues with this legend on the box: "This box normally contains 125 sheets. Our 25 percent FREE BONUS OFFER gives you 150 sheets at no increase in price—a true bonus value." The retail price was $0.38.

What had happened was that in the previous six months the manufacturer had raised the wholesale price of the 125-count box of tissues three times, or a total of 6.4 cents. The manufacturer then provided the bonus offer of 150 sheets for the new price of 125 sheets. When the bonus offer expired, customers paid $0.38 for a box of 125 tissues. The astute reader has perhaps also noticed that the "25 percent bonus" offer was only 20 percent $[100(\frac{25}{125})]$.

Figure 12-2 illustrates the way the price increase was concealed. The issue of deception arises in respect to the comparative frame of reference for claiming a "free bonus offer." From the seller's perspective, the representation is true when comparing the offer at time t with the *planned* offer at time $t + 1$. But, from the buyer's perspective, the representation is false, when comparing the offer at time t with the *previous* offer at time $t - 1$.

To counteract such difficulties, the Federal Trade Commission has published guidelines and regulations governing "cents-off," "economy-size," and other savings representations. Tables 12-1 and 12-2 give examples of these published and proposed guidelines and the appendix to this chapter reproduces the FTC's guidelines on deceptive pricing.

A PRICE PROMOTION MODEL

The above problems coupled with the increased use of price deals have led to questions regarding the optimum discount to offer, when it is best to offer the deal, and how frequently it should be offered. Additional parameters of the strategy are the optimum duration of the deal, the quantity of units to offer at the reduced price, and whether dealers as well as ultimate consumers should be offered a discount at the time of the deal.

Goodman and Moody have considered the problem of how many units a manufacturer should offer at the reduced price during the promotional period.[16] They suggest that the decision be treated as an inventory management problem through the channels of distribution.

Opportunity costs of two types are viewed as the relevant decision variables: (1) lost sales due to stock outs at the retail level and (2) excessive sales to the channel

[16] David Goodman and Kavin Moody, "Determining Optimum Price Promotion Quantities," *Journal of Marketing*, 34 (October 1970), 31–39.

Table 12-1 FTC Guides on Cents-Off Promotions

FOR CENTS-OFF PROMOTIONS, the key aspects of the regulations for any food, drug, cosmetic, or device which bears on the label a representation that the consumer commodity is being offered for retail at a reduction in price are the following:

—An ordinary and customary selling price must have been previously established at the retail level.

—The selling price must have been reduced by the manufacturer and all middlemen by at least the savings differential represented on the package or label.

—Invoices or other records by manufacturers and all wholesalers and retailers must be kept for one year on all items so promoted.

—Phraseology by the retailer must indicate the amount of cents-off, such as: "Price marked is 8¢ off the regular price" or "Price marked is 8¢ off the regular price of this package."

—The retailer also must conspicuously display the regular price, either on the product itself or on a sign or shelf market contiguous to the retail display. (The sponsor promoting the product must supply the retailer with such signs.)

TO QUALIFY AS A REGULAR PRICE, the commodity must have been sold openly for a minimum of 30 days in each store selling the item at a reduction. For commodities that fluctuate in price, the ordinary and customary price, from which the reduction is to be based, is the lowest price at which substantial sales were made during the previous 30 days.

Shipments of commodities bearing the savings representations to a given geographical trade area shall be in no greater volume than 50 percent of the total units distributed in that area during the previous 12 months.

A maximum of three cents-off promotions are allowed during any calendar year with a minimum of one month between each and a maximum of six months for any one promotion.

THE KEY RULES FOR PACKAGE SIZE savings are:

—Only one package size of a product may bear a representation of economy, and only if the product is also available in at least one other size.

—Reduction in price to warrant an *economy size* representation must be substantially reduced (that is, at least 5 percent) from actual price of all other packages of the same brand.

Source: The Marketing News, 5 (March 1, 1972), 5.

at the reduced price. Let C_s represent the marginal shortage cost (opportunity cost of having an additional promoted unit left in inventory at the end of the promotion period) and let C_I be the inventory carrying cost. If P is the probability of making a retail sale and $(1 - P)$ is the probability of not making that sale, then marginal decision analysis suggests selling promoted units to the channel until the expected opportunity costs are equal.

$$PC_s = (1 - P)C_I \qquad (12\text{-}1)$$

The probability level which will minimize the total expected opportunity costs can be derived from Eq. (12-1):

$$P^* = \frac{C_I}{C_s + C_I} \qquad (12\text{-}2)$$

Table 12-2   FTC Proposed Guides on Price Comparisons

These guides are to apply to price comparisons that merchants or manufacturers use in their advertising. The purpose of the proposed guides is to make sure the advertiser tells the truth—clearly—when the asking price is stated, and to ensure the advertiser does not deceive consumers by using sales gimmicks.

Advertisers should stop:

—Using the words "sale" or "reduced to" unless the reduction is recent and the immediately preceding price is disclosed;

—Advertising a "sale" or other temporary change in prices unless consumers are told approximately how long the sale will last;

—Comparing the price of one article with that of another article unless the price for the article is explicitly identified as to whether it is a manufacturer's list price, advertiser's own price, competitor's offering price, etc.;

—Advertising lowered prices—such as "special purchase," "exceptional purchase," "clearance," "manufacturer's close-out"—unless the prices actually are lower than the advertiser's usual prices; and

—Using the term "wholesale" in their advertising price unless they make substantial bona fide sales to retailers at those prices.

Source: The Marketing News, 7 (August 15, 1974), 11.

Marginal theory suggests that as long as the probability of selling an additional unit of the price-deal item at retail is greater than P^*, the seller should ship the unit through the distribution network.

As noted above, the shortage cost (C_s) is the opportunity loss of not selling an additional item at the deal price due to inadequate retail inventory. Conversely, the opportunity cost of inventory (C_I) is the difference in revenues from selling an additional unit at the regular price and selling it at the deal price. Thus

$$C_s = p_d - C_v \tag{12-3}$$

and

$$C_I = p_r - p_d$$

where p_d = special deal price

C_v = unit variable cost of production

p_r = regular price

Substituting these expressions into Eq. (12-2) yields

$$P^* = \frac{p_r - p_d}{p_r - C_v} \tag{12-4}$$

Application of this solution requires estimates of the average and standard deviation quantity of the item to be sold if a discount were not to be offered. The authors suggest methods of forecasting from past data and adjustments to make in the forecast to reflect current conditions as a means to obtain these estimates. If S denotes the estimated quantity to be distributed, then there is a value S^* which corresponds to P^*, where S^* is the optimal amount of price-deal items to ship through the channel. Assuming the forecast error is distributed normally, S^* can be transformed into a standard unit normal deviate, k^*:

$$k^* = \frac{S^* - \overline{S}}{\sigma_S} \qquad\qquad (12\text{-}5)$$

where $\overline{S}$ = estimated average sales figure for this time period

$\quad\ \sigma_S$ = standard deviation of estimated sales for this time period

and S^* is as defined above. Solving for S^* yields

$$S^* = \overline{S} + k^*\sigma_S \qquad\qquad (12\text{-}6)$$

which is the quantity of price-deal items to offer during the price-promoted period.

To illustrate this model, assume that a consumer products firm is planning a special deal for the month of May. The deal will be offered to distributors in anticipation that retailers will reduce the retail price to induce greater consumer demand. The product is normally sold to distributors in cases at a price of $8.00 per case. Direct variable costs are $5.85 per case. The special price to distributors for this deal is $6.75 per case. Sales to distributors without the deal are estimated to be 80,000 cases for this time period.

To determine the optimum quantity to promote, it is first necessary to determine the probability level that will minimize total expected opportunity costs. Using Eq. (12-4)

$$P^* = \frac{p_r - p_d}{p_r - C_v} = \frac{\$8.00 - \$6.75}{\$8.00 - \$5.85} = 0.58$$

The probability of 0.58 on the standard normal curve corresponds to the point $k^*\sigma_S = 0.2\sigma_S$. Assume that σ_S, the standard deviation of estimated sales for May, is 8,000 cases. Therefore, using Eq. (12-6) the quantity of price-deal items to offer during May can be determined.

$$S^* = \overline{S} + k^*\sigma_S = 80{,}000 + 0.2(8{,}000) = 80{,}000 + 1{,}600$$

$$= 81{,}600 \text{ cases}$$

It would not be economical to offer more than 81,600 cases for the price promotion. It is likely that orders will exceed this amount as dealers attempt to stock up on the special. However, an excessive inventory buildup in May will reduce shipments in June, when dealers will be depleting their excessive inventories at regular prices. Thus, it is necessary to determine an amount to offer during the deal that balances the shortage cost (C_s) with the inventory opportunity cost (C_I).

This model appears to assume that the magnitude of the price discount and the duration of the promotion are independently determined. The justification for this approach may be that the model was developed for a specific firm, Corning Glass Works, which has historically behaved in this pattern. However, the degree to which this model can be generalized must be assessed. It is reasonable to assume that the magnitude of the price discount influences the effective length of the promotional period and thus the quantity of items to be sold in that period. Therefore, the general appropriateness of the model is a function of the degree to which this interaction exists.

The model represents an interesting approach to maximizing short-run profits. However, little consideration is given to possible long-run effects of the price promotion. Regular customers of the product may take advantage of the price deal to inventory the product at a lower cost. In such a case, sales of the product at the regular price are lost. The unit opportunity cost in this case is the difference between the regular price and the deal price. However, this cost is not treated by the model. The opportunity cost may be offset by inducing nonloyal patrons of competing brands to switch to the deal brand and become loyal or habitual purchasers of it. The cost may also be balanced by bolstering lagging support for the brand from particular market segments. The model does not treat the extent to which these factors are relevant because it assumes a homogeneous market. Useful extensions of the model lie in defining particular market segments and the influence price deals will have on them.[17]

SALES COMPENSATION PLANS

Not only must the manufacturer be concerned with obtaining cooperation from distributors, but care must also be exercised to gain the sales forces' cooperation. Many companies have indicated that greater care is needed when explaining changes in prices or price policy to the sales force than when explaining these changes to customers.

As pointed out in Chap. 1, many pricing changes recently enacted by business firms have reduced the flexibility of the sales force and have increased sales force dissatisfaction. Moreover, the increased accent on profit margins and pruning products and services makes it incumbent on management to develop compensation plans that reward rather than penalize the sales force.

Using the costing principles developed in earlier chapters, a sales compensation plan can be developed that rewards salespeople in terms of their contributions to profit. The segment contribution analysis developed in Chap. 6 may be used to evaluate the economic rationale of sales compensation plans.

A compensation plan that more companies are turning to, particularly in the current inflationary economy, is one based on contribution to profits. Such a plan rewards a salesperson to the degree that he or she helps the firm reach its profit goal,

---

[17]Additional discussion on price promotion models may be found in Kent B. Monroe and Albert J. Della Bitta, "Models for Pricing Decisions," *Journal of Marketing Research*, 15 (August 1978), 413-428.

and helps motivate salespersons to put less effort into easy-to-sell, low-margin products. Moreover, when companies move away from a varying-price policy to a one-price policy, such a compensation plan gives the salesperson incentive to avoid shading or reducing prices as a means of soliciting sales. Finally, a compensation plan based on profit contributions will influence salespersons to restrict selling expenses, since doing so will improve their sales performance.

A compensation plan that properly motivates the sales force can be effective in managing the product-sales mix. Again, it is important to recognize that pricing policy is intricately related to all parts of the marketing management function.

SUMMARY

This chapter has shown the relationship of the pricing function to the three major marketing decision variables—distribution and channel decisions, promotion management, and sales force management. Previously, Chaps. 9 and 10 linked the pricing decision to product management and Chap. 11 discussed the linkage between pricing and transportation decisions.

As the reader may recall, pricing was defined in Chap. 1 by considering price as a ratio between the quantity of goods and services provided by the seller to the quantity of goods and services given up by the buyer. There are many options available to the seller when price must be changed. The seller can change the product in terms of its performance or attached services, the discount structure, the methods of distribution, or the sales promotion methods. Thus, price as the only revenue-generating marketing variable is intimately linked to the other marketing variables. The seller, therefore, has many alternatives available when making either short-term or permanent price changes.

As a final note, it should be remembered that the ultimate objective of a pricing decision is to influence buyer behavior. Thus, the decision should come less from traditional practice than from the analysis of what pricing alternatives will positively influence buyers. The purpose of this chapter has been to demonstrate that the underlying rationale for pricing decisions is also useful when making distribution, promotion, or sales management decisions.

DISCUSSION QUESTIONS

1 a Discuss the problem of controlling prices through the distribution channel.
   b What are some legal ways of developing price controls?
   c Why would a manufacturer be concerned with controlling the price through the channel?
2 a Distinguish between single-function and dual-function buyers.
   b Why is this distinction important?
3 What should a manufacturer do to establish a legally valid functional discount pricing structure? Why?
4 a Why would a firm use temporary price reductions?
   b What are some alternative ways to temporarily reduce prices?
   c What are some of the problems of establishing a special price promotion?

5 If a manufacturer paid close attention to the behavioral aspects of price as discussed
   in Chap. 3, what behavioral principles would you suggest be used when developing a
   price-deal strategy?
6 a What are some ways in which a seller might use price deals deceptively?
   b Can you formulate any prescriptions for avoiding such deceptions?
7 a Look through several magazines, particularly magazines such as *Readers' Digest*,
      Ladies Home Journal, *Woman's Day*, *Family Circle*. List the number of different
      types of deals—coupons, refunds, premiums—that you find.
   b Look through several Sunday newspapers, and the Wednesday or Thursday food
      sections of your newspaper. List the number of different types of deals—cou-
      pons, refunds, premiums—that you find.
   c If you took advantage of all the coupons you found, how much would you save?
   d Compare the weekly advertisements of several grocery stores in your area for
      at least a month. Are any national brands featured as specials by rival super-
      markets? Are they the same brands?
   e Why do you suppose rival supermarkets would feature the same national brands
      as price specials?

SUGGESTED READINGS

Beringer, William E.: "The Validity of Discounts Granted to Dual Function Buyers
   under the Robinson-Patman Act," *The Business Lawyer*, 31 (January 1976), 783–
   800.
Goodman, David, and Kavin Moody: "Determining Optimum Price Promotion Quanti-
   ties," *Journal of Marketing*, 34 (October 1970), 31–39.
Hinkle, Charles: "The Strategy of Price Deals," *Harvard Business Review*, 43 (July–
   August 1965), 75–85.
Monroe, Kent B., and Albert J. Della Bitta: "Models for Pricing Decisions," *Journal of
   Marketing Research*, 15 (August 1978), 413–428.
Warshaw, Martin R.: "Pricing to Gain Wholesalers' Selling Support," *Journal of Mar-
   keting*, 26 (July 1962), 50–54.

APPENDIX: FTC Guides against Deceptive Pricing

(January 8, 1964)

INTRODUCTION

These Guides are designed to highlight certain problems in the field of price advertising which experience has demonstrated to be especially troublesome to businessmen who in good faith desire to avoid deception of the consuming public. Since the Guides are not intended to serve as comprehensive or precise statements of law, but rather as practical aids to the honest businessman who seeks to conform his conduct to the requirements of fair and legitimate merchandising, they will be of no assistance to the unscrupulous few whose aim is to walk as close as possible to the line between legal and illegal conduct. They are to be considered as *guides*, and not as fixed rules of "do's" and "don'ts" or detailed statements of the Commission's enforcement policies. The fundamental spirit of the Guides will govern their application.

The basic objective of these Guides is to enable the businessman to advertise his goods honestly, and to avoid offering the consumer nonexistent bargains or bargains that will be misunderstood. Price advertising is particularly effective because of the universal hope of consumers to find bargains. Truthful price advertising, offering real bargains, is a benefit to all. But the advertiser must shun sales "gimmicks" which lure consumers into a mistaken belief that they are getting more for their money than is the fact.

GUIDE I—FORMER PRICE COMPARISONS

One of the most commonly used forms of bargain advertising is to offer a reduction from the advertiser's own former price for an article. If the former price is the actual, *bona fide* price at which the article was offered to the public on a regular basis for a reasonably substantial period of time, it provides a legitimate basis for the advertising of a price comparison. Where the former price is genuine, the bargain being advertised is a true one. If, on the other hand, the former price being advertised is not *bona fide* but fictitious—for example, where an artificial, inflated price was established for the purpose of enabling the subsequent offer of a large reduction—the "bargain" being advertised is a false one; the purchaser is not receiving the unusual value he expects. In such a case, the "reduced" price is, in reality, probably just the seller's regular price.

A former price is not necessarily fictitious merely because no sales at the advertised price were made. The advertiser should be especially careful, however, in such a case, that the price is one at which the product was openly and actively offered for sale, for a reasonably substantial period of time, in the recent, regular course of his business, honestly and in good faith—and, of course, not for the purpose of establishing a fictitious higher price on which a deceptive comparison might be based. And the advertiser should scrupulously avoid any implication that a former price is a selling, not an asking price (for example, by use of such language as, "Formerly sold at $___"), unless substantial sales at that price were actually made.

Inquiries concerning these Guides and requests for copies should be addressed to the Bureau of Industry Guidance, Federal Trade Commission, Washington, D.C. 20580.

The following is an example of a price comparison based on a fictitious former price. John Doe is a retailer of Brand X fountain pens, which cost him $5 each. His usual markup is 50% over cost; that is, his regular retail price is $7.50. In order subsequently to offer an unusual "bargain," Doe begins offering Brand X at $10 per pen. He realizes that he will be able to sell no, or very few, pens at this inflated price. But he doesn't care, for he maintains that price for only a few days. Then he "cuts" the price to its usual level—$7.50—and advertises: "Terrific Bargain: X Pens, Were $10, Now Only $7.50!" This is obviously a false claim. The advertised "bargain" is not genuine.

Other illustrations of fictitious price comparisons could be given. An advertiser might use a price at which he never offered the article at all; he might feature a price which was not used in the regular course of business, or which was not used in the recent past but at some remote period in the past, without making disclosure of that fact; he might use a price that was not openly offered to the public, or that was not maintained for a reasonable length of time, but was immediately reduced.

If the former price is set forth in the advertisement, whether accompanied or not by descriptive terminology such as "Regularly," "Usually," "Formerly," etc., the advertiser should make certain that the former price is not a fictitious one. If the former price, or the amount or percentage of reduction, is not stated in the advertisement, as when the ad merely states, "Sale," the advertiser must take care that the amount of reduction is not so insignificant as to be meaningless. It should be sufficiently large that the consumer, if he knew what it was, would believe that a genuine bargain or saving was being offered. An advertiser who claims that an item has been "Reduced to $9.99," when the former price was $10.00, is misleading the consumer, who will understand the claim to mean that a much greater, and not merely nominal, reduction was being offered.

GUIDE II—RETAIL PRICE COMPARISONS; COMPARABLE VALUE COMPARISONS

Another commonly used form of bargain advertising is to offer goods at prices lower than those being charged by others for the same merchandise in the advertiser's trade area (the area in which he does business). This may be done either on a temporary or a permanent basis, but in either case the advertised higher price must be based upon fact, and not be fictitious or misleading. Whenever an advertiser represents that he is selling below the prices being charged in his area for a particular article, he should be reasonably certain that the higher price he advertises does not appreciably exceed the price at which substantial sales of the article are being made in the area—that is, a sufficient number of sales so that a consumer would consider reduction from the price to represent a genuine bargain or saving. Expressed another way, if a number of the principal retail outlets in the area are regularly selling Brand X fountain pens at $10, it is not dishonest for retailer Doe to advertise: "Brand X Pens, Price Elsewhere $10, Our Price $7.50."

The following example, however, illustrates a misleading use of this advertising technique. Retailer Doe advertises Brand X pens as having a "Retail Value $15.00, My Price $7.50," when the fact is that only a few small suburban outlets in the area charge $15. All of the larger outlets located in and around the main shopping areas charge $7.50, or slightly more or less. The advertisement here would be deceptive, since the price charged by the small suburban outlets would have no real significance to Doe's customers, to whom the advertisement of "Retail Value $15.00" would suggest a prevailing, and not merely an isolated and unrepresentative, price in the area in which they shop.

A closely related form of bargain advertising is to offer a reduction from the prices being charged either by the advertiser or by others in the advertiser's trade area for other merchandise of like grade and quality—in other words, comparable or competing merchandise—to that being advertised. Such advertising can serve a useful and legitimate purpose when it is made clear to the consumer that a comparison is being made with other merchandise and the other merchandise is, in fact, of essentially similar quality and obtainable in the area. The advertiser should, however, be reasonably certain, just as in the case of comparisons involving the same merchandise, that the price advertised as being the price of comparable merchandise does not exceed the price at which such merchandise is being offered by representative retail outlets in the area. For example, retailer Doe advertises Brand X pen as having "Comparable Value $15.00." Unless a reasonable number of the principal outlets in the area are offering Brand Y, an essentially similar pen, for that price, this advertisement would be deceptive.

GUIDE III—ADVERTISING RETAIL PRICES WHICH HAVE BEEN ESTABLISHED OR SUGGESTED BY MANUFACTURERS (OR OTHER NON-RETAIL DISTRIBUTORS)

Many members of the purchasing public believe that a manufacturer's list price, or suggested retail price, is the price at which an article is generally sold. Therefore, if a reduction from this price is advertised, many people will believe that they are being offered a genuine bargain. To the extent that list or suggested retail prices do not in fact correspond to prices at which a substantial number of sales of the article in question are made, the advertisement of a reduction may mislead the consumer.

There are many methods by which manufacturers' suggested retail or list prices are advertised: large scale (often nation-wide) mass-media advertising by the manufacturer himself; pre-ticketing by the manufacturer; direct mail advertising; distribution of promotional material or price lists designed for display to the public. The mechanics used are not of the essence. These Guides are concerned with *any* means employed for placing such prices before the consuming public.

There would be little problem of deception in this area if all products were invariably sold at the retail price set by the manufacturer. However, the widespread failure to observe manufacturers' suggested or list prices, and the advent of retail discounting on a wide scale, have seriously undermined the dependability of list prices as indicators of the exact prices at which articles are in fact generally sold at retail. Changing competitive conditions have created a more acute problem of deception than may have existed previously. Today, only in the rare case are *all* sales of an article at the manufacturer's suggested retail or list price.

But this does not mean that all list prices are fictitious and all offers of reductions from list, therefore, deceptive. Typically, a list price is a price at which articles are sold, if not everywhere, then at least in the principal retail outlets which do not conduct their business on a discount basis. It will not be deemed fictitious if it is the price at which substantial (that is, not isolated or insignificant) sales are made in the advertiser's trade area (the area in which he does business). Conversely, if the list price is significantly in excess of the highest price at which substantial sales in the trade area are made, there is a clear and serious danger of the consumer being misled by an advertised reduction from this price.

This general principle applies whether the advertiser is a national or regional manufacturer (or other non-retail distributor), a mail-order or catalog distributor who deals directly with the consuming public, or a local retailer. But certain differences in the responsibility of these various types of businessmen should be noted. A retailer competing in a local area has at least a general knowledge of the prices being charged in his area. Therefore, before advertising a manufacturer's list price as a basis for comparison with his own lower price, the retailer should ascertain whether the list price is in fact the price regularly charged by principal outlets in his area.

In other words, a retailer who advertises a manufacturer's or distributor's suggested retail price should be careful to avoid creating a false impression that he is offering a reduction from the price at which the product is generally sold in his trade area. If a number of the principal retail outlets in the area are regularly engaged in making sales at the manufacturer's suggested price, that price may be used in advertising by one who is selling at a lower price. If, however, the list price is being followed only by, for example, small suburban stores, house-to-house canvassers, and credit houses, accounting for only an insubstantial volume of sales in the area, advertising of the list price would be deceptive.

On the other hand, a manufacturer or other distributor who does business on a large regional or national scale cannot be required to police or investigate in detail the prevailing prices of his articles throughout so large a trade area. If he advertises or disseminates a list or pre-ticketed price in good faith (i.e., as an honest estimate of the actual retail price) which does not appreciably exceed the highest price at which substantial sales are made in his trade area, he will not be chargeable with having engaged in a deceptive practice. Consider the following example:

> Manufacturer Roe, who makes Brand X pens and sells them throughout the United States, advertises his pen in a national magazine as having a "Suggested Retail Price $10," a price determined on the basis of a market survey. In a substantial number of representative communities, the principal retail outlets are selling the product at this price in the regular course of business and in substantial volume. Roe would not be considered to have advertised a fictitious "suggested retail price." If retailer Doe does business in one of these communities, he would not be guilty of a deceptive practice by advertising, "Brand X Pens, Manufacturer's Suggested Retail Price, $10.00, Our Price, $7.50."

It bears repeating that the manufacturer, distributor or retailer must in every case act honestly and in good faith in advertising a list price, and not with the intention of establishing a basis, or creating an instrumentality, for a deceptive comparison in any local or other trade area. For instance, a manufacturer may not affix price tickets containing inflated prices as an accommodation to particular retailers who intend to use such prices as the basis for advertising fictitious price reductions.

GUIDE IV—BARGAIN OFFERS BASED UPON THE PURCHASE OF OTHER MERCHANDISE

Frequently, advertisers choose to offer bargains in the form of additional merchandise to be given a customer on the condition that he purchase a particular article at the price usually offered by the advertiser. The forms which such offers may take are numerous and varied, yet all have essentially the same purpose and effect. Representative of the language frequently employed in such offers are "Free," "Buy One—Get One Free," "2-For-1 Sale," "Half Price Sale," "1¢ Sale," "50% Off," etc. Literally, of course, the seller is not offering anything "free" (i.e., an unconditional gift), or ½ free, or for only 1¢, when he makes such an offer, since the purchaser is required to purchase an article in order to receive the "free" or "1¢" item. It is important, therefore, that where such a form of offer is used, care be taken not to mislead the consumer.

Where the seller, in making such an offer, increases his regular price of the article required to be bought, or decreases the quantity and quality of that article, or otherwise attaches strings (other than the basic condition that the article be purchased in order for the purchaser to be entitled to the "free" or "1¢" additional merchandise) to the offer, the consumer may be deceived.

Accordingly, whenever a "free," "2-for-1," "half price sale," "1¢ sale," "50% off" or similar type of offer is made, all the terms and conditions of the offer should be made clear at the outset.

GUIDE V—MISCELLANEOUS PRICE COMPARISONS

The practices covered in the provisions set forth above represent the most frequently employed forms of bargain advertising. However, there are many variations which appear from time to time and which are, in the main, controlled by the same general principles. For example, retailers should not advertise a retail price as a "wholesale" price. They should not represent that they are selling at "factory" prices when they are not selling at the prices paid by those purchasing directly from the manufacturer. They should not offer seconds or imperfect or irregular merchandise at a reduced price without disclosing that the higher comparative price refers to the price of the merchandise if perfect. They should not offer an advance sale under circumstances where they do not in good faith expect to increase the price at a later date, or make a "limited" offer which, in fact, is not limited. In all of these situations, as well as in others too numerous to mention, advertisers should make certain that the bargain offer is genuine and truthful. Doing so will serve their own interest as well as that of the public.

These Guides supersede the Guides Against Deceptive Pricing adopted October 2, 1958.

Adopted: December 20, 1963.

Joseph W. Shea
Secretary

Section Five

Special Topics
on Pricing

Chapters 13 through 16 discuss some specific types of pricing problems. These include the problems of setting price when a specific target rate of return is desired, when a firm wishes to determine the bid price for a specific project, and when the firm has a shortage of a resource necessary to produce its products. In addition, the problems of developing justifiable price differentials are dealt with.

Often, profit objectives are stated in terms of rate of return on investment. The traditional approach is to determine the necessary profit per unit sold that will permit achieving the target return if actual demand equals forecasted demand. However, such an approach ignores the differences in capital investment required to produce various products. Chapter 13 extends contribution analysis to include considerations of return on investment. The particular technique developed in Chap. 13 is being used by a major chemical company.

Chapter 14 presents a brief overview of the problem of developing bids for providing products or services on an order basis. The chapter provides applications of costing and discusses specific considerations of competitive strategy. It concludes by introducing the problem of pricing with capacity constraints, which is discussed in detail in Chap. 15.

The problem of the multiple-product firm operating at or near capacity is discussed in Chap. 15. Capacity limitations may be due to limited production facilities, scarce materials, or even cash flow difficulties. Given these limitations, the firm must decide how to allocate the scarce resource so as to maximize contribution to fixed costs and profits. Chapter 15 discusses this problem, develops a decision criterion using contribution analysis, and illustrates the solution with applications to product-line pricing and the pricing of special orders.

One of the most complex and frustrating problems of pricing is that of justifying price differentials. The need to justify price differentials may arise from litigations initiated by a customer, a competitor, or the government. However, particularly during inflationary periods, customers may request (demand) justification for a recent price increase. Because it has been traditional to use cost-plus pricing that incorporates arbitrary overhead allocations, the cost defense has rarely been successful in a legal proceeding. Moreover, during the recent inflationary period of our country, many firms were hard pressed to justify price increases to their customers. (In fact, the firms' sales personnel were often the least satisfied by such justification attempts.) Using the costing approach developed in Chaps. 5, 6, and 7, guidelines for justifying prices are presented in Chap. 16.

Chapter 13

Pricing for Return on Product Investment

In the 1920s, Donaldson Brown, an early vice-president of General Motors, developed a formula for pricing. According to this formula, prices are based on an average sales estimate or "standard volume." The overall pricing objective was to determine a standard volume large enough to cover fixed costs and variable production costs at a price customers were willing to pay, while still permitting the firm to earn a target return on investment. It was Brown's contention that the pricing objective was to obtain the highest rate of return on capital consistent with attainable volume.[1] A popular pricing method commonly called *target-return pricing* has been developed from this initial pricing concept. In the classic study of pricing practices, "target return on investment was probably the most commonly stressed of company pricing goals."[2]

The purpose of this chapter is to review the traditional approach to determining a target-return price, which is to determine the necessary profit per unit sold that will permit achieving the target return if actual demand equals forecasted demand. However, it will be shown that such an approach ignores the differences in capital investment required to produce various products. Some investment, e.g., in materials, is more current and requires a different rate of return. To handle this problem of different types of capital, contribution analysis will be extended to include considera-

---

[1] See "Detroit's Dilemma on Prices," *Business Week*, January 20, 1975, p. 82.
[2] A. D. H. Kaplan, Joel B. Dirlam, and Robert F. Lanzillotti, *Pricing in Big Business* (Washington, D.C.: The Brookings Institution, 1958), p. 130.

tions of return on investment. The technique developed in this chapter is being used by a major chemical company.

TARGET-RETURN PRICING

Target-return pricing is the development of a set of product prices designed to provide a predetermined return on capital employed in the production and distribution of the products involved.[3] In this pricing method, both costs and profit goals are based on standard volume. *Standard volume* is the volume or quantity expected to be produced in the following year or an average volume expected to be produced over a number of future years. For an expected volume, the firm determines what its unit labor and materials costs must be, and allocates its fixed costs over the expected volume to obtain a fixed cost per unit figure. To these standard costs is added a percentage of capital employed per unit volume to arrive at selling price. In equation form, the pricing rule is

$$P_r = \text{DVC} + \frac{F}{X} + \frac{rK}{X} \tag{13-1}$$

where P_r = selling price determined when the target-return formula is used
$\quad\;\;$ DVC = direct unit variable costs
$\qquad F$ = fixed costs
$\qquad X$ = standard unit volume
$\qquad r$ = profit rate desired
$\qquad K$ = capital (total operating assets) employed

The effect of target-return pricing is to help prevent cyclical or seasonal changes in volume from affecting prices unduly. That is, the firm expects that averaging the changes in cost and demand over seasons or business cycles will enable the firm to realize a desired rate of return on investment. However, as in full-cost pricing, pricing decisions based on target returns are not thought to be responsive to demand or shifts in demand. Target-return pricing provides some stability in making pricing decisions, since standard volume and standard costs are usually based on expected volume over a planning period. However, it makes little allowance for price competition. Perhaps the major reason for this pricing approach is management's increasing concern with allocating scarce capital resources over many alternative uses.

To illustrate the application of this method, assume the data given in Table 13-1A. From this data, the selling price of each product can be obtained using Eq. (13-1):

$$P_A = \$8.00 + \frac{\$400,000}{200,000} + \frac{0.15(\$1,000,000)}{200,000} = \$10.75$$

$$P_B = \$6.00 + \frac{\$800,000}{400,000} + \frac{0.15(\$2,400,000)}{400,000} = \$\;8.90$$

[3] Robert Lanzillotti, "Pricing Objectives in Large Companies," *American Economic Review*, 48 (December 1958), 921–940.

Table 13-1 Target-Return Pricing

	Product A	Product B
A Planning data		
1. Direct variable cost per unit	$ 8.00	$ 6.00
2. Total fixed cost	$ 400,000	$ 800,000
3. Expected volume (units)	200,000	400,000
4. Desired rate of return	15%	15%
5. Total capital employed	$1,000,000	$2,400,000
B Summary data		
6. Selling price	$10.75	$8.90
1. Direct variable cost	8.00	6.00
7. Contribution (6 – 1)	$ 2.75	$2.90
8. Return on sales (7 + 6)	25.6%	32.6%
9. Markup on cost (7 ÷ 1)	34.4%	48.3%
10. Return on capital {[(7 × 3) – 2] ÷ 5}	15%	15%

Table 13-1B summarizes the data for each product for comparison purposes. If the company makes only these two products, and the expected volume of the product mix is realized, the target return is achieved. However, this approach ignores a number of factors, which may result in one or both products failing to achieve the desired return.

Disadvantages of the Target-Return Approach

First, the above approach assumes the product sales mix will remain in a 2:1 proportion, ignoring market acceptance of the formularized prices. As discussed in Chap. 10, acceptance of a product line's prices depends on price differentials within the line as well as the price differentials with competitive offerings. Thus, the prices as formularized may not lead to the desired rates of return. For example, if actual sales volume, at these prices, is 180,000 units for A and 400,000 units for B, then the return on capital for A is only 9.5 percent, and overall the firm will have a rate of return of 13.38 percent.

A second difficulty is that markup is based on fully allocated costs. As noted in earlier chapters, a full-cost approach distorts the effects from a shift in activities or demand. Indeed, no out-of-pocket costs were developed, and it is not possible to analyze the effect on contributions of setting lower prices.

Third, the approach summarized above assumes that each product in the product line carries capital investments in the same proportions. That is, no distinction is made in production costs between materials cost and conversion cost. Presumably, a materials-intensive product will require relatively more capital investment than a product for which the major proportion of costs are for conversion (see Fig. 5-1). As shown below, the materials aspect of the capital assets structure develops the firm's rate of return differently than a piece of fixed equipment.

The Example of the Auto Industry

The target-return approach to pricing produces a startling paradox in pricing theory. When a firm is intent on maintaining a desired rate of return, then, if demand slackens and expected volume fails to materialize, the firm must raise its prices. Notice that in Eq. (13-1), both fixed costs and the desired dollar return on capital are divided by X, the standard unit volume. If, however, actual demand is less than X, then the expressions F/X and rK/X increase in value, leading to a higher price, P_r. To illustrate, assume that demand for product A is only 180,000 units. Applying this value to the formula (13-1) produces

$$P_A = \$8.00 + \frac{\$400,000}{180,000} + \frac{0.15(\$1,000,000)}{180,000} = \$11.06$$

During the recession of 1974-1975, the automobile industry faced such a dilemma. During 1974-1975, auto prices rose an average $1,000 while sales fell by 25 percent.[4] Yet, the automobile industry, as shown above, could not reduce prices. Part of the industry's reluctance to reduce prices comes from the belief that demand for automobiles is either price inelastic or barely price elastic. And, as shown in Chap. 9, when pricing a mature product, demand must be sufficiently elastic for a price reduction to increase revenues more than the increase in variable costs due to increased demand. (See also the economic argument of this point in Chap. 2.)

However, the automobile industry also faced this pricing dilemma because of its inflexible, formularized method of pricing. Indeed, there had been some shift in demand to smaller, less profitable cars, but the automobile industry was unable to analyze either the significance of the shift in the product mix or the effect on contributions of a change in prices. "The next step in the industry's long and sometimes lacerating evaluation may be a more flexible pricing formula. This would require a whole new line of industry thinking, however. The problem is that change comes slowly in Detroit—as slowly, in fact, as a price cut."[5]

ELEMENTS OF CAPITAL

As noted above, pricing for return on investment utilizes the concept of capital as a means of determining the proper markup for pricing decisions. But, we have not defined what constitutes capital. First, it is important to recognize that *total capital* is composed of current assets and fixed assets. *Current assets* or *variable capital* represents cash, accounts receivable, and inventories. The amount of variable capital employed in producing and marketing a product varies according to changes in output and sales. *Fixed capital* represents the book value of fixed facilities, equipment, land, and machinery used to produce and market a product. The amount of fixed capital

---

[4]See "Detroit's Dilemma on Prices," *Business Week*, January 20, 1975, pp. 82–83.
[5]Ibid., p. 83.

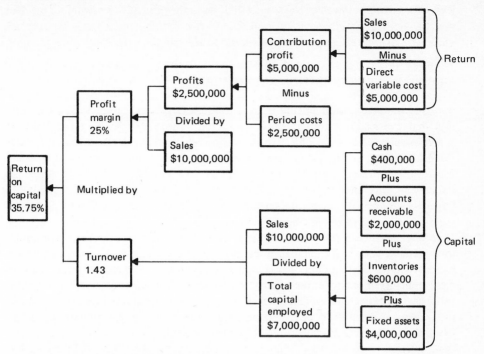

Figure 13-1 Return on capital. *(Adapted from Sam R. Goodman, Techniques of Profitability Analysis (New York: Wiley, 1970), p. 117.)*

employed does not vary with output and sales. The value of fixed capital changes over time due to depreciation and investment in new capital.

The relationship of these elements of capital to sales and the concept of return on investment is illustrated in Fig. 13-1. As the figure shows, total capital employed is $7,000,000, of which $3,000,000 is in current assets. The figure also shows that a return on capital can be improved if the turnover can be improved, either by increasing sales with the same capital base or maintaining sales with a smaller capital base. In the short run, the firm can obtain a smaller capital base by reducing the average investment in current assets.

For example, in the figure, the sales to inventory ratio is 16.67. Or, inventory turns on the average 16.67 times during the planning period. If the average inventory could be reduced to $250,000, the sales to inventory ratio would be 40, and the overall return on capital would become 37.6 percent. If, through better management of cash, credit, and inventory, the current assets could be reduced by a million dollars, the capital turnover would become 1.67 and the overall return on capital would become 41.7 percent.

However, different products make different uses of the various elements of capital, and, as noted above, variable capital varies with output and sales. We have already discussed in Chap. 11 the role of the price structure in influencing the cash flow and level of accounts receivable. Now, we will develop the principle of pricing for product investment: *The development of a product's price should consider how the product makes use of the various elements of capital used to produce and market the product.*

PRICING FOR CONTRIBUTION AND RETURN

The goal of target-return pricing is to establish a target price to provide a contribution that will enable a firm to obtain a desired return on capital invested. From an analytical perspective, the objective is to establish a pricing method that facilitates the achievement of this pricing goal, while incorporating the pricing principle established earlier in this chapter. Caution must be exercised in that, as with the automobile industry, a price that allows for a desired rate of return may not be acceptable to buyers or competitive in the market place. Thus, the method we will now develop is only the beginning of the pricing decision process.

In the production and sale of manufactured products two types of capital are used—variable and fixed capital. The variable capital includes cash, accounts receivable, and inventories. The amount of cash available is normally determined by cash management policy. For example, the controller may strive to maintain a cash balance equal to 15 days of expected cash disbursements. The amount of capital invested in accounts receivable is influenced by cash discount and credit policy. Inventory levels are generally planned to cover a predetermined number of production days for in-process and raw materials, and a normal number of "selling days" for finished products. For example, the automobile industry tries to maintain new-car inventories between 40 and 60 days, assuming a normal rate of demand.

Generally, a manufactured product uses materials, labor, and equipment in the production process. From a cost perspective these inputs are segregated into material costs and conversion costs (see Fig. 5-1). Material costs usually constitute a variable investment in that they are more liquid, can be turned over faster, and can be adjusted as output demand varies. On the other hand, a significant portion of conversion costs relates to fixed operating facilities representing a longer-term investment that turns over at a slower rate.

For example, in Fig. 13-1, the amount of capital invested in cash is $400,000. Assume that this amount of cash represents a 20-day period of cash expenditures. Assume also that the firm wishes to earn a return of 25 percent on its capital. Therefore, $400,000 \times \frac{20}{360} \times 0.25 = \$5,555.56$ is the amount the firm must earn from this cash amount. As a percentage of the cash balance, the amount earned is 1.39 percent ($5,555.56/$400,000). Therefore, every 20 days, a cash balance of $400,000 must generate (earn) the amount of $5,555.56 if the firm is to receive a 25 percent return on its cash investment on an annual basis.

On the other hand, the fixed assets of $4 million are held throughout the operating year and must earn $1,000,000 if the 25 percent return is to be achieved. Hence, it is necessary to develop a means of pricing the variable assets in a product differently than the fixed assets. The key component of such a method is to segregate capital turnover into its fixed and variable elements rather than having one turnover ratio for all capital (see Fig. 13-1). Thus, the specific cost elements that comprise the direct variable costs should be marked up individually to reflect their investment differences.

Table 13-2 Basic Data for Target-Return Pricing

Variable- cost elements	Product A	Product B
Materials	$15	$ 5
Conversion costs	3	13
Total variable costs	$18	$18

Developing the Markups[6]

To illustrate this method of target-return pricing, see Table 13-2. Since both product A and product B have the same direct variable costs, they will make the same contribution if they are priced the same. However, product A is materials-intensive and requires relatively little labor and machine time. But, product B requires more labor and machine time. In most industries, product B would require considerably more investment in fixed capital than product A because it requires more than four times the amount of conversion effort needed for product A.

If products A and B are priced equally, then, ignoring market and competitive factors, at least one of the prices is incorrect from a target-return pricing perspective. Unless a distinction is made for differences in capital requirements, material-intensive products are likely to be overpriced and fixed-capital-intensive products underpriced.

To develop separate markups for the different types of capital employed in producing a product, the first step is to develop an annual profit plan. As shown in Table 13-3, this annual plan consists of a statement of capital and desired rate of return, a forecast of unit sales, and an operating plan. It should be noted that, under this approach, the required sales revenue is derived from the plan, given the target profit objective, period expenses, and estimated sales volume. Clearly, the prices that result are derived from the sales revenue constraint developed in the annual profit plan.

Materials Cost Markup

The desired markup on materials cost is found by dividing the target return by the number of times the materials will turn over during the year. If, for the example, the turnover is four times a year, then the markup on material investment is $\frac{20}{4}$, or 5 percent. Thus, each turn of material will provide a 5 percent return, and for the year a 20 percent return will be obtained. As shown in Table 13-4, the materials invested in each product will be marked up 5 percent.

Conversion Cost Markup

On an annual basis, the selling price of materials is 1.05 × ($7,500,000 + $4,000,000), or $12,075,000. Since required revenues are $25,700,000, the markup on conversion costs must cover these costs, plus target contribution, so that $13,625,000 are generated ($25,700,000 - $12,075,000). To avoid the distortion of marking up period

---

[6] This section is adapted from Spencer A. Tucker, *Pricing for Higher Profit* (New York: McGraw-Hill, 1966), pp. 159–178.

Table 13-3 Annual Profit Plan

A Statement of capital and desired return

1. Total capital employed	$4,000,000
2. Desired return (pretax)	20%
3. Target earnings (1 × 2)	$ 800,000
4. Period expenses	$1,500,000
5. Target contribution (3 + 4)	$2,300,000

B Forecasts

	Product A	Product B
6. Estimated sales (units)	500,000	800,000
7. Estimated materials cost	$7,500,000	$ 4,000,000
8. Estimated conversion costs	1,500,000	10,400,000
9. Total direct variable costs	$9,000,000	$14,400,000

C Operating plan

9. Total direct variable costs	$23,400,000
5. Target contribution	2,300,000
10. Required sales revenue (5 + 9)	$25,700,000

costs, only the direct conversion costs are marked up. To determine this markup, the required revenues are divided by the total conversion costs:

$$\frac{\$13,625,000}{\$1,500,000 + \$10,400,000} = 1.145$$

As shown in Table 13-4, conversion costs will be marked up 14.5 percent to provide a return on fixed capital invested in manufacturing.

Table 13-4 Pricing for Target Return

Cost element	Cost	×	Markup	=	Price
Product A					
Materials cost	$15		1.05		$15.75
Conversion cost	3		1.145		3.44
Price to provide 20% return on capital					$19.19
Product B					
Materials cost	$ 5		1.05		$ 5.25
Conversion cost	13		1.145		14.89
Price to provide 20% return on capital					$20.14

Table 13-5 Contribution Summary

	Product A	Product B
Target price	$19.19	$20.14
Direct variable costs	18.00	18.00
Contribution	$ 1.19	$ 2.14
PV	0.062	0.106

Applying the Separate Markups

Table 13-4 shows the application of these separate markups in determining target selling prices. Although both products have the same direct variable costs, the target prices differ because of the different types of capital investment necessary to produce each product. As Table 13-5 shows, each product has a different contribution and PV ratio. If actual sales volume equals the sales estimate, then the target return is achieved. But, regardless of the different PV ratios, each product will earn the same return on total capital employed.

SUMMARY

This chapter has discussed the problems of target-return pricing and has illustrated a variation of the target-return method. The primary advantage of the new method is it recognizes variations in the type and amount of capital employed to produce different products. As a result of these variations, some products require larger markups to produce the same percent return on capital. Using this method will lead to a set of target prices that reflect the different types of investment needed for different products.

However, if final selling prices are set without consideration of market and competitive factors, this revised approach to target-return pricing will have the same disadvantages of the traditional approach. Moreover, the method relies on a unit-sales forecast that is developed without knowing the final selling price. Thus, this method should be used primarily to analyze the profit implications of alternative price-quantity estimates. As Table 13–5 indicates, neither dollar contributions nor PV ratios have to be equal for products to earn the same return on capital employed. Firms must also consider the different ways capital is employed to produce different products.

DISCUSSION QUESTIONS

1 a Briefly describe the traditional approach to target-return pricing.
   b What are the advantages and disadvantages of this approach?
2 a What is the pricing paradox that results when using the target-return approach to pricing?
   b Illustrate this paradox by describing the problem of pricing automobiles.

3 Define
   a Variable capital
   b Fixed capital
   c Turnover
   d Return on capital
4 a What is the principle of pricing for product investment?
   b What cautions must be exercised when using a rate-of-return pricing approach?
5 Describe how markups for variable capital differ from markups for fixed capital.
6 The Delmarva Manufacturing Company is developing its operating plans for 1980. The vice-president of finance recommends that the firm plan for a pretax return on capital of 25 percent. Further, his report indicates that the firm currently has total assets of $10,000,000. The director of marketing research indicates that forecasts predict unit sales for product A of about 800,000 units and for product B about 1,200,000 units. The vice-president of production estimates that the above sales forecasts mean that production costs will be, per unit,

	A	B
Materials cost	$10	$ 5
Conversion costs	5	15

Fixed costs are estimated to be $2,500,000 for 1980.
   a Develop a profit plan for Delmarva.
   b Develop a target price for products A and B. Assume materials turn over five times a year.
   c What prices would you recommend? Why?

SUGGESTED READINGS

Deakin, Michael D.: "Pricing for Return on Investment," *Management Accounting*, 57 (December 1975), 43–44, 50.
"Detroit's Dilemma on Prices," *Business Week*, January 20, 1975, pp. 82–83.
Edson, Harvey O.: "The Application of Return on Investment to Product-Pricing," *The Controller*, (October 1959), 464–469.
Finerty, James J.: "Product Pricing and Investment Analysis," *Management Accounting*, 53 (December 1971), 15–18.
Lanzillotti, Robert: "Pricing Objectives in Large Companies," *American Economic Review*, 48 (December 1958), 921–940.
Weston, J. Fred: "Pricing Behavior of Large Firms," *Western Economic Journal*, 10 (March 1972), 1–18.

Chapter 14

Developing Competitive Bids

In industrial marketing and in selling to the government, firms often compete by submitting bids that detail the services and product specifications to be offered at a stated price. Sealed or closed bidding takes place when two or more bidders submit independent bids for the rights to property or to render a service.

Competitive bidding is a fascinating, challenging, and difficult job involving judgmental assessment of customers and competitors as well as scientific analysis. The theory of competitive bidding has received considerable attention from management scientists and covers such situations as (1) deciding what to bid when the number of competitor bidders is known and when it is known who these competitors are, (2) deciding what to bid when the number is unknown and when the competitors are unknown, (3) deciding whether to submit a bid at all, and (4) deciding how many contracts to bid on simultaneously when a company cannot afford to win them all.

Normally, when all other factors such as quality and service are equal, the low bidder is awarded the contract. Thus, the decision problem is to submit a bid that will help the firm achieve its objectives, while at the same time be lower than the competing bids. What to bid depends largely on the objectives the firm is striving for. Some possible objectives are

1 To maximize immediate profits
2 To maximize long-run profits

3 To achieve a minimum return on investment
4 To minimize risk of losses
5 To minimize the profits of competitors

In the basic decision models, it is generally assumed the firm is interested in achieving immediate profits. Since it is also assumed that the lowest bid gets the award, the chances of the firm winning the bid decrease as the bid price increases. Yet, if the firm does not get the bid its profits are zero. Thus, the amount of profits to be earned from any particular bid is uncertain and probability theory is used to determine the optimal bid. The theory of competitive bidding assumes the bidder's objective is to maximize expected profits.

An example would perhaps make this point clearer. Suppose that on a particular contract a firm determines that its costs for fulfilling the contract would amount to $50,000. Further, assume that the probability of being awarded the contract is 0.70 if the bid is $60,000 but only 0.40 if the bid is $90,000. Which bid should the firm submit if it wishes to maximize expected immediate profits? If a bid of $60,000 is submitted, expected immediate profits are $7,000 [0.70 X ($60,000 - $50,000]. If a bid of $90,000 is submitted, expected immediate profits are $16,000 [0.40 X ($90,000 - $50,000)]. Thus, in this simple example, the firm should bid $90,000 on the contract. Table 14-1 shows this example in greater detail.

In practice, the greatest difficulty in competitive bidding is to develop the required information to estimate the probabilities of winning the contract at various prices. Usually a firm has some idea of the costs that will be incurred if the bid is awarded. It must also estimate the number of bidders submitting a bid since the probability of winning a bid is also a function of this number. The firm must also estimate what competitors are likely to bid since competitors will keep their intentions as secret as possible. Therefore, the company must rely on past bidding information when relevant, on conjecture, and, perhaps, on trade rumors.

Table 14-1 Competitive Bidding Example

Bid (B)	Cost (C)	Immediate profits (B - C)	Probability of contract (P)	Expected immediate profits [P X (B - C)]
$ 30,000	$50,000	$-20,000	1.00	$-20,000
40,000	50,000	-10,000	0.90	- 9,000
50,000	50,000	0	0.80	0
60,000	50,000	10,000	0.70	7,000
70,000	50,000	20,000	0.60	12,000
80,000	50,000	30,000	0.50	15,000
90,000	50,000	40,000	0.40	16,000
100,000	50,000	50,000	0.30	15,000
110,000	50,000	60,000	0.20	12,000
120,000	50,000	70,000	0.10	7,000
130,000	50,000	80,000	0	0

The purpose of this chapter is to present an overview of the problem of developing bids for providing products or services on an order basis. After discussing a procedure for determining whether to submit a bid, the chapter considers cost estimation, determining the probability of winning the contract, and determining the best bid. The chapter concludes by introducing the problem of pricing with capacity constraints.

PREBID ANALYSIS

When offered a contract opportunity, a firm should first perform an analysis to determine whether to prepare a bid. By being selective in its bidding, a company can save time and money that would be spent on bid activities such as cost estimation, engineering proposals, purchasing (there will be fewer requests for subcontract quotes), and printing the bids. The Cleveland Pneumatic Tool Company developed a procedure for screening bid opportunities that permits it to avoid costly bid proposals.[1]

The Cleveland Pneumatic Tool Company has a screening committee that evaluates a bid opportunity in terms of potential growth, engineering capability and facilities needed, and potential competition. As an executive of the firm pointed out, "The important thing is developing a philosophy of the kind of business you're in, where you want to be, and what your sales curve growth should be. Look at your present capabilities and future markets . . . in determining whether to bid."[2]

Determine Bid Objectives

Whether to bid and what to bid depends largely on the firm's objectives. As already indicated, the objective may be the typical economic objective of profit maximization, either in terms of return on investment or absolute profits, or it may be to keep labor busy, gain an entree into a new business, or overcome a survival crisis. A bidder should define objectives carefully before evaluating bid opportunities. Whenever possible, the objectives of potential competitive bidders should also be analyzed. This latter information will be useful in assessing the chances of winning the contract.

Develop Evaluation Criteria

To evaluate a bid opportunity the firm needs benchmarks or criteria. Among these criteria would be

1 Labor skills and engineering capability required
2 Available plant capacity
3 Followup bid opportunities
4 Design content
5 Competition
6 Degree of familiarity with the bid project
7 Delivery requirement
8 Experience curve factor

[1] "Evaluation System Boosts Job Shop's Bidding Average," *Steel*, September 21, 1964, pp. 46–47.
[2] Ibid., p. 47.

It is necessary to determine whether the firm has the *necessary labor skills and engineering capability* to complete the bid project as specified. If major extensions of skills are required, the firm must consider the cost of acquiring these capabilities.

Available plant capacity is an important factor. To bid on a contract requiring 20 percent of a firm's capacity when the firm is already operating at 90 percent would not usually be considered appropriate. On the other hand, a company operating at 60 percent capacity would probably be quite interested in the bid opportunity.

The firm should also consider whether it has capacity for future business that might result from winning the contract. For example, if the firm's business has been growing normally, it might not be able to accommodate this normal growth in the next few years if current slack capacity is devoted to the contract.

Many bid opportunities provide the possibility that *followup orders* will be secured after the first contract has been fulfilled. Winning a federal government contract, for example, to develop a new defense system, gives the winning bidder an expertise that would be important in future bids to supply more components for the defense system. Moreover, winning a contract may make other potential buyers aware of the firm's expertise and capability.

Jobs with low *design content* may not fully utilize a company's design engineering talent. A precision, design-oriented company would want to keep its engineers occupied developing new processes or special materials and would be less interested in jobs requiring little design effort.

To determine the chances of winning a bid, it is important to consider the number and identity of *probable competitors* for the contract. In general, the more profitable a bid opportunity seems to be, the greater the number of competitive bids that will be submitted.

In high technology fields, a high degree of significance is placed on the *degree of familiarity* the firm has with the bid project. Often, the firm's degree of competency is an important factor in winning an award. It is known that aerospace companies prepare for future bids by adding skills and experience in advance.[3]

A fundamental factor in awarding contracts is whether a bidder can *deliver the project on time*. Indeed, the federal government will invalidate a bid if it appears that the bidder may not be able to deliver as specified. The firm must also consider the effects on permanent customers if an awarded contract is given priority in production.

Finally, the firm should consider whether the quantity of items specified in the bid will allow a cost savings due to the *experience curve*. For example, if the contract results in a doubling of cumulative production volume, then the cost savings will extend to all similar products. Hence, the contract could make the firm more cost competitive in its traditional markets.

Develop a Screening Procedure[4]

The eight criteria outlined above must be analyzed to measure the value of a bid opportunity. One procedure would be to assign a weight to each of these factors

---

[3] Stephen Paranka, "The Pay-Off Concept in Competitive Bidding," *Business Horizons*, 12 (August 1969), 77–81.

[4] This procedure is adapted from Stephen Paranka, "Competitive Bidding Strategy," *Business Horizons*, 14 (June 1971), 39–43.

according to their relative importance to the firm. Then, for a particular bid, the relative merits of each factor could be assigned a rating of high, medium, or low. These ratings might then be assigned quantitative values, for example, 10, 5, 0. For example, if the project used existing labor skills, it would get a rating of 10. The product of each factor's weight and rating could be summed to provide an overall score. The firm can then compare the score to other previous bids, or to a predetermined minimum acceptable value. If the bid opportunity passes this prebid analysis, then the firm would proceed to develop a bid.

Table 14-2 illustrates this screening procedure. In this case, a minimum score of 650 is necessary before the firm will prepare a bid. In the bid opportunity presented in the table, the firm would be able to use existing labor skills and design engineers. Moreover, the firm is familiar with the project requirements because of past and present projects, and could obtain cost reductions of current projects because of the experience factor. Hence, each of these criteria receives a high evaluation and a weight of 10. Thus, despite the lack of followup opportunities, the bid opportunity scored high on a sufficient number of factors to warrant preparing a bid. The development of such a screening procedure has improved the bidding success of the Cleveland Pneumatic Tool Company.[5]

COST ESTIMATION

Cost estimation involves the familiar procedures for costing discussed in Chaps. 4 through 8. It is vitally important that the components of cost as illustrated in Fig. 5-1 be classified and separated to permit an analysis of the implications of alternative bids. As discussed earlier, the direct cost data set a price floor below which the firm will not want to make a bid. A firm operating well below capacity may choose to bid less than a full cost, whereas, when operating near capacity, it may choose to submit a full-cost-plus-profit bid. In any event, the firm should avoid arbitrary cost estimating formulas, and instead prepare careful cost estimates based on realistic activity levels.

ESTIMATING THE PROBABILITY OF WINNING

As the example at the beginning of this chapter indicated, the theory of competitive bidding involves the use of probabilistic models. A key factor in submitting a bid is to estimate the chances of winning the contract. Assuming that the lowest bid will win the contract, as is true in most governmental bidding situations, then the problem is predicting how competitors will bid. Probabilistic bidding models assist a firm in determining a bid price that optimizes the combination of probability of winning and profit if it does win. Evidence shows that firms that use probabilistic bidding models have a better record of successful bids than firms that do not.[6]

[5]"Evaluation System Boosts Job Shop's Bidding Average," *Steel*, September 21, 1964, p. 47.

[6]Stephen Paranka, "The Pay-Off Concept in Competitive Bidding," *Business Horizons*, 12 (August 1969), 77–81.

Table 14-2   Evaluation of a Bid Opportunity

Prebid factor	Weight	Rating High, 10	Rating Medium, 5	Rating Low, 0	Score
Labor skills	20	10	. . .	. . .	200
Plant capacity	20	. . .	5	. . .	100
Followup	10	. . .	. . .	0	0
Design content	5	10	. . .	. . .	50
Competition	10	. . .	5	. . .	50
Familiarity	15	10	. . .	. . .	150
Delivery	10	. . .	5	. . .	50
Experience	10	10	. . .	. . .	100
Total	100				700

Minimum acceptable score: 650

There are a number of approaches to estimating the chances of winning. The *winning bid approach* simply uses the history of competitors' winning bids. The *average opponent approach* uses the history of competitors' winning and losing bids to represent the bidding behavior of an average opponent. The *specific opponent approach* uses the past bidding behavior of specific competitors. Each of these approaches will now be illustrated.

The Winning Bid Approach[7]

The estimation of the probability of winning is based on two assumptions: (1) that there is a constant relationship between competitors' estimates of direct costs and the bidder's direct cost estimates and (2) that competitors will act in the future as they have in the past. The second assumption can be relaxed by allowing decision makers to incorporate their subjective feelings in the analysis. To reflect the first assumption in the following discussion, all bids will be expressed as a percentage of the bidder's estimated direct costs. For example, with direct costs of $100,000, a bid of 120 percent is actually a bid of $120,000.

To utilize the winning bid approach requires only a knowledge of the history of previous winning bids. As shown in Table 14-3, the first step is to calculate the ratio of each winning bid to the firm's direct costs on that bid. Then, for selected bids, the fraction of competitors' winning bids that exceeds these bids is determined. Figure 14-1 illustrates the development of the data in step two into a probability curve. For example, a bid of 115 percent would have a 0.50 probability of winning.

As shown, the winning bid approach is a relatively simple way of estimating the probability of winning [$P(B)$]. Since it utilizes only the history of winning bids, it is best used when this history is the only available information.

[7]Discussion of these approaches to estimating the chances of winning are based on John F. Kottas and Basheer M. Khumawala, "Contract Bid Development for the Small Businessman," *Sloan Management Review*, 14 (Spring 1973), 31–45.

Table 14-3 Winning Bid Approach

Bid as a percent of direct cost (B)	Number of competitors' winning bids exceeding B	Fraction of competitors' winning bids exceeding B
90	100	$\frac{100}{100} = 1.00$
95	100	$\frac{100}{100} = 1.00$
100	95	$\frac{95}{100} = 0.95$
105	88	$\frac{88}{100} = 0.88$
110	75	$\frac{75}{100} = 0.75$
115	50	$\frac{50}{100} = 0.50$
120	30	$\frac{30}{100} = 0.30$
125	16	$\frac{16}{100} = 0.16$
130	5	$\frac{5}{100} = 0.05$
135	2	$\frac{2}{100} = 0.02$
140	0	$\frac{0}{100} = 0$

The Average Opponent Approach

The average opponent approach is more sophisticated in that it considers the number of competitors presenting bids. Although it does not require knowledge about specific competitors, it does consider all past winning and losing bids. The probability of underbidding the average opponent $[P_A(B)]$ is determined by calculating the fraction of all previous bids which exceeded selected bid values, as shown in Table 14-4. Figure 14-2 illustrates the development of this data into the probability curve for $P(B)$.

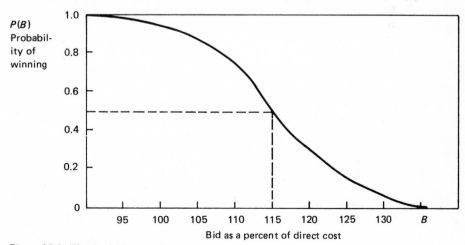

Figure 14-1 Winning bid approach.

Table 14-4 Average Opponent Approach

Bid as a percent of direct cost B	Fraction of previous bids exceeding B	Probability of underbidding N average opponents $[P_A(B)]^N$ (Number of opponents = N)				
		1	2	4	8	16
		$P_A(B)$	$P_A(B)^2$	$P_A(B)^4$	$P_A(B)^8$	$P_A(B)^{16}$
95	$\frac{100}{100}$	1.00	1.00	1.00	1.00	1.00
100	$\frac{95}{100}$	0.95	0.90	0.81	0.66	0.44
105	$\frac{90}{100}$	0.90	0.81	0.66	0.43	0.19
110	$\frac{85}{100}$	0.85	0.72	0.52	0.27	0.07
115	$\frac{75}{100}$	0.75	0.56	0.32	0.10	0.01
120	$\frac{60}{100}$	0.60	0.36	0.13	0.02	0
125	$\frac{40}{100}$	0.40	0.16	0.03	0	0
130	$\frac{20}{100}$	0.20	0.04	0	0	0
135	$\frac{5}{100}$	0.05	0	0	0	0
140	$\frac{2}{100}$	0.02	0	0	0	0

As Table 14-4 and Fig. 14-2 show, the probability of winning (underbidding) decreases as the number of competitors increases. By assuming each opponent to be average, the $P(B)$ is equal to the product of the chances of underbidding each of the N opponents with a bid of B:

$$P(B) = [P_A(B)]^N \tag{14-1}$$

Indeed, as the number of opponents increases, there is a rapid decrease in the chance of winning. For example, if the bid, B, is 115 and if there is only one other bidder, then the probability of winning the bid is $P(B) = P_A(B) = 0.75$. But if there are two opponents, then $P(B) = P_A(B)^2 = (0.75)^2 = 0.56$. With four opponents, then $P(B) = P_A(B)^4 = (0.75)^4 = 0.32$. Table 14-4 and Fig. 14-2 show these results and also the $P(B)$ for $N = 8$ and 16.

It should also be noted that the fewer the opponents, the greater is the opportunity for a winning bid to contribute to profit and overhead. For example, when there is only one opponent, four bids greater than 100 percent have better than a 50 percent chance of winning (120, 115, 110, 105). However, with four opponents, only bids of 110 and 105 have better than a 50 percent chance of winning and making a contribution to profits.

If, for a particular contract, it is not known exactly how many competitors will bid, the probability of the number of different opponents must be estimated. One approach is to calculate the proportion of times that different numbers of competitors have bid on a contract. If f_i is the proportion of time and there are i competitors, the chances of winning may be estimated using

$$P(B) = f_0 + f_1 P_A(B) + f_2 [P_A(B)]^2 + \ldots + f_N [P_A(B)]^N \qquad (14\text{-}2)$$

where f_0 is the estimated probability that there will be no competitors. (The sum of the f_i should equal one.) Suppose it is calculated that $f_0 = 0.1, f_1 = 0.4, f_2 = 0.3$, and $f_3 = 0.2$, and as given in Table 14-4, $P_A(120) = 0.60$. The chances of winning the contract with a bid of 120 is

$$\begin{aligned} P(120) &= 0.2 + 0.4(0.60) + 0.3(0.60)^2 + 0.2(0.60)^3 \\ &= 0.2 + 0.4(0.60) + 0.3(0.36) + 0.2(0.22) \\ &= 0.2 + 0.24 + 0.11 + 0.04 = .59 \end{aligned}$$

The advantage of the average opponent approach is that it allows for consideration of the number of bidders for a contract. When economic conditions are slow or when the contract is lucrative, generally the expected number of bidders increases. This, plus the fact that $P(B)$ is sensitive to the number of bidders, makes the average opponent approach more refined than the winning bid approach. However, a more sophisticated approach would be to consider the bidding behavior of specific competitors.

The Specific Opponent Approach

If the firm knows both the specific opponents that will bid on a contract and their history of previous bidding behavior, the specific opponent approach may be used. It is now necessary to estimate the chances of underbidding each opponent. Thus, the fraction of each competitor's bids that exceeds selected bid values must be calculated.

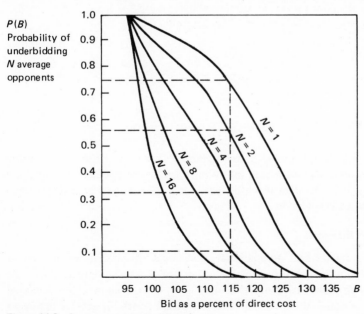

Figure 14-2 Average opponent approach.

To win the contract, the firm must bid lower than all competitors. The probability of underbidding all competitors is determined by multiplying the probabilities of underbidding each competitor.

$$P(B) = P_1(B) \times P_2(B) \times P_3(B) \times \ldots \times P_N(B) \qquad (14\text{-}3)$$

Table 14-5 and Fig. 14-3 illustrate the specific opponent approach when there are three rival competitors. Table 14-5 is constructed by computing the ratio that a specific bid was exceeded by a given competitor relative to the total number of times the opponent was a competitor.

In the usual bidding situation, potential bidders file an intention to bid and pay a fee for the project specifications by a specific date. Competitors who fail to file by the specified date are not eligible to bid. However, it is not certain that all eligible bidders will actually submit a bid. Thus, Eq. (14-3) needs to be modified by

$$P(B) = P_{S_1}(B) \times P_{S_2}(B) \times P_{S_3}(B) \times \ldots \times P_{SN}(B) \qquad (14\text{-}4)$$

where

$$P_{Si}(B) = p_i P_i(B) + (1 - p_i) \qquad i = 1, 2, \ldots, N \qquad (14\text{-}5)$$

The $P_{Si}(B)$ is the probability of underbidding specific competitor i with bid B. p_i is the fraction of times potential competitor i has submitted bids in previous similar situations. For example, suppose there are three potential competitors and that the fraction of times they have previously submitted bids are $p_1 = 0.5, p_2 = 0.8, p_3 = 0.6$. The probability of winning with a bid of 120 is determined using Table 14-5:

$$P_{S_1}(B) = 0.5(0.60) + (1 - 0.5) = 0.80$$
$$P_{S_2}(B) = 0.8(0.65) + (1 - 0.8) = 0.72$$
$$P_{S_3}(B) = 0.6(0.62) + (1 - 0.6) = 0.77$$
$$P(B) = 0.80(0.72)(0.77) = 0.44$$

Each of the above three approaches uses historical data only. However, often the decision maker has subjective feelings or intuition about the contract situation that are not revealed in the historical data. Each of these approaches may be modified by subjective estimates as described below.

Utilizing Subjective Estimates

An experienced contractor will normally have additional information about the prevailing economic conditions, the slack plant capacity of potential competitors, or the relative advantages an individual competitor may have, or may know about potential new competitors for which there are no historical data. In both the average opponent

Table 14-5 Specific Opponent Approach

Bid as a percent of direct costs B	Probability of underbidding competitor i (i = 1,2,3)			Overall probability of underbidding
	1	2	3	
95	1.00	1.00	1.00	1.00
100	0.95	0.98	0.95	0.88
105	0.90	0.95	0.85	0.73
110	0.85	0.88	0.80	0.60
115	0.75	0.80	0.70	0.42
120	0.60	0.65	0.62	0.24
125	0.40	0.45	0.40	0.07
130	0.20	0.22	0.15	0.01
135	0.05	0.10	0.05	0
140	0.02	0.05	0.01	0

or specific opponent approaches the decision maker may modify the f_i or the p_i to reflect the perceptions of the current bidding situation. Moreover, the bidder may modify the $P_A(B)$ or the $P_{Si}(B)$ to reflect the perceptions of the bidding situation.

For example, when economic conditions are slack and plant capacity utilization is low, a firm can expect more competitive bids at or near estimated direct costs. But when many or all competitors are operating close to plant capacity, the firm can expect fewer bids and these bids are more likely to be higher than estimated direct costs. Again, the estimation procedure outlined in Chap. 2 can be used effectively. Sewall[8] has described the use of a similar procedure for a New York contractor.

Combining the Specific and Average Opponent Approaches

Often the firm knows some of its potential competitors but has reason to believe other, unknown competitors will enter the bidding competition. The chances of underbidding the specific, known competitors can be determined using Eq. (14-4) or (14-5). The other, unknown competitors' behavior must be estimated using Eq. (14-1) or (14-2). To win, the firm must underbid all competitors. The probability of doing this can be estimated using[9]

$$P(B) = P_{NC}(B) \times P_{UC}(B) \tag{14-6}$$

where $P_{NC}(B)$ = probability of underbidding all specific, known competitors
$P_{UC}(B)$ = probability of underbidding all unknown competitors considered as an average opponent

[8]Murphy Sewall, "A Decision Calculus Model for Contract Bidding," *Journal of Marketing*, 40 (October 1976), 92–98.
[9]See ibid. for an application of this approach.

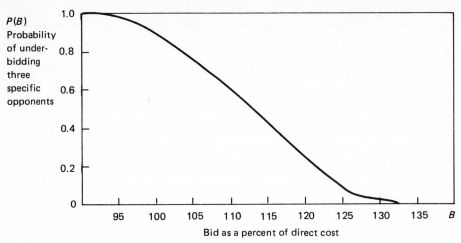

Figure 14-3 Specific opponent approach.

DETERMINING THE BEST BID

As mentioned above, probabilistic bidding models assist the firm in determining a bid
price that optimizes the combination of the probability of winning and of making a
profit if the bid wins. The optimum bid is the bid that offers the highest expected contribution to profit and overhead. The expected contribution of a bid $E(B)$ is determined by multiplying the probability of winning with a bid, $P(B)$, by the difference
between the bid price and the estimated direct costs $(B - C)$:

$$E(B) = (B - C) \times P(B) \tag{14-7}$$

Table 14-6 and Fig. 14-4 illustrate the relationship between the probability of winning and expected contribution. As indicated in Table 14-6 and Fig. 14-4, the maximum expected profit occurs with a bid of 115. The expectation curve in Fig. 14-4
shows the expected profit contribution corresponding to each bid. The optimum bid is
115, or 15 percent above direct cost. Zero expectation will always occur at a bid equal
to direct cost. A bid below direct costs will always have a negative expectation and
bids above direct costs will range upward from zero to an upper value, and then taper
off, reaching zero again for bids far above direct costs.

Sometimes a firm may wish to maximize expected contributions, but only with
some minimum probability of winning the bid. For example, assume that a firm
wishes to have at least a probability of 0.60 of winning the contract. The firm is in
need of some work, has sufficient short-term financial resources, and does not feel
the need to maximize its expected contributions. As shown in Table 14-6, a bid of
110 is the best bid since the expected contribution of 6 percent is the best under the
probability of winning constraint.

On the other hand, the firm may already be operating near capacity and will only
consider new business if it has higher than usual contributions. If, for example, the
firm decides that a contribution of 20 percent is the lowest it will accept, then a bid

Table 14-6 Expected Contributions in Relation to Size of Bid

Bid as a percent of direct cost B	Probability of bid winning P(B)	Contribution margin, percent, (B - C)	Expected contribution from bid, percent, E(B)
80	1.00	-20	-20
85	1.00	-15	-15
90	1.00	-10	-10
95	1.00	- 5	- 5
100	0.88	0	0
105	0.73	5	3.65
110	0.60	10	6.00
115	0.42	15	6.30
120	0.24	20	4.80
125	0.07	25	1.75
130	0.01	30	0.30
135	0	35	0
140	0	40	0

of 120 maximizes the expected contribution subject to the contribution margin constraint.

As these examples indicate, frequently a firm will change its bidding objectives depending on the overall bidding situation. Regardless of the objective selected, the firm ultimately must trade off the chances of winning against maximizing expected contributions to select the best bid. The procedures outlined above allow management to consider the firm's objectives, its market and financial positions, current and future

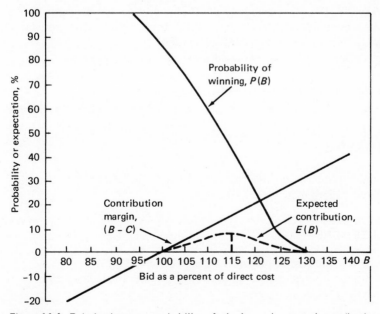

Figure 14-4 Relation between probability of winning and expected contribution.

competition, and current and future opportunities to select the best bidding strategy. Moreover, these procedures also allow for management to *subjectively* change the data to reflect current perceptions of the bidding situation.

BIDDING WITH CAPACITY CONSTRAINTS

As briefly indicated above, a firm may be offered the opportunity to bid on a project when it is operating near full capacity. In such a situation, the contribution margin criterion is insufficient to help the firm set its bidding strategy. When operating at or near full capacity, the firm is in a position to allocate its resources to *maximize contributions per resource unit*. Chapter 15 develops this criterion and shows its application to pricing. When capacity constraints exist, the bidding firm should substitute the contribution per resource unit criterion for contribution margin in the analytical procedures developed in this chapter, and then proceed as usual.

SUMMARY

This chapter has presented an overview of the problem of developing bids for providing products or services on an order basis. Applications of direct costing and considerations of competitive strategy have been explored. Finally, the problem of pricing with capacity constraints has been briefly considered. Pricing with scarce resources will be developed in Chap. 15.

The most serious limitation of a probabilistically developed bidding strategy is the assumption that competitors will follow the same bidding behavior in the future as they have followed in the past. There is no guarantee that this assumption will prevail. Hence, it is important that any analytical procedure provide for management to change the data based on subjective criteria that reflect its perceptions. The procedures outlined in this chapter permit such subjective adaptation.

Overall, a probabilistic bidding model provides a guide for management in

1 Evaluating the chances of winning a particular contract
2 Recognizing the profit potential that can be expected under various bidding situations
3 Identifying projects in which the expense of preparing and submitting a bid is not economically justified

Competitive bidding models provide management with useful and objective procedures for developing appropriate pricing strategies.

DISCUSSION QUESTIONS

1 What is the most difficult part of preparing a competitive bid? Why?
2 Why should a firm perform an analysis to determine whether to prepare a bid?

3 a Describe the steps involved in prebid analysis.

   b Assume that a prebid analysis has produced the result given in Table 14-2. To what extent should this prebid analysis influence the bid that will eventually be made? Why?

   c Suppose that the evaluation shown in Table 14-2 led to an assigned weight of 10 for the followup factor. What would be the total score for the bid now? Would this high score on followup affect your answer on how the prebid analysis might influence the bid that will eventually be made? Why or why not?

4 A firm was preparing a bid on a government contract for an electronic part in a new missile guidance system. The contract was for 10,000 units. The company has also determined that it is likely that five other companies will bid on the contract. Two of these potential bidders have never bid against the firm before, but management believes that these new bidders will be similar to previous opponents on other government contracts. Direct costs for producing one of these electronic parts is estimated to average $100 if the firm wins the contract. Moreover, it is likely that the government will ask for another round of bids on this electronic part within 18 months after this current contract is settled. The firm believes that the 10,000 units can be produced and delivered within 15 months of the contract award. Assume that the data given in Tables 14-4 and 14-5 are relevant for this firm's initial bid. Prepare an analysis for this bid opportunity. What bid would you recommend? Why?

SUGGESTED READINGS

Edelman, Franz: "Art and Science of Competitive Bidding," *Harvard Business Review*, 43 (July–August 1965), 53–66.

Kottas, John F., and Basheer M. Khumawala: "Contract Bid Development for the Small Businessman," *Sloan Management Review*, (Spring 1973), pp. 31–45.

Paranka, Stephen: "The Pay-Off Concept in Competitive Bidding," *Business Horizons*, 12 (August 1969), 77–81.

_____: "Competitive Bidding Strategy," *Business Horizons*, 14 (June 1971), 39–43.

Sewall, Murphy: "A Decision Calculus Model for Contract Bidding," *Journal of Marketing*, 40 (October 1976), 92–98.

Chapter 15

Pricing with
Scarce Resources

During the past few years, a number of economic problems have occurred that businesspeople and economists did not expect: shortages of critical materials, uncontrollable inflation even during a recession, and a lack of sufficient amounts of new capital to overcome material shortages. During 1973 and 1974 the world demand for materials overtook supply. Suddenly, there were shortages of metals, wood products, and agricultural products.[1] "Typical of the problems faced by industry were those of Del Monte where the company faced shortages of fruits and vegetables, glass for jars, tinplate for cans, fibreboard for boxes, and labels for the jars and cans."[2]

To cope with these shortages and with other economic problems, it has been suggested that the marketing manager assume new responsibilities and develop alternative marketing strategies.[3] As often happens when an unexpected problem occurs, many different marketing strategies have been tried out, with varying degrees of success. Within the area of pricing, it has become readily apparent that firms must develop a positive and responsive approach to cope with the many new economic uncertainties.

[1] "The 1970's: A Second Look," *Business Week*, September 14, 1974, pp. 50–162.
[2] "The Two-Way Squeeze on New Products," *Business Week*, August 10, 1974, pp. 130–132.
[3] Philip Kotler, "Marketing during Periods of Shortage," *Journal of Marketing*, 38 (July 1974), 20–29; Nessim Hanna, A. H. Kizinbash, and Albert Smart, "Marketing Strategy under Conditions of Economic Scarcity," *Journal of Marketing*, 39 (July 1975), 63–67; Avraham Shama, "Marketing Management during Periods of Stagflation," *Journal of Marketing*, forthcoming.

Tightening credit policies, reducing or eliminating quantity and cash discounts, refusing to quote a "firm" price at the time of bids on contracts, pricing services separately from the product, and establishing "one-price policies" are some of the pricing strategies that have been used.[4]

The problem of scarce resources has led some companies to prune their product lines by eliminating slow-moving and low-margin products. However, the elimination of products on the basis of the size of margin is primarily a defensive strategy and ignores the role price may play. When a firm is operating at or near full capacity, or when key resources are scarce, the firm must determine how scarce resources can be allocated to its products so as to maximize contribution to fixed costs and profits.

This chapter discusses the special pricing problem that arises when a multiple-product firm is operating at or near capacity or when key resources are scarce. The purposes of the chapter are (1) to demonstrate the inadequacy of the gross margin criterion when resources are scarce; (2) to develop a new criterion using contribution analysis; and (3) to illustrate applications of the new decision criterion.

THE PROBLEM OF COMMON RESOURCES[5]

The multiproduct firm typically uses joint or common resources to produce various product lines. The same plant and equipment may be used, as well as similar research and development facilities. Likewise, the same selling, administrative, and warehousing facilities may be used in the production and sale of the various products. Moreover, a critical or scarce resource may be used in the production of these products.

Because product prices must reflect the competitive situation and the reactions of buyers, as well as costs and corporate objectives, not all products make the same use of resources per dollar of revenue or per dollar of out-of-pocket costs. However, when determining prices, it is important to consider the degree to which products (or special orders) use available facilities (capacity) and consume available resources. Otherwise, the firm may be short of the necessary resources to obtain the desired level of contribution.

Indeed, pricing special orders or composing the product line strictly on contribution (gross margin) may result in the exhaustion of available resources without obtaining the target contribution. In Table 15-1A, the basic price and cost data for a product line are provided. Table 15-1B provides the demand forecasts, cost estimates, and required supply of a common resource material to meet the demand forecast.

As shown in Table 15-1A, product C contributes $1.00 per unit sold to cover fixed expenses and profits. This unit contribution by product C is $0.24 larger than B's unit contribution, and $0.41 larger than A's unit contribution. However, in Table 15-1B it

---

[4]Joseph P. Guiltinan, "Risk-Aversive Pricing Policies: Problems and Alternatives," *Journal of Marketing*, 40 (January 1976), 10–15; Joseph P. Guiltinan and Kent B. Monroe, "Making Sound Pricing Decisions in the Current Economic Environment," *Executive Scene*, 3 (October 1974), 11–16; "Pricing Strategy in an Inflation Economy," *Business Week*, April 6, 1974, pp. 43–49.
[5]Much of the material in this chapter is adopted from Kent B. Monroe and Andris A. Zoltners, "Pricing the Product Line during Periods of Scarcity," working paper, 1978.

can be seen that because of total expected demand, the total dollar contribution is larger for product B, with product C ranked second, and product A ranked third.

In this illustration, two common resources are required to produce the three products; labor and material. However, the mix of labor and material required to produce a unit of each product is quite different. Indeed, product A is a relatively labor-intensive product since 74.5 percent of its direct variable costs are due to labor. However, products B and C owe only 32.3 and 20 percent, respectively, of their direct costs to labor. Hence, products B and C require much more material input.

Now suppose that this common material resource currently is scarce and the firm has been advised that it can acquire no more than 3,000 tons during the planning period. Furthermore, the supply of this material is expected to be below demand for at least several years. The firm must now consider the alternatives of reducing the production of each product, eliminating a product and reducing the production of the other products, or some reasonable combination of these two choices. Clearly, the firm has a problem of allocating the scarce resource to its products in the product line.

RESOURCE ALLOCATION CRITERIA

A number of criteria have been used to make this decision. Some firms allocate the scarce resource according to the *unit contributions* (gross margin) of each product.

Table 15-1   Product-Line Contribution Analysis

		Product		Total
	A	B	C	
A. Unit data				
1. Price	$2.20	$3.00	$4.00	
Variable costs:				
2. Direct labor	$1.20	$ .70	$ .60	
3. Direct materials	.41	1.54	2.40	
4. Total	$1.61	$2.24	$3.00	
5. Contribution (1 – 4)	$ .59	$ .76	$1.00	
B. Data for planning period				
6. Demand (units)	6,200	8,100	5,000	
7. Revenue (1 × 6)	$13,640	$24,300	$20,000	$57,940
8. Direct labor (2 × 6)	$ 7,440	$ 5,670	$ 3,000	$16,110
9. Direct materials (3 × 6)	$ 2,542	$12,474	$12,000	$27,016
10. Contribution (5 × 6)	$ 3,658	$ 6,156	$ 5,000	$14,814
11. Tons of material required	500	2,500	2,400	5,400
12. Units per ton (6 ÷ 11)	12.4	3.24	2.083	
13. Tons per unit (11 ÷ 6)	0.081	0.309	0.480	

Since product C has the largest unit contribution, the first 2,400 tons would be allocated to C and the remaining 600 tons to B. As Table 15-2 shows, the total contribution for the planning period would be $6,477, or $8,337 less than total contributions with no scarce resource.

Other firms make their allocations on the basis of *total contributions*. Since product B has the largest total contribution, product B would be allocated 2,500 tons. Product C would be allocated 500 tons because its total contribution is second in amount for the period. The total period contribution under this plan improves to $7,197, but still is $7,617 less than period contributions with no scarce resource. If the firm adopted either of these two plans, it would be necessary to eliminate product A from the line.

A third alternative would be to allocate the scarce material *proportionately on the basis of resource requirements*. Since product A requires 500/5,400 or 9 percent of the scarce resource if no constraints are present, it would be allocated 9 percent or 270 tons of material. The material would be allocated to B and C in similar fashion and total period contribution improves to $8,197.

As is apparent from Table 15-2, the contribution or margin criteria are inferior to the third allocation criterion. Moreover, contribution to overhead and profits is greater under the third alternative and it is not necessary to eliminate a product from the line.

As demonstrated above, pricing a product line strictly on gross contribution or margin may result in the exhaustion of available resources without obtaining the largest contribution to profits possible. Essentially, the margin approach does not consider how much of the scarce resource is consumed per unit of output.

The data in Table 15-1 demonstrate that a ton of the resource material is necessary to produce 12.4 units of A, 3.24 units of B, and 2.083 units of C. As shown in

Table 15-2 Alternative Resource Allocations

Criterion	Resource units	Units produced	Total contribution
Contribution per unit:			
A	0	0	$ -0-
B	600	1,944	$1,477
C	2,400	5,000	5,000
			$6,477
Total contribution:			
A	0	0	$ -0-
B	2,500	8,100	6,156
C	500	1,041	1,041
			$7,197
Proportion of resources required:			
A	270	3,348	$1,975
B	1,410	4,568	3,472
C	1,320	2,750	2,750
			$8,197

Table 15-2, a resource allocation method that allocates less resources to C and B and more to A improves contribution. Hence, what is necessary is to develop a criterion that utilizes the information on how products consume scarce resources.

THE CONTRIBUTION PER RESOURCE UNIT CRITERION

As the data in Table 15-1B indicate, it requires 0.081 ton of the scarce resource to produce a unit of product A, 0.309 ton to produce a unit of product B, and 0.48 ton to produce a unit of product C. At the current prices (Table 15-1A), each unit of A produces $0.59 contribution. Thus, 0.081 ton of scarce material helps produce a $0.59 contribution. Therefore, a ton of the material produces $0.59/0.081 or $7.28 contribution per ton. Similarly, for product B, the contribution per ton is $0.76/0.309, or $2.46. And for product C, the contribution per ton is $1.00/0.48 or $2.08. These calculations can also be made using the period planning data from Table 15-1B and are shown in Table 15-3.

What the data of Table 15-3 indicate is that the first 500 tons of the scarce material should be allocated to product A since each ton used in product A contributes more to profits and to covering fixed costs. This allocation procedure is followed because product A has the highest *contribution per resource unit* (ton). And, when the resource is in limited supply, the decision criterion is to allocate resources to the profit segments with the highest contribution per resource unit (CPRU). Following this decision criterion, Table 15-4 shows that product C, the highest priced, largest unit margin product, is a candidate for elimination.

This illustration provides a fundamental principle: *When the volume of products that could be sold is greater than the resource capacity to produce them, the largest contribution (and profit) results from producing those products and orders that generate the greatest contribution per resource unit used.* The factors that cause the bottleneck could be machines, equipment, time, skilled labor, materials, or cash.

PRICING THE PRODUCT LINE USING CPRU

If the firm wishes to maintain the prices shown in Table 15-1, then the best decision is to use the CPRU criterion and suspend production of product C. However, from a marketing viewpoint it may be desirable to keep product C in the line. For example, demand for product C may be expected to grow in the near future or the product

Table 15-3   Contribution per Resource Unit (CPRU)

	Product		
	A	B	C
1. Contribution	$3,658	$6,156	$5,000
2. Resource units	500	2,500	2,400
3. CPRU (1 ÷ 2)	$ 7.28	$ 2.46	$ 2.08

Table 15–4   Resource Allocation using CPRU

Product	Resource units	Units produced	Total contribution
A	500	6,200	$3,658
B	2,500	8,100	6,156
C	0	0	-0-
			$9,814

may be necessary to complete the product line. The firm should then consider re-pricing products C and B to increase their relative CPRUs. Initially, the analytical question is "What should the prices of C and B be so as to equalize contributions?" Table 15–5 shows that the price of C must be $6.49 and the price of B must be $4.49. However, it is unlikely that the original demand forecast will be valid at these prices. Hence, a lower production volume would be required, which would reduce some of the firm's demand for the scarce material. Thus, what is needed is a solution technique that incorporates price-volume relationships as well as cost-volume relationships. We will now describe such a solution technique.

If the firm desires to reprice some or all of the products in the line, then, assuming a constant price of the scarce material, higher prices will improve the contribution per resource unit consumed. But raising the prices of some or all of the products in the line can naturally be expected to reduce demand, and the pricing decision may be used to allocate demand. (Some executives have confided to the author that they followed such a pricing policy during the oil crisis of the mid-1970s.) Also, the reduction of product-line demand due to price increases leads to lower production requirements, which reduces the firm's demand for the scarce material.

It should be apparent that, to do further pricing analysis, one must know the demand curve for each product in the line. Generally, executives may follow the operational approach described in Chap. 2 to develop subjective estimates of the price-volume relationships. Given the ability to obtain reasonable price-volume estimates for each product, the pricing problem becomes amenable to solution using a computerized technique.[6]

To illustrate, assume the price-volume relationship is linear for each product, as shown in Fig. 15–1. The prices that will enable the firm to achieve maximum total contribution subject to the scarce resource constraint are given in Table 15–6. Given the demand relationship depicted in Fig. 15–1, the prices shown in Table 15–6 enable the firm to maximize contributions.

However, management may feel that such relatively large price increases are not desirable because of potential loss of customer goodwill, relative competitive prices, and potential government intervention. Further, such a large price increase may dampen long-run demand, particularly if one or more of the products is in the growth stage of its life cycle. The firm may also wish to have wider price differentials to maintain perceptual differences in the product line. Hence, the solution technique should

[6]The solution technique is described in Kent B. Monroe and Andris A. Zoltners, ibid.

Table 15-5 Pricing to Equalize CPRU

		Product	
		B	C
1.	Desired CPRU	$ 7.28	$ 7.28
2.	Total resources required	2,500	2,400
3.	Desired contribution (1 × 2)	$18,200	$17,472
4.	Variable costs	$18,144	$15,000
5.	Total revenue required (3 + 4)	$36,344	$32,472
6.	Original demand forecast	8,100	5,000
7.	New selling price (5 ÷ 6)	$ 4.49	$ 6.49

be used to find the optimum solution; the firm can then estimate the profit implications of moving to another solution because of realistic, but unquantifiable, marketing considerations.

The effect of adjusting the optimal prices may be assessed using the CPRU criterion with a different set of prices. For example, a firm may believe that the prices should be no higher than $5, $5, and $6 respectively; the product manager feels that these prices are realistic and suitable for both the firm's long-run objectives and environmental considerations. Total demand at these prices will exceed the firm's production capacity. The solution shown in Table 15-7 is the best product mix using the CPRU criterion relative to the prices stated. Table 15-7 shows that the price constraint causes the total contribution to profit to decline by $1,347.04. In general, the CPRU criterion provides the best solution when there are resource constraints and price ceilings.

PRICING SPECIAL ORDERS

The contribution per resource unit criterion may be used even when a firm is not operating at capacity or is faced with the shortage of critical resources. Essentially, use of the CPRU when establishing prices provides a means of maintaining consis-

Table 15-6 Optimal Solution, Linear Price-Volume Function, and Resource Constraints

	Product		
	A	B	C
Price	$ 5.03	$ 5.27	$ 6.18
Volume	3,370	4,468	2,820
Contribution	$11,525.40	$13,538.04	$8,967.60
Resources required (tons)	271.77	1,379.01	1,353.82

Total contribution: $34,031.04
Total resources required: 3,004.6 tons*

*Excess due to rounding the prices.

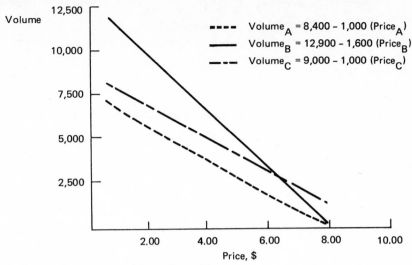

Figure 15-1 Linear price-volume relationship.

tency over customers, product lines, or special orders. A special order arises when an established customer places an order for a quantity different from the normal one, when a nonregular customer makes a one-time-only order for a substantial quantity, or when an order is placed for a product not usually produced by the firm, but which the firm has capability for producing. In each of these situations, the firm must establish a price that is consistent with prices for regular products and customers and is acceptable to the originator of the special order. The CPRU criterion is useful in pricing such a special order.

To illustrate the application of the CPRU to pricing special orders, assume that the firm normally sells a product in a standard order of 500 units. Further, the basic cost and contribution data for a standard order are given in Table 15-8A. On a standard order of 500 units, the firm spends 10 hours to set up the production equipment to

Table 15-7 Optimum Price Solution: Resource and Price Constraints

	Product		
	A	B	C
1. Price	$ 5.00	$ 5.00	$ 6.00
2. Variable cost	1.61	2.24	3.00
3. Contribution (1 − 2)	$ 3.39	$ 2.76	$ 3.00
4. Demand (units)	3,340	4,900	3,000
5. Units produced	3,400	4,900	2,528
6. Resources required (tons)	274.19	1,512.34	1,213.47
7. Contribution (3 × 5)	$11,526	$13,524	$7,584
8. CPRU (7 ÷ 6)	$ 42.04	$ 8.94	$ 6.25

Total contribution: $32,634
Total resources required: 3,000 tons

Table 15–8
CPRU Pricing of a Special Order

A. Data for standard order (500 units)

1. Revenue at $10.00 selling price.		$5,000
2. Variable costs		
Setup cost (10 hours @ $7/hour).	$ 70	
Machine cost (100 hours @ $4.50/hour).	450	
Materials ($3.00 per unit).	1,500	
Total.		2,020
3. Contribution		$2,980
4. Total hours (10 hours + 100 hours)		110
5. CPRU per hour (3 ÷ 4).		$27.09

B. Data for 1,000-unit orders

1. Desired CPRU per hour	$ 27.09	
Time required (hours):		
Setup	10	
Machine (100 × 2).	200	
2. Total hours	210	
3. Required order contribution (1 × 2).		$5,688.90
4. Variable costs		
Setup cost (10 hours @ $7/hour).	$ 70.00	
Machine cost (200 hours @ $4.50/hour).	900.00	
Materials (3.00 per unit).	3,000.00	
Total.		3,970.00
5. Required sales volume for 1,000 units (3 + 4)		$9,658.90
6. Unit selling price (5 ÷ 1,000)		$ 9.66

make the production run. Labor costs per hour for a production setup are $7.00. The standard hourly rate for the machines used in the process is $4.50 and five units can be produced per hour. Therefore, an order of 500 units requires 100 hours of machine time. A standard order of 500 units currently is priced at $10.00 per unit or $5,000 per order.

Suppose a nonregular customer approaches the firm with an offer for a one-time-only order for 1,000 units. This potential customer is aware that a standard order is 500 units at a price of $10.00. However, the customer asks for a price quotation. Obviously, the customer is seeking a lower price than $10.00 per unit. The firm has the capacity to handle this special order but wishes to be consistent in its price quotation to be able to justify such a lower price to regular customers should they object.

The data of Table 15–8A indicate that the CPRU per production hour is $27.09 for a standard production run (order) of 500 units. The data of Table 15–8B show the calculations for determining the selling price that meets the two objectives of (1) a lower per unit price and (2) maintaining the CPRU. The price that satisfies these objectives is $9.66 per unit for an order size of 1,000 units.

It is important to note that this price will not necessarily be attractive to the buyer. Nor does the price of $9.66 imply that the seller could not get more from the customer for a 1,000 unit order. But, the price does provide to management information on the costs and the necessary markup to achieve a specific profit objective. Other alternative selling prices can be developed that take into consideration specific demand, competitive and other market factors. Essentially, the CPRU criterion as applied to the pricing of special orders gives management a specific price alternative for a given profit contribution objective.

SUMMARY

Noting that during times of scarcity the firm is faced with problems of determining the optimum product mix and a set of profit-maximizing prices, this chapter has developed a criterion for these decisions. It has been shown that the largest contribution per resource unit (CPRU) criterion should be used. Further, as many firms have recognized, it has been shown that price may be used effectively to shift demand to the products with the largest CPRUs. However, when prices are changed, the quantity demanded changes and a new optimum product mix results.

The structure of this decision problem is amenable to analysis using computer programming procedures. Taking a specific product-line example, the chapter has briefly illustrated the use of the CPRU principle. Any price-volume relationship that can be readily estimated by a product manager may be used in the analysis. If a linear relationship is used, the manager needs to provide only two price-volume estimates for each product in the product line. If other types of demand functions are used, the manager must provide several price-volume relationships. In any event, a firm's periodic planning efforts typically provide and utilize such price-volume estimates.

Additional reasons for focusing on maximizing contribution are to minimize data requirements for the solution technique and to observe the dynamic price-volume-cost relationships as the product mix changes. As long as fixed or period costs do not change when the product or sales mix is altered, then maximizing contribution will provide the optimum strategy. The accounting data required are the direct product cost and the amount of scarce resource needed to produce an order or product. Such data are normally available from the firm's cost accounting system.

The contribution per resource unit criterion is best used when productive capacity is constrained by a bottleneck. Factors that may cause the bottleneck are machines, equipment, time, skilled labor, materials, or cash. Any industry or product line that depends heavily on a single resource would be particularly suited to the use of the CPRU criterion and the analysis outlined in this chapter. For example, product lines heavily dependent on petrochemicals, the paper industry, drugs, and fertilizers all are dependent on critical materials. Several years ago the candy industry could obtain sugar, but because of high prices, did not have the cash resources to acquire the necessary sugar tonnage to meet demand. More recently, the high price of cocoa beans produced a chocolate constraint on the candy industry.[7]

This chapter has demonstrated the inadequacy of the gross margin criterion for product-mix and pricing decisions when the firm is operating at capacity due to resource constraints. It has been shown that the contribution per resource unit is a

---

[7] See "Inflation Bites Chocolate Again," *Business Week*, August 29, 1977, p. 28.

superior criterion and that pricing and production decisions may be enhanced using this criterion.

It has also been shown that the CPRU criterion is applicable to the pricing of special orders when management wishes to have a consistent pricing approach. When a particular resource is in short supply, thereby creating a production bottleneck, or the firm is operating at or near full productive capacity, or there is a special pricing situation, application of the CPRU criterion gives management the information on costs and markups needed to achieve a specific objective. But, as with any other approach developed in this book, the CPRU criterion does not necessarily specify the correct price for the particular situation. Management, in the final analysis, must still make that decision.

DISCUSSION QUESTIONS

1 When a firm is faced with scarce resources or is operating at productive capacity, what are some of the pricing problems that may result?
2 What problems are created by simply raising prices when the demand for a firm's output is greater than the firm can supply?
3 Why is the CPRU criterion superior to other criteria when a firm is operating with scarce resources?
4 a When a common resource is used to produce multiple products, what problems result when a firm tries to reprice its product line?
  b Would these problems be similar if the firm added a new product to the line that was produced using a resource common to the product line?
  c Would your answer to part b differ if the common resource was not in scarce supply?
5 What information is necessary when repricing a product line under conditions of scarce common resources?
6 a What are the problems of pricing special orders?
  b How may the CPRU be used to analyze the special-order pricing problem?

SUGGESTED READINGS

Guiltinan, Joseph P.: "Risk-Aversive Pricing Policies: Problems and Alternatives," *Journal of Marketing*, 40 (January 1976), 10–15.
Hanna, Nessim: "10 Ways Inflation-Recession Challenge Marketers with Pricing Responsibilities," *Marketing News*, 8 (February 28, 1975).
Kniffen, Fred: " 'Stagflation' Pricing—Seven Ways You Might Improve Your Decision," *Marketing News*, 8 (November 15, 1974).
Kotler, Philip: "Marketing during Periods of Shortage," *Journal of Marketing*, 38 (July 1974), 20–29.

Chapter 16

Justifying Price Differentials

One of the most complex and frustrating areas of pricing is the problem of justifying price differentials. This problem may arise (1) when a customer believes that he or she has been illegally charged a price higher than the price charged to other customers for the same product; (2) when a competitor believes that a rival's prices are lower in markets where they both compete than in markets where they do not compete; (3) when the government believes that competing customers of a seller are charged different prices; and (4) when price increases must be justified to customers, sales force, or a price control board. Conditions (1), (2), and (3) generally arise as a result of legal proceedings after a charge of illegal price discrimination. The fourth condition prevails primarily during inflationary periods. For example, when double-digit inflation was present during the early 1970s, price increases had to be cost-justified to a price control commission, and even when the price control commission approved such price increases, firms often found it necessary to justify price changes both to their sales force and to their customers. "We ask them to justify [every price increase]," says Peter Tremblay, purchasing agent for Gillette Co.[1] (And the firm's sales personnel were often the least satisfied by such justification attempts.)

The purpose of this chapter is to illustrate how price differentials may be justified when a firm is faced with either litigation or disgruntled customers and sales force.

[1] Terry Kirkpatrick: "Purchasing for a Corporation: Buyer Fights Nightmare of Inflation," *Roanoke Times and World-News*, August 13, 1978, p. D1.

249

The main emphasis will be on developing a cost justification for price differentials. Although other legally defensible approaches will be discussed, cost justification of price differentials seems to have wider application than these other approaches. A valid cost justification can be used to prevent further litigation as well as to soothe disgruntled customers. Other legal defenses are suitable only within the legal arena.

The chapter begins by discussing the nature of price discrimination. Then the provisions of the Robinson-Patman Act will be summarized, along with a brief interpretation of its litigation history. A specific section on the cost justification defense including guidelines for a cost justification study will follow. The chapter concludes with a case example of justifying differential prices.

THE NATURE OF PRICE DISCRIMINATION

Both the Clayton Act (1914) and the Robinson-Patman Act (1936) prohibit illegal price discrimination. But neither Act prohibits price differences, as is so often believed. In fact, price discrimination can be found in many markets. First, price discrimination in selling to ultimate consumers is assumed by the Federal Trade Commission, the courts, lawyers, and marketers to be legal. Many cases of permissible and accepted price discrimination involve ultimate consumers (see Table 16-1). Secondly, in the situation with businesses selling to businesses, the Robinson-Patman Act does indicate when it may be lawful to discriminate on the basis of price.

Economically, price discrimination occurs whenever there are price differences for the same product or service sold by a single seller that are not justified by cost differences or by changes in the level of demand. Price discrimination also occurs when two or more buyers of the same product or service are charged the same price despite differences in the cost of serving these buyers.[2] Thus, to know whether price discrimination exists, in the economic sense, between two or more buyers, it is necessary to know both the price and the total relevant costs applicable in each instance of possible discrimination.

As indicated by the way price was defined in Chap. 1, price discrimination may arise in a variety of ways. The product sold to some buyers may be physically different—of different quality. There may be differences in services that accompany the products, for example, delivery, storage, credit extension, sales force efforts. Some buyers may qualify for volume, cash, or trade discounts. Hence, whether there is price discrimination in the economic sense depends on analyzing the factual detail surrounding the involved transactions.

However, the legal basis for price discrimination goes beyond the economic tests mentioned above. Indeed, the Robinson-Patman Act sets out conditions beyond cost differences in which price discrimination may legally exist. We turn now to an overview of the Robinson-Patman Act.[3]

---

[2] *The Attorney General's National Committee to Study the Antitrust Laws*, (Washington, D.C.: Office of the *Federal Register*, National Archives and Records Service, 1955), pp. 333–336.

[3] For an excellent presentation of economic and legal bases for price discrimination in utility rate-making, see *Legal Memorandum of Assistant General Counsel*, Litigation Division on Discriminatory and Preferential Practices under the Postal Reorganization Act, Washington, D.C., Postal Rate Commission, Docket No. *mc*73-1, April 15, 1974.

Table 16-1 Types of Price Discrimination

Class	Bases of discrimination	Examples
Personal	Buyer's income or earning power	Doctor's fees, royalties paid for use of patented machines, professional association dues
Group	Age, sex, military status or student status of buyer	Children's haircuts, ladies days, airline tickets, magazine subscription rates, theater admission charges, senior citizen rates
	Location of buyers	Zone prices ("prices slightly higher west of the Rockies"), in-state vs. out-of-state tuition
	Status of buyers	New magazine subscriptions, quantity discounts to large volume buyers
	Use of product	Railroad rates, public utility rates
Product	Qualities of products	Deluxe vs. regular models
	Labels of products	National, private, or unbranded
	Product size	Family, economy, giant size
	Peak–off peak services	Off-season resort rates, airline excursion rates, evening and holiday telephone rates

Source: Adapted from Donald Watson, *Price Theory and Its Uses*, 1st ed. (Boston: Houghton Mifflin, 1963), p. 312.

PROVISIONS OF THE ROBINSON–PATMAN ACT

Section 2 of the Clayton Act sought to prevent sellers from cutting prices in areas where strong competition existed while maintaining higher prices in areas with no or little competition. Essentially, the Act was aimed at preventing local price cutting. However, Section 2 was also interpreted as applying to price discrimination among competing buyers.

During the 20 years following passage of the Clayton Act in 1914, chain stores grew rapidly and increased their buying power. As the chain's buying power increased, some chain buyers began coercing price concessions to their advantage. This type of price discrimination behavior was thought to threaten the survival of independent wholesalers and retailers, and Section 2 was insufficient to protect these independent distributors. Hence, in 1936, Congress passed the Robinson-Patman Act as an amendment to the Clayton Act.

Section 2 of the Robinson-Patman Act amends Section 2 of the Clayton Act and is divided into six parts. Section 2 of the Robinson-Patman Act contains civil prohibitions and Section 3 lists criminal prohibitions.

Section 2(a) is the backbone of the Act. It prohibits sellers from charging different prices to different buyers for similar products where the effect might be to injure, destroy, or prevent competition, in either the buyers' or sellers' market. It also provides a defense when a price discrimination can be cost-justified by the seller, and other limited defenses and exceptions.

Section 2(b) is related to 2(a) and places the burden of proof on the person charged with a price discrimination violation under 2(a). Section 2(b) also provides a defense if the seller can prove that the lower price was made to equal a lawful, low price of a competitor.

Section 2(c) prohibits the seller from paying and the buyer from receiving any brokerage fee, commission, or other form of compensation for a transaction.

Sections 2(d) and 2(e) prohibit a seller from granting discriminatory allowances 2(d), or services and facilities 2(e), unless such allowances or services are available on proportionately equal terms to all competing customers.

Section 2(f) makes it unlawful for a buyer knowingly to induce or receive an illegal price discrimination.

Section 3 prohibits a seller from providing secret allowances to a favored buyer. The section also forbids territorial price reductions or sales at unreasonably low prices for the purpose of destroying competition or eliminating a competitor. Section 3 is a criminal statute in that it makes it a crime for any person to be a party to its prohibitions. Maximum penalties include a $5,000 fine and imprisonment for a year. However, the U.S. Supreme Court has held that Section 3 is not an antitrust statute, and therefore does not provide for liability for treble damages by private litigants if a conviction occurs.

Jurisdictional Defenses—Section 2(a)[4]

Unlike economic price discrimination, a price differential is not, per se, illegal price discrimination unless certain requirements specified in Section 2(a) are met. In any price discrimination litigation, the seller first may attempt to prove that the Act does not apply to the price differences at issue. Primarily, a *jurisdictional issue* is a legal matter and does not include the actual issue of the price differentials.

Before a violation of Section 2(a) can be shown, the following jurisdictional requirements must be present. It must be shown that

1 The same seller
2 Charged different prices
3 To two or more different purchasers
4 For use, consumption, or resale within the United States or any territory

Furthermore, it must be shown that

5 There were two or more sales
6 Reasonably close in time
7 Involving commodities
8 Of like grade, quality, and quantity
9 And that at least one sale was "in commerce"

---

[4]In the commentary that follows, specific court cases will not be cited. Excellent overviews of the Robinson-Patman Act that include case citations are Earl W. Kinter, *A Robinson-Patman Primer* (New York: Macmillan, 1970); and Paul H. LaRue, "Meeting Competition and Other Defenses under the Robinson-Patman Act," *The Business Lawyer*, 25 (April 1970), 1037-1051. The material in this chapter has been drawn primarily from these sources.

Each of these jurisdictional requirements will be discussed below.

The Same Seller Although this requirement seems uncomplicated, it has presented some thorny problems. Primarily the problems occur when parent corporations sell through independent subsidiaries or distributors, and when at least one of the purchasers bought directly from the parent, while unfavored customers bought from an independent distributor or subsidiary.

Legally, it must be shown that the distributor or subsidiary possesses sufficient autonomy insofar as distribution policies are concerned. That is, ownership per se is not the issue, but rather whether there is sufficient managerial autonomy in the marketing activities of the subsidiary or distributor. There are no specific guidelines on how a firm can determine whether sufficient marketing control resides with the distributor or subsidiary to qualify legally the parent and the distributor or subsidiary as separate sellers. However, if legal autonomy is proved, then the alleged discrimination did not result *from sales by the same seller* and illegal price discrimination is not present.

A Price Difference Within the legal setting, price has been defined simply as what the buyer has actually paid the seller as consideration, i.e., what the seller gives up to acquire the goods and services. Thus, the U.S. Supreme Court has held that a difference in price is prima-facie (at face value) evidence of price discrimination. Thus, if the seller has one price for all customers and they pay transportation expenses, there is no violation of Section 2(a).

Because, legally, price discrimination is equivalent to price differentiation, equal prices are not unlawful. As was indicated in Chap. 12, a firm may sell at the same price to wholesalers, retailers, and consumers. However, when there are differing terms or conditions of sale, an illegal, indirect price discrimination may occur.

As observed in our definition of price in Chap. 1 and as has been discussed in Chaps. 11 and 12, there are many ways to differentiate price besides the direct dollar quotation. Promotional, trade, cash, and quantity discounts, rebates, premiums, or free goods, guarantees, provision of delivery, warehousing, or credit all affect how much the buyer actually receives. Differences in these terms and conditions of sale have been held to result in indirect price discrimination within the domain of Section 2(a). Moreover, under Sections 2(d) and 2(e), these terms and conditions of sale must be available to all competing customers on proportionately equal terms.

Two or More Purchasers Similar to the requirement that there be a single seller, it must also be shown that the alleged price discrimination was between two or more purchasers. Again, this issue arises when a manufacturer uses more than one channel of distribution. That is, the manufacturer may sell direct to some customers and through distributors or subsidiaries to other customers who compete on the same level as the direct-buying customers.

It has been held that in some cases in which the manufacturer also deals directly with the distributor's or subsidiary's customers, these customers are also *indirect purchasers* of the manufacturer in the eyes of the law, and they may therefore pay a higher, discriminatory price than competing direct-buying customers. As in the situation of the same seller, this legal issue revolves on the question of managerial control. But, although a subsidiary or distributor may be legally autonomous within the purview of the same seller requirement, it is possible that the manufacturer may have sufficient contact with the indirect customers to establish the requirement of two or more purchasers. Indeed, this was one of the legal issues prevailing against Purolator as discussed in Chap. 12.

Perhaps the safest approach is to have no contact between a manufacturer and its distributor's customers. Such an approach would rule out the use of missionary salespeople who arrange store displays, check retailer's inventory, and occasionally take orders. Furthermore, this "hands off" approach would prevent controlling wholesalers' or retailers' selling prices. The legal precedents in this area are inconclusive, and, at this time, raise more questions about what is legally acceptable distribution control.

Geographical Requirement   Section 2(a) cannot be applied to sales made for use, consumption, or resale in a foreign country. That is, export sales are exempt but import sales are not exempt from the provisions of Section 2(a). However, Sections 2(c), 2(d), and 2(e) have been applied to export sales.

Two or More Sales   The different purchasers requirement has also been interpreted to mean that both sets of transactions consist of sales. It has been held that consignments are not "sales" for the application of the Act. The issuance of a loan, the making of a gift, and terms of leases are not "sales." Furthermore, refusing to sell is not, per se, an unlawful price discrimination. Hence, when price discrimination involves nonsale transfers of property, or refusal to sell, it is not prima-facie evidence of unlawful price discrimination.

Contemporaneous Sales   Since discrimination occurs when there is a price differential for similar transactions under comparable conditions, then the Act is operative only if sales are reasonably close in time. The courts have ruled that price differences must be reasonably close in time and must involve delivery of the products also reasonably close in time. Thus, two contracts for future delivery at different times will not necessarily be in violation since delivery does not occur at the time of the contract agreement.

Also, Section 2(a) permits "price changes from time to time . . . in response to changing [market] conditions." Included in such price changes are obsolescence of seasonal goods, perishable products, going-out-of-business sales, closing-out-a-line sales, and court-sanctioned distress sales.

Tangible Commodities   It has consistently been found that Section 2(a) applies only to tangible products and does not encompass price differences for real estate, services, contract rights or privileges. Thus, the courts have said that the word *commodity* is restricted only to products, merchandise, or other tangible goods.

Products of Like Grade and Quality   Jurisdiction is not present when it is demonstrated that the products involved are of different grade and quality. Basically, the defendant must show that there are substantial physical differences affecting consumer preference or marketability. However, brand differences alone are not a sufficient defense.

Recently, the courts have seemingly applied some current marketing thinking and have considered customer preferences for the products in question. Thus, if there is substantial customer preference for a variation in design, and if the customer is willing to pay a higher price for the product, then the two products are not of like grade and quality. These design variations should not be decorative features that have no demonstrable effect on consumer demand.

The effect of using different labels or brand names was argued in the landmark Borden case.[5] The Borden Company had been producing private brand evaporated milk for about 20 years when the FTC issued a compaint on April 22, 1958. Borden was charged with price discrimination by selling milk of "like grade and quality" to different purchasers at higher prices than to the private label purchasers. It was readily admitted that there were no physical differences between the Borden brand and the private brands of evaporated milk. However, Borden contended that the Borden brand commanded a higher market price because of consumer acceptance. Hence, the Borden brand of evaporated milk was a different product than the private brands.

The hearing examiner, the full Federal Trade Commission, and the U.S. Supreme Court all concluded that Borden's evaporated milk and the private brands that Borden produced were of like grade and quality. However, the U.S. Supreme Court remanded the case back to the Appeals Court to make a final determination of the issues of injury to competition and cost justification.

The Fifth Circuit Court of Appeals rendered the final decision on July 4, 1967. It was the Court's opinion that Borden's policy of selling private brand milk did not result in injury to competition, and the case was resolved in favor of Borden. The Court did not take a position on the cost justification issue.

In finding no competitive injury the Court recognized the value of a premium brand:

> Where a price differential between a premium and nonpremium brand reflects no more than a consumer preference for the premium brand, the price difference creates no competitive advantage to the recipient of the cheaper private brand . . . [the price difference] represents merely a rough equivalent of the benefit by way of the seller's national advertising and promotion which the purchaser of the more expensive branded project enjoys.[6]

Thus, the Court recognized that when the buyer perceives there is a difference between two branded products, then there is a valid difference, so long as the "price difference is reasonable." It has not been established what constitutes a reasonable price difference.

---

[5] This case has spawned a number of articles including Jacky Knopp, Jr., "Branding and the Robinson-Patman Act," *The Journal of Business*, 39 (January 1966), 24–34; Morris L. Mayer, Joseph B. Mason, and Einar A. Orbeck, "The Borden Case—A Legal Basis for Private Brand Price Discrimination," *MSU Business Topics*, 18 (Winter 1970), 56–63; Thomas F. Schutte, Victor J. Cook, Jr., and Richard Hemsley, "What Management Can Learn from the Borden Case," *Business Horizons*, 9 (Winter 1966), 23–30.

[6] *The Borden Company v. FTC*, 381 F.2d 175 (5th Cir. 1967).

One Sale in Commerce Section 2(a) provides "that it shall be unlawful for any person engaged in *commerce*, in the course of such *commerce* . . . to discriminate in price . . . where either or any of the purchasers . . . are in *commerce*." (Italics added.) Hence, it is a jurisdictional defense that the alleged discrimination did not involve a sale "in commerce." Generally, the courts have held that for a sale to be "in commerce" the product must cross a state line. Legally, a firm is not engaged in commerce if it sells its products only in the state where they are produced. Thus, the use of local plants selling their products only in the producing state has become a recognized way of avoiding the prohibitions of Section 2(a).

The "No Statutory Injury" Defense

Section 2(a) provides another jurisdictional defense in that price discrimination is illegal if the effect is to injure, destroy, or prevent competition. As pointed out in the discussion on the Borden case, the Appeals Court determined that no competitive injury had resulted from the price differentials. As with Borden, many Robinson-Patman defendants have prevailed by showing no injury to competition.

The "Guidelines for Setting Functional Discount Policy" included in Chap. 12 contained a recommendation for knowing the buyer's position in the distribution sequence. One reason for this prescription is to enable the seller to know whether differential prices to different channel members would have the effect of injuring competition. For example, suppose manufacturer M sells to two distributors, D_1 and D_2. However, D_1 in turn sells to retailer R_1, who sells to final consumers. But, D_2 sells direct to final consumers in competition with R_1, and D_2 also sells to retailer R_2, who sells to final consumers in a separate market area. Figure 16-1(a) illustrates this possibility.

If M charges D_1 and D_2 the same price, then, there is no discrimination at the distributor level and no competitive injury. However, since D_2 competes with R_1, it is possible that D_2 could sell to consumers in market A at a price lower than R_1's price. If the price advantage harms the competitive position of R_1, then illegal price discrimination exists.

If the price to D_1 was lower than the price to D_2, then there is no illegal price discrimination since D_1 and D_2 do not compete for the same customers. However, if the lower price to D_1 permits R_1 to sell in market A at a price lower than D_2's price, *and* if D_2's competitive position is harmed, then there is illegal price discrimination by the manufacturer. Note, however, that if prices to R_1 and R_2 differ because of the manufacturer's pricing policy, there is no illegal price discrimination to these two retailers, since R_1 and R_2 do not compete with each other.

Each of the above situations in which a possible competitive injury existed is called a *secondary-line injury case*. That is, competitive injury due to a manufacturer's pricing policy occurs somewhere in the distributive sequence. For secondary-line injury to occur at some level of distribution, it is necessary that competing buyers purchase the same product at different prices, and that the disadvantaged buyer's competitive position has been injured. The important issue here is whether competition has been injured.

Now, consider the situation depicted by Fig. 16-1(b). M_1 competes with M_2 for the purchases of D_2. There is no other competition at lower levels of the distribution system. Suppose M_1's price to D_2 is lower than the price to D_1. Since M_2 does not sell to D_1, it is possible that M_2's competitive position can be harmed. Indeed, it is not necessary that M_1's price to D_2 be lower than M_2's price to D_2 for a possible finding of competitive injury to prevail. This second example is called a *primary-line injury case*.

Primary-line cases usually involve area price reductions at the seller's level of competition. Normally, injury may be shown whenever predatory intent can be proved or inferred.

Thus, even if one or more of the nine jurisdictional requirements discussed in the previous section are present for a determination of price discrimination, the defendant may prevail by proving no competitive injury. As we have discussed, injurious price discrimination can occur at the seller's level (primary-line injury), or at a lower level in the distribution sequence (secondary-line injury). Furthermore, a seller's attempt to match a lower competitive price in one market area while maintaining higher prices

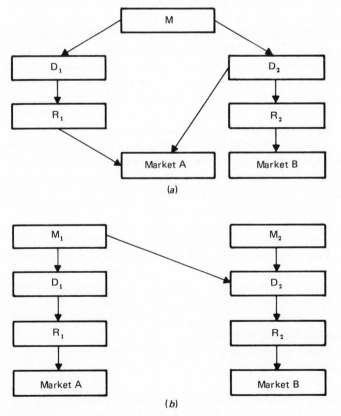

Figure 16-1 Hypothetical distribution systems.

elsewhere may lead to an inference of predatory intent to harm competition. Clearly, the legal complexities of establishing the presence of price discrimination within the domain of Section 2(a) makes pricing a difficult managerial task.

The Affirmative Defenses

Even when an alleged price discrimination charge has withstood the jurisdictional defenses outlined above, the seller may still show justification using one of three affirmative defenses: meeting competition, changing market conditions, cost justification. These defenses may be utilized when it has been established that the price differences constitute price discrimination under the Robinson-Patman Act. Since it has been established that the Act has jurisdiction over the price differences, then there is a prima-facie case of price discrimination, that is, the seller is guilty until proven innocent.

Defense of Meeting Competition A seller may reduce prices in a good-faith attempt to meet an equally low and lawful price of a competitor. The meeting of competition is a complete defense under Section 2(b) but there are strict rules for when such a defense should be used.

First, the defense is not available if the defendant knew, or should have known, that the competitor's price was unlawful. The seller must show that there was reason to believe that the competitor's price was lawful.

Second, the seller's price discrimination must have been temporary, and not part of a permanent price schedule. That is, the seller may reduce a price to hold a customer, or gain a new customer, but this new, lower price must be temporary and not part of a plan to systematically charge higher prices to some customers.

Third, "an equally low price of a competitor" must be for a given quantity. The competitor's product need not be of like grade and quality, but the products in question must be competitive, and the prices must be for similar quantity.

Fourth, the seller's lower price must be available to specific customers. That is, the price concession must be limited to those specific customers to whom a competitor has offered a lower price.

Fifth, the statute expressly permits reducing prices to *meet* a competitor's lower price, but the competitor's price cannot be beat. That is, the seller's price cannot be reduced below the competitor's price. As simple as this condition seems, it becomes complicated when the products are premium and nonpremium products, for example, beer or gasoline. Where historically there has been an established range of price differences between a premium and a nonpremium product, then meeting competition means preserving the established price differentials.

For a seller facing a price discrimination charge, the evidence necessary for a successful meeting competition defense includes

1 Existing market conditions and foreknowledge of competitors' low prices
2 A good-faith effort to verify the competitors' low prices
3 Facts indicating it was reasonable to believe the reports of competitors' low prices to be true
4 A belief that the business would be lost without the price reduction

Changing Conditions Defense   Section 2(a) provides that prices may be changed to reflect changing market conditions or changes in the marketability of the product. The section also lists a number of applicable examples: "actual or imminent deterioration of perishable goods, obsolescence of seasonal goods, distress sales under court process, or sales in good faith in discontinuance of business in the goods concerned."

Few defendants have attempted to use this defense. As with the meeting competition defense, there are two strict rules for using the changing conditions defense.

1   The specific market change or change in marketability must be a departure or variation from usual market conditions. These market changes must not be due to behavioral changes by a competitor or by the defendant.

2   The market must resemble the provisions of the statute, that is, the defense is confined to sales of products whose marketability has been affected by obsolescence or by changes in buyer preferences.

Cost Justification Defense   At the beginning of this chapter, it was observed that price differences not warranted by cost differences constituted economic price discrimination. Section 2(a) provides for a complete defense if the price differentials "make only due allowance for differences in the cost of manufacture, sale, or delivery resulting from the differing methods or quantities in which such commodities are to such purchasers sold or delivered." Thus, the Robinson-Patman Act provides for a defense based on economic principles.

Despite congressional intent, it has not been easy for a seller to justify price differentials on the basis of cost differences. Cost defenses have been successful, and many investigations by the Federal Trade Commission have been closed upon showings of cost justification. Yet the cost justification case has infrequently been used relative to the total number of cases litigated under the Act.

There are a number of reasons why the cost justification defense has had limited use. First, there are limited areas of business operations that provide recognizable cost savings of serving particular customers. If a manufacturer produces to maintain inventory and sells from inventory, there are no demonstrable savings due to manufacturing. Since it is impossible to causally relate any order, large or small, to the manufacturing process, volume discounts cannot be justified because of "production economies of scale." Only if the seller produces to fill specific orders can manufacturing costs be a part of the cost justification.

Second, the Federal Trade Commission has consistently accepted only actual costs. Incremental or marginal costs have been unacceptable, as have investment and opportunity costs.

Third, there is a lack of officially sanctioned accounting standards for performing a cost justification study. As noted above, manufacturing costs usually will not permit cost justification of price differences. Thus, the primary area of study is marketing and distribution. However, as shown in Chap. 6, little attention has been devoted to developing and utilizing standards for marketing cost analysis.

Fourth, a cost justification defense has usually been expensive and, because of the inexactness of marketing cost analysis, unpredictable. Also, the cost studies used as a defense invariably have been made after the discrimination citation. Hence, there was an obvious lack of good faith in setting price differentials based on cost differences.

AN EXAMPLE OF A COST JUSTIFICATION STUDY

As the above summary of available defenses to a price discrimination charge indicates, there are a number of ways to defend price differentials successfully. However, a careful reading of the litigation history of the Robinson-Patman Act reveals a woeful lack of attention to the pricing function by many firms. Most defenses to a price discrimination charge have relied on hastily developed studies that, when subjected to cross-examination, have failed to justify the price differentials.

Despite its relative lack of use, the cost justification defense remains one of the most viable defenses available. However, it is necessary for firms to develop cost accounting techniques for analyzing marketing expenditures and to refrain from lumping marketing costs into a general overhead category such as selling, general, and administrative overhead. The basic approach to marketing cost accounting was outlined in Chap. 6. We now illustrate how one company studied its volume discount schedule and determined that the discount schedule lacked cost justification.

The Company[7]

The company in question produced and sold a product in a very competitive market. There were a number of variations of the product, which resulted from selling a basic unit plus a number of different modifying assemblies at the time of dealer installation. The product was distributed through manufacturers' agents to distributors. The distributors sold to retailers who sold the product to the final customers. The manufacturers' agents were paid sales commissions after the distributors' discounts were deducted.

Original Discount Structure

The distributors were categorized into three classes depending on minimum-order size. A Class I distributor was required to order a minimum of one item and received no discount. Typically, a Class I distributor ordered three items per order. A Class II distributor was required to order a minimum of six items and typically did order six items each time. A Class II distributor was quoted a price 3 percent less than a Class I distributor. A Class III distributor's minimum and usual order size was 18 items. The price quoted to Class III distributors was 6 percent less than the Class I price. Table 16-2 shows a typical price list.

Identifying Relevant Costs

As Table 16-2 indicates, all prices were quoted f.o.b. manufacturer's factory. Further, all products were made for inventory. Consequently, neither differences in freight costs nor manufacturing costs could be used to justify price differences. It was deter-

---

[7]This example is adapted from James C. Cohrs, "A Cost Justification Study," *Management Controls*, 12 (November 1965), 230–235.

Table 16-2 Sample Price List

Item	Distributor class		
	I	II	III
Basic unit	$100.00	$97.00	$94.00
Modifying assembly A	75.00	72.75	70.50
Modifying assembly B	50.00	48.50	47.00
Modifying assembly C	25.00	24.25	23.50
Minimum order size	1	6	18
All prices f.o.b. manufacturer's factory.			

mined that only those costs incurred in the following departments could be used to justify price differences:

1 Ordering and billing
2 Traffic (bills of lading)
3 Accounts receivable
4 Credit and collection
5 Shipping

Preliminary Analysis

Initially, the treasurer and sales manager were asked to estimate the average cost of processing and filling minimum orders for each distributor class. After considerable discussion and some analysis of departmental records it was estimated that the order costs per order were:

I	II	III
$10.00	$12.50	$15.00

It was also determined that sales commissions paid to the manufacturer's agents were (on sales after discounts):

I	II	III
7%	5%	4%

Using the above estimates, order processing costs were calculated for a sale of 18 units of modifying assembly A to each distributor class as shown in Table 16-3. The order processing costs were based on the usual order size for each distributor class. Hence, for Class I, 18 items would require six orders at three items per order, or $10.00 per order times 6 equals $60.00.

A summary of the price and cost differences are shown in Table 16-4. Based on the preliminary analysis, the excess of a price difference over cost differences of $3.28

Table 16-3 Price Differences and Assumed Cost Differences—Modifying Assembly A

Item	Distributor class		
	I	II	III
Sales value of assembly A (unit)	$ 75.00	$ 72.75	$ 70.50
Sales value of assembly A (18 units)	1,350.00	1,309.50	1,269.00
Price differences			
Versus Class I	....	40.50	81.00
Versus Class II	....	....	40.50
Differential costs for 18 items			
Order filling and processing	$ 60.00	$ 37.50	$ 15.00
Sales commissions	94.50	65.48	50.76
Total	$ 154.50	$ 102.98	$ 65.76
Assumed cost differences			
Versus Class I	....	$ 51.52	$ 88.74
Versus Class II	....	....	37.22

represented an apparent lack of cost justification. However, it was believed that a detailed study of the actual order processing and filling costs would lead to a discount schedule that could be cost justified.

The Cost Study

A detailed cost study was undertaken to determine what activities were involved in order processing and shipping. It also determined who performed these activities and the time spent performing them. The study program and results are outlined below.

A Data collection
  1 Analyzed the company's organization to determine the departments involved in order filling and processing.
  2 Determined the personnel and time spent in order filling and processing.
  3 Obtained data on orders, back orders, and items processed.
  4 Accumulated direct and overhead costs for each department involved in order filling and processing.
  5 Determined typical times required to ship various size orders.
  6 Developed hourly cost rates for the shipping department (direct and overhead) for different annual volumes of shipments.
  7 Determined sales and marketing activities that were transaction identifiable.

Table 16-4 Summary of Price and Cost Differences

Distributor class	Price difference	Cost difference	Excess of cost difference over price difference
I vs. III	$81.00	$88.74	$ 7.74
I vs. II	40.50	51.52	11.02
II vs. III	40.50	37.22	(3.28)

Table 16-5 Order Processing and Filling Costs

Fixed costs per order	
Order department	$3.64
Accounts receivable	0.35
Credits and collection	0.30
Traffic	1.71
	$6.00

Variable costs per order		
Number of units	Shipping	Order department
1	$1.84	$0.05
3	1.95	0.07
6	2.27	0.08
18	3.25	0.22

8 Allocated corporate overhead expenses to the order processing and filling function.

9 Computed the costs of filling various sized orders.

10 Determined whether distributors were ordering in specified quantities.

Table 16-6 Price Differences and Estimated Cost Differences
Assembly A

Item	Distributor class		
	I	II	III
Sales value (18 units)	$1,350.00	$1,309.50	$1,269.00
Price differences			
Versus Class I	....	40.50	81.00
Versus Class II	....	....	40.50
Differential costs (18 units)			
Order processing—fixed	$ 36.00	$ 18.00	$ 6.00
Order processing—variable	0.42	0.24	0.22
Shipping	11.70	6.81	3.25
Sales commissions (7%, 5%, 4%)	94.50	65.48	50.76
Total	$ 142.62	$ 90.53	$ 60.23
Cost differences			
Versus Class I	....	$ 52.09	$ 82.39
Versus Class II	....	....	30.30
Excess of cost differences over price differences			
Versus Class I	....	11.59	1.39
Versus Class II	....	....	(10.20)

B Results

1 About 70 percent of all shipments to each distributor class were for less than five components each. Therefore, cost justification of the price list differences would not justify *actual* pricing practices.
2 The fixed cost of processing an order was $6.00.
3 Some order processing activities and shipping room time did not increase proportionately with order size. Therefore, these activities provided a source of differential costs.
4 Concluded that there was substantial lack of cost justification of list prices.
5 Estimated actual cost (Table 16-5).
6 Determined price and cost differences (Table 16-6).

Table 16-7 Quantity Discount and Sales Commission Schedule

Sales value at list per order	Quantity discount as percent of list	Sales commission, %
Less than $450	None	7
$450–$675	2	6
$675–$1,125	3	5
Over $1,125	4	4

Table 16-8 Price and Cost Differences: New Discount Schedule

| Item | Quantity discount class | | | |
	None	2%	3%	4%
Sales at list	$225.00	$450.00	$675.00	$1,125.00
Quantity discount	. . . .	9.00	20.25	45.00
Net sales	$225.00	$441.00	$654.75	$1,080.00
Differential costs				
Order processing—fixed	$ 6.00	$ 6.00	$ 6.00	$ 6.00
Order processing—variable	0.07	0.08	0.11	0.17
Order filling	1.95	2.27	2.52	3.02
Sales commissions (7%, 6%, 5%, 4%)	15.75	26.46	32.74	43.20
Total	$ 23.77	$ 34.81	$ 41.37	$ 52.39
Differential costs (% of sales at list)	10.6	7.7	6.1	4.7
Versus no discount	. . . .	2.9	4.5	5.9
Versus 2% discount	. . . .	. . . .	1.6	3.0
Versus 3% discount	. . . .	. . . .	. . . .	1.4
Excess of cost differences over price differences (% of sales at list)				
Versus no discount	. . . .	0.9	1.5	1.9
Versus 2% discount	. . . .	. . . .	0.6	1.0
Versus 3% discount	. . . .	. . . .	. . . .	0.4

Recommendations

Because the distributors were not ordering according to the minimum-order requirements and because not all price differences were cost-justified, it was recommended that another discount policy be adopted. The new pricing policy was recommended to provide for cost-justified price differences and to encourage customers to increase their average order size. It was also recommended that the discount schedule be based on dollar value of shipments rather than number of items shipped.

The discount schedule adopted is shown in Table 16-7. The sales commission of 6 percent was added to encourage the manufacturer's agents to make regular sales calls to smaller distributors averaging around $500 per order. Table 16-8 shows the cost justification for the new discount schedule.

GUIDELINES FOR JUSTIFYING PRICE DIFFERENTIALS[8]

Any seller who, in the normal course of business, charges different customers different prices should not leave to chance the matter of complying with the Robinson-Patman Act. From a policy perspective it is necessary to have clearly defined policies and procedures.

Administrative Guidelines

Minimally, these policies and procedures should

1　Provide a published price list that includes the price breaks and discount eligibility criteria
2　Establish all discount schedules on a cost-justified basis
3　Communicate to all sales personnel the policy of adhering to the established price lists and discount schedules
4　Provide for specific procedures when departing from the established prices and discount schedules
5　Develop a program for cost-justifying discount schedules and other sources of price differentials
6　Instruct sales personnel to obtain, whenever possible,
　a　Copies of competitor's offers, price lists, discount schedules, invoices from customers
　b　Signed statements from customers about claimed price concessions provided by competitors
　c　Memoranda of conversations with customers who report competitive offers
　d　A list of customers lost because of lower competitive offers
7　Provide for periodic review of all price concessions granted to meet competition

---

[8]These guidelines are adopted from Ronald M. Copeland, "The Art of Self-Defense in Price Discrimination," *Business Horizons,* 9 (Winter 1966), 71–76; Paul H. LaRue, "Meeting Competition and Other Defenses under the Robinson-Patman Act," *The Business Lawyer,* 25 (April 1970), 1037–1051; John E. Martin, "Justifying Price Differentials," *Management Accounting,* 47 (November 1965), 56–62.

Cost Justification Guidelines

To cost-justify price differences the seller should develop a marketing cost accounting system. Such an accounting system should utilize the computer to prepare reports showing the cost and price differences of serving different types of customers. Marketing costs should not be averaged, but traced objectively and directly to the activities that give rise to these costs.

Cost justification studies should

1 Be made before price lists and discount schedules are established
2 Be periodically reviewed to determine effects of cost changes
3 Analyze only those costs that vary among customers
4 Include marketing, accounting, and legal personnel
5 Include only the seller's costs
6 Group customers according to similarities of marketing to them and according to similarities of their purchasing behavior
7 Classify relevant costs into their variable and fixed components
8 Compare cost differences to the price lists and discount schedules to determine the legal basis of the price differentials

In addition to providing for a legal defense to a price discrimination charge, these administrative and cost-justification guidelines provide management with useful knowledge for making pricing decisions. The value of good intelligence reports from salespeople and the value of marketing cost studies is that they provide useful guidance for developing overall marketing strategies.

SUMMARY

This chapter has provided an overview of the legal environment for managing the pricing function. The history of litigation under the Robinson-Patman Act provides few clear guidelines for developing lawful price schedules except to be prepared. Indeed, those firms that have prevailed against price discrimination charges often could demonstrate an underlying analytical foundation for their pricing practices. At the very least, price analysis of a firm's pricing practices is a good-faith attempt to comply with the requirements of the Robinson-Patman Act.

This chapter has also integrated material from Chaps. 6, 11, and 12. It has been shown that it is important to know both the direct and traceable costs of manufacturing and marketing activities. Arbitrary allocation of marketing costs without a clear understanding of how these costs vary when serving different types of customers, usually fails to justify price differentials. In Chaps. 11 and 12, we repeatedly argued against tradition as a basis for establishing discount policies. Given the dynamic nature of our economy, the guidelines in this chapter also stress a planned, periodic review of all prices and underlying analyses. Regardless of the legal benefits of such control, such reviews are simply sound management practice.

Another benefit of an analytical base for making pricing decisions is that it becomes easier to explain the necessity of price changes to sales personnel, customers, or a price control board. During periods of inflation, prices generally are increased. While some price increases are expected, often the frequency and amount of these increases exceed the expectations of salespeople and customers. To help these people adapt to the price increases, a reasoned justification is useful. Additional prescriptions for pricing management are given in Chap. 17.

DISCUSSION QUESTIONS

1 Contrast the meaning of price discrimination from the economic point of view with the legal view represented in the Robinson-Patman Act.
2 Using Table 16-1 as a guide, develop additional examples of permissible price discrimination.
3 What is a jurisdictional defense? What are the 10 jurisdictional requirements for price discrimination as set forth in the Robinson-Patman Act?
4 What is the importance of the Borden case for marketing?
5 What is a primary-line injury case? What is a secondary-line injury case?
6 Explain the meaning of the "no statutory injury" jurisdictional defense.
7 What are the affirmative defenses to a charge of price discrimination?
8 What are the necessary conditions for the following defenses to a charge of price discrimination:
  a Meeting competition
  b Changing conditions
  c Cost justification
9 What is the rationale for the proposed administrative and cost justification guidelines given in the chapter? How do these guidelines help a pricing administrator manage the pricing function?

SUGGESTED READINGS

Copeland, Ronald M.: "The Art of Self-Defense in Price Discrimination," *Business Horizons*, 9 (Winter 1966), 71–76.

Kinter, Earl W.: *A Robinson-Patman Primer* (New York: Macmillan, 1970).

LaRue, Paul H.: "Meeting Competition and Other Defenses under the Robinson-Patman Act," *The Business Lawyer*, 25 (April 1970), 1037–1051.

Martin, John E.: "Justifying Price Differentials," *Management Accounting*, 47 (November 1965), 56–62.

Mayer, Morris L., Joseph B. Mason, and Einar A. Orbeck, "The Borden Case—A Legal Basis for Private Brand Price Discrimination," *MSU Business Topics*, 18 (Winter 1970), 56–63.

Recommendations

This last section of the book offers some prescriptions for improving pricing decisions. Chapter 17 first outlines four basic rules for developing a positive approach to pricing. These rules summarize the analytical prescriptions contained in Chaps. 2 through 8. The chapter also discusses the different types of data that can be used when considering the profit implications of pricing alternatives and suggests when it is appropriate to use each type.

The chapter also suggests that pricing be included in a firm's marketing planning in an adaptive manner. An adaptive approach to pricing is necessary to help firms adjust to current and future economic pressures. Finally, the chapter provides a set of guidelines for developing and maintaining an effective approach to solving pricing problems.

Chapter 17

Guidelines for Better Pricing Decisions

The objective of this book has been to provide a systematic presentation of the factors to consider when setting price and to show how pricing alternatives can be developed and analyzed. As was observed in Chap. 1, many contemporary pricing practices are reactions to environmental pressures that have been developing over a number of years. Today, in reaction to these environmental pressures, we have been witnessing changes in pricing practices that are a little less than "a revolution in pricing practices that will have ramifications for capital spending, the inflation rate, industrial concentration, and the application of existing antitrust laws."[1]

As the reader may have perceived, the emphasis has been less on describing current or past pricing practices, than on prescribing new approaches to the setting of prices. Indeed, many businesses are now changing their approach to pricing. Perhaps the foremost change has been the elevating of the pricing decision to a more central position in corporate headquarters. Moreover, price has been recognized to be a key influence on investment decisions because of the direct link between price and net cash flow into the organization.

---

[1] "Flexible Pricing," *Business Week*, December 12, 1977, pp. 78–88.

The purpose of this chapter is to review some of the basic prescriptions for improving the pricing function of the organization and to present a set of guidelines for developing and maintaining an effective organizational approach to solving pricing problems. The chapter first summarizes the analytic framework provided in Chaps. 2 through 8, then presents some criteria for making pricing decisions. It concludes with a set of guidelines for improving the pricing function of the organization.

FOUR BASIC RULES FOR PRICING

The four rules listed below are intended to capture the essence of the analysis necessary to determine and evaluate pricing alternatives. The order in which the rules are presented does not imply a hierarchy of importance—each rule is equally important.

1. Know Your Costs

An initial prescription is to determine the basic cost data necessary for the pricing decision. As stated in Chaps. 4, 5, and 6, it is necessary to know which costs vary directly with changes in levels of activity, and the underlying causes of the changes in costs. It is also necessary to identify the costs that are directly related to the product being costed, but do not vary with activity levels—direct period or fixed costs. Furthermore, marketing costs should be objectively traced to the products and not simply lumped into a general overhead category.

Valid cost data provide an objective basis for choosing between pricing alternatives, determining discounts, and establishing differential pricing alternatives. Furthermore, objective cost studies that are completed before the pricing decisions provide the firm with a valid legal justification for its price structure. The direct costing approach developed in this book provides a mechanism for obtaining objective, valid cost data. Finally, as shown in Chap. 7, when it is necessary to develop full-cost data, the firm should avoid arbitrary allocation formulas based on inappropriate allocation bases. Again, well-executed cost studies will usually provide a more valid way of allocating period expenses not directly related to the appropriate activity levels.

2. Know Your Demand

This second prescription suggests that the firm understand fully the factors influencing the demand for its products and services. Demand analysis is not as objective or as quantifiable as cost analysis, but it is no less important. The emerging discipline of buyer behavior has provided considerable information on consumer behavior and has begun to provide information on industrial buying behavior. From the perspective of this book, the key question is the role of price in the purchaser's decision process. As Chap. 3 indicated, price and price differentials influence buyer perceptions of value. In fact, many companies have achieved positive results from differentially pricing their products and services. A vice-president of a large data processing company has observed "... we try to find a proprietary enclave where our product has a unique application. ..."[2]

[2]Ibid., p. 81.

Coupled with knowing how price influences buyers' perceptions of value, it is necessary to know how buyers use the product or service. Is the product used as an input in the buyer's production process? If so, does the product represent a significant or insignificant portion of the buyer's manufacturing costs? If the product is a major cost element in the buyer's production process, then small changes in the product's price may significantly affect the buyer's costs and the resulting price of the manufactured product. If the final market is sensitive to price increases, then a small price increase to the final manufacturer may significantly reduce demand to the initial seller of the input material.

Further, as was suggested in Chaps. 12 and 16, the seller should also know the different types of distributors and their function in the distribution channel. This prescription is particularly important when the manufacturer sells both to distributors and to the distributors' customers.

3. Know Your Competition and Your Market

In addition to the influence of buyers, there are a number of other significant market factors influencing demand. It is important to understand the operations of both domestic and foreign competitors, their rate of capacity utilization, and their products and services. As described in Chap. 8, the current rate of capacity influences product supply. In many markets, the dynamic interaction of supply and demand influences prices. Moreover, changes in capacity availability due to capital investment programs will influence supply and prices.

A second important aspect of knowing the market is the need to determine price-volume relationships. Chapters 2 and 3 have discussed methods of estimating demand and behavioral influences on demand. Chapters 9 and 14 have shown the importance of knowing price-volume relationships when setting prices or determining competitive bids. Finally, as shown in Chap. 15, when scarcity of resources and/or capacity is present, knowing price-volume relationships facilitates the use of price to allocate these scarce resources over products and to customers.

4. Know Your Corporate Targets

As demonstrated in Chap. 13, many firms stress the profit objective of return on investment. Other firms stress the objective of maintaining specified profit margins while still other firms seek to achieve market share goals. As shown in Chap. 13, it is not necessary for each product to maintain the same profit margin in order to achieve a particular return on investment. Similarly, different margins on products may still produce an overall desired corporate profit goal. Finally, firms stressing market share may utilize the experience curve factor developed in Chap. 8 and build profits by reducing prices.

The important point to remember is that differences in corporate profit targets eventually will lead to differences in prices and the role of price in influencing actual profits. Thus, imitating or following the pricing practices of other companies is not necessarily in the best interests of any firm. Many firms are, in fact, departing from this type of pricing practice.[3]

[3]Ibid., pp. 78–88.

CRITERIA FOR PRICING DECISIONS[4]

Following the above four rules should enable a firm to have a balanced approach to pricing. That is, costs, demand, competition, and corporate profit objectives will all have a place in the analysis. Hence, when a firm is operating at normal capacity, and internal and external environmental factors are stable, prices can be determined with a degree of confidence. However, as observed in Chaps. 1 and 15, the current economic environment has made pricing a more complex and important decision. The price setter, therefore, must develop a more analytical decision process.

Throughout this text, a contribution approach to pricing has been emphasized. A contribution analysis produces several types of data: profit-volume ratio, contribution dollars, contribution per scarce resource unit, target selling price. In this section, the appropriateness of each of these types of data is evaluated for situations in which a firm is not operating under normal conditions.

When Operating below Normal Capacity

As suggested when discussing whether to submit a bid and at what price, a firm operating at 55 percent capacity needs additional business that can make some contribution to overhead and profits. Hence, maximizing contribution dollars represents the key criterion for pricing new orders or for increasing the demand for existing products. The primary concern of management should be to generate enough contribution dollars to bring its operating level above the break-even point.

By using either a minimum PV ratio or gross margin, a firm may turn away business because its prices are too high. Adhering to a target selling price may also lead to overpricing the market. When operating below normal capacity, the goal is to generate sufficient product volume to cover all costs and also earn a profit. By stressing the dollars of contribution earned, the firm is in a position to achieve some minimal level of profits.

When Operating at or near Maximum Capacity

When a firm is operating at capacity, its situation is essentially the same as when resources are scarce. And, as demonstrated in Chap. 15, the appropriate decision criterion is to maximize the contribution per scarce resource unit. Any other criterion may produce lower contributions to profit.

When Operating at Normal Capacity

Under normal operating conditions, a firm should seek primarily to maximize dollar contributions consistent with target return on investments. As shown in Chap. 13, because of the different ways variable and fixed capital are mixed to produce different products, it is not necessary for each product to have equal profit-volume ratios or contribution margins. And since there are no scarce resource constraints in normal circumstances, the CPRU criterion is also inappropriate.

[4] This section has been adapted from Spencer A. Tucker, *Pricing for Higher Profit* (New York: McGraw-Hill, 1966).

Summary

It is important to realize there is no one right way to determine price. Pricing simply cannot be reduced to a formula—there are too many interacting factors. Successful pricing requires considering all internal and external factors and adapting to changes as they occur. Successful pricing is adaptive pricing.

ADAPTIVE PRICING

Adaptive pricing explicitly recognizes the role of costs, corporate goals, and competition, as well as the effect of price and the total interaction of the marketing mix variables on demand when making pricing decisions. Moreover, adaptive pricing provides for a formal mechanism to adapt to environmental changes.

Adaptive pricing provides for the formal use of (1) plans and standards of controls, (2) review and analysis of deviations between planned and actual results, and (3) an information feedback system providing for revisions of plans, standards, and policies.[5] The decision to commit resources involves analyzing a variety of variables that interact with price: (1) product characteristics, (2) price-product quality relationships, (3) the distribution organization for marketing the products, (4) advertising and other communicative efforts, (5) the quality and nature of services to offer with the products.

Changes in demand, legal and regulatory changes, and changes in competitor strategies and products influence the firm to develop adaptive policies with respect to product, quality, price, personal selling, advertising, and service. These decisions influence the quantity and type of fixed investments and the level and behavior of other costs. The decision process involving these variables must consider several alternative dimensions for each variable. To limit the costs of generating, processing, and transmitting information, goals and tasks are determined for each of several levels in the firm. That is, operating divisions are given targets to reach for, and if these targets are reached, the overall position of the firm is enhanced. For example, a product manager may be given a market share target determined by considering the market potential and the managerial judgment of the share of the market the product may be expected to capture. Given the market potential and the target market share, the expected sales volume can be determined leading to a determination of the necessary capacity and, therefore, necessary investment.

The major features of adaptive pricing are

1 Demand and the responsiveness of demand to the marketing mix variables are explicitly considered
2 The constraining influences of competitive products and services and legal and regulatory forces are recognized
3 The necessity to develop a mechanism for adapting to changing market and environmental forces is considered

[5] J. Fred Weston, "Pricing Behavior of Large Firms," *Western Economic Journal*, 10 (March 1972), 1–18.

Hence, a pricing goal per se exists only in the context of an adaptive marketing plan. The adaptive marketing plan should determine investments and cost behavior rather than existing investments and cost behavior determining pricing and marketing decisions.

PROVIDING A BASIS FOR PRICING DECISIONS[6]

The discussion in Chap. 1 detailed reasons why many firms' current pricing strategies may be inappropriate. Firms can perform a number of activities to develop strategies that may be more consistent with the actual decision environment.

Determine Consistent Objectives

As suggested above, objectives such as improving margins, avoiding bottlenecks, and improving cash flows may not be mutually consistent. As shown in Chap. 15, focusing on high-margin products may increase bottlenecks because of the resources required and may lead to cash flow reductions because of the sales decline of low-margin, high-volume products. A clear and consistent statement of pricing objectives is necessary in order to select appropriate pricing strategies.

In addition, the impact of short-run objectives on long-run profits must be recognized. When identifying "weak" products, managers should consider potential sales growth and the annual cash flow generated per dollar of assets invested in the product. Further, if shortages are expected to persist in the long run, the appropriate objective would be to maximize contributions per critical resource unit.

Establish a Pricing Research Program

In terms of applied marketing research, the effect of price changes is the least understood and the least researched. The lack of data in this area has led to many inappropriate pricing strategies. A pricing research program should minimally determine the demand and cost effects of price changes.

Demand Effects of Price Changes The objective of this research is to determine the sensitivity of the market to price changes. Clearly, the seller should know the sensitivity of buyers to price changes, but the seller should also know the sensitivity of buyers' customers to price changes. The seller should be concerned about how buyers use price in their purchasing decisions, whether they impute quality from price, and whether perceived end prices affect the evaluation of the product line. Further, considerations of cross-elasticity of demand for the product line, including the behavioral perception of complementarity, should be investigated. (See Chaps. 3 and 10.)

Cost Effects of Price Changes Whereas the effect of price changes on demand concerns market or external reactions, the cost effects of price changes are internal

---

[6]This section is based on Joseph P. Guiltinan and Kent B. Monroe, "Making Sound Pricing Decisions in the Current Economic Environment," *Executive Scene*, 3 (Fall 1974), 11–16.

considerations. As discussed in Chap. 10, a multiple-product firm has cost and demand interdependencies. Dropping low-margin products or curtailing volume by increasing prices can have unanticipated results. First, eliminating a product shifts its common cost burden to other products. Second, severe reductions in output demand may remove the firm's eligibility for quantity discounts when purchasing production inputs. Therefore, it is important that the firm properly classify costs into the ones that are tangibly traceable to and generated by a given product and the ones that are common. Furthermore, since for pricing purposes only future costs are relevant, the firm must develop adequate bases for forecasting future costs. (See Chap. 8.)

GUIDELINES FOR BETTER PRICING DECISIONS

The purpose of this book has been to develop a consistent, analytical approach to pricing. The emphasis has been on developing positive attitudes toward the pricing decision and to demonstrate that price is a critical decision variable in the marketing mix. Further, it has been shown how appropriate pricing strategies may be developed with the help of adequate information and analysis. The following guidelines are offered for those firms interested in improving their pricing decisions.

Set Consistent Objectives

1 Make sure that objectives are clearly stated, operational, and mutually consistent

2 When there are several objectives, develop priorities, or otherwise clarify the relationships between the objectives.

3 Make sure that everyone concerned with a pricing decision, at any level in the firm, understands the relevant objectives.

Identify Alternatives

1 Identify enough alternatives to permit a sensible choice between courses of action

2 Avoid traditional thinking, encourage creativity.

Acquire Relevant Information

1 Be sure that information about buyers and competitors is current and reflects their current and future situations.

2 Make sure information is for the future, not just a report of the past.

3 Involve market research people in the pricing problem.

4 Make sure cost information identifies which costs will be affected by a particular pricing alternative.

5 Communicate with and involve accounting people with the cost aspects of a pricing decision.

6 Analyze the effect a particular alternative will have on scarce resources, inventories, production, cash flows, market share, volume, and profits.

Make the Pricing Decision

1 Make full use of the information available.
2 Correctly relate all the relevant variables in the problem.
3 Use sensitivity analysis to determine which elements in the decision are most important.
4 Consider all human and organizational problems which could occur with a given pricing decision.
5 Consider the long-run effects of the pricing decision.
6 Base the pricing decision on the life cycle of each product.
7 Consider the effect of experience in reducing costs as the cumulative production volume increases.

Maintain Feedback and Control

1 Develop procedures to ensure that pricing decisions fit into the firm's overall marketing strategy.
2 Provide for a feedback mechanism to ensure that all who should know the results of individual price decisions are fully informed.

To summarize, pricing decisions should be logically made and should involve rigorous thinking, with minimum difficulty from human and organizational factors. Further, it should be recognized that judgment and prediction are needed about the future, not the past. Finally, pricing decisions should be made within a dynamic, long-run marketing strategy.

DISCUSSION QUESTIONS

1 Assume that you are the price administrator for a corporation and you wish to implement the four basic rules for pricing given in this chapter. What steps would you take to put these rules into action?
2 Comment on the applicability of the following types of data for pricing purposes:
   a Profit-volume ratio
   b Contribution dollars
   c Contribution per scarce resource unit
   d Target selling price
3 What is "adaptive pricing"?
4 Review the "Guidelines for Better Pricing Decisions" given in this chapter. Explain the rationale for each guideline.

SUGGESTED READINGS

"Flexible Pricing," *Business Week*, December 12, 1977, pp. 78–88.
Guiltinan, Joseph P.: "Risk-Aversive Pricing Policies: Problems and Alternatives," *Journal of Marketing*, 40 (January 1976), 10–15.

_____, and Kent B. Monroe: "Making Sound Pricing Decisions in the Current Economic Environment," *Executive Scene*, 3 (Fall 1974), 11–16.

Oxenfeldt, Alfred R.: "A Decision-making Structure for Price Decisions," *Journal of Marketing*, 37 (January 1973), 48–53.

Weston, J. Fred: "Pricing Behavior of Large Firms," *Western Economic Journal*, 10 (March 1972), 1–18.

Index

Index